Women in America

FROM COLONIAL TIMES TO THE 20TH CENTURY

Women in America

FROM COLONIAL TIMES TO THE 20TH CENTURY

Advisory Editors
LEON STEIN
ANNETTE K. BAXTER

A Note About This Volume

The articles, pamphlets and studies included in this anthology attempt to indicate the tremendous scope of feminine experience in America. They are details from a far larger canvas that is now beginning to be filled through the rediscovery of that part of American history concerned with the accomplishments of its women. These few examples muster a small army of printers, educators, frontierswomen and rangers, literary figures, political agitators and industrial entrepreneurs. Their accomplishments are all the more extraordinary for having been achieved despite obstacles to equal opportunity.

Lives to Remember

Edited by

LEON STEIN

ARNO PRESS

A New York Times Company

NEW YORK – 1974

Reprint Edition 1974 by Arno Press Inc.

"Kate Chopin" by Robert Cantwell was reprinted
   by permission of The Georgia Review
"Four Sisters" by Norma Kidd Green was reprinted
   by permission of The Nebraska State Historical
   Society

WOMEN IN AMERICA
From Colonial Times to the 20th Century
ISBN for complete set: 0-405-06070-X
See last pages of this volume for titles.

Publisher's Note: This volume was reprinted
from the best available copies.

Manufactured in the United States of America

—————◆—————

Library of Congress Cataloging in Publication Data

Stein, Leon, 1912-   comp.
   Lives to remember.

   (Women in America: from colonial times to the 20th
century)
   CONTENTS: Gundy, H. P. Molly Brant--loyalist.--
Oldham, E. M. Early women printers of America.--
Small, E. W. and M. R. Prudence Crandall: champion of
Negro education. [etc.]
   1. Women in the United States--Biography. I. Title.
II. Series.
HQ1412.S74   301.41'2'0973 [B]   74-3984
ISBN 0-405-06109-9

CONTENTS

Haddock, Emma
WOMEN AS LAND-OWNERS IN THE WEST (Reprinted from the *Proceedings of the Association for the Advancement of Women,* Louisville, Ky., Oct. 1886)

Diggs, Annie L.
THE WOMEN IN THE ALLIANCE MOVEMENT (Reprinted from *The Arena,* Vol. 6, July 1892)

McKelway, A. J.
"KATE," THE "GOOD ANGEL" OF OKLAHOMA (Reprinted from *American Magazine,* Vol. 66, No. 6, Oct. 1908)

Altman, Addie R.
JULIA RICHMAN (Reprinted from *Julia Richman: Two Biographical Appreciations of the Great Educator* by Her Sisters). New York, 1916

Cantwell, Robert
"THE AWAKENING" BY KATE CHOPIN (Reprinted from the *Georgia Review,* Winter 1956)

Wolcott, Robert W.
A WOMAN IN STEEL — REBECCA LUKENS (1794-1854). Princeton, N. J., 1940

Dwyer, James L.
LADY WITH THE HATCHET (Reprinted from *The American Mercury,* Vol. 7, No. 27, March 1926)

de Ford, Miriam Allen
POETESS OF PASSION (Reprinted from *The American Mercury,* Vol. 32, No. 128, Aug. 1934)

Gold, Louis
LAURA JEAN LIBBEY (Reprinted from *The American Mercury,* Vol. 24, No. 93, Sept. 1931)

Steele, Zulma
FANNIE FARMER AND HER COOK BOOK (Reprinted from *The American Mercury,* Vol. 59, No. 247, July 1944)

MOLLY BRANT—LOYALIST

H. Pearson Gundy

MOLLY BRANT - LOYALIST

H. Pearson Gundy

The fame of Joseph Brant, widely celebrated, has all but obscured the remarkable life of his sister Mary—Miss Molly, as she was universally known. Scattered references to her appear in the Sir William Johnson Papers and other pre-revolutionary records. The biographers of Sir William pay passing tribute to her, repeating the few known facts and legends that have been handed down. With a wealth of invented detail, she appears as a character in several historical novels[2] for the most part without biographical authenticity. Mr. W. Max Reid, local historian of the Mohawk Valley, says of her: "The fact is that with the exception of the date of her death (1805) she appears to have dropped out of the pages of history entirely after her flight to Niagara in 1779."[3] In point of fact she fled to Niagara in 1777, and died in Kingston in 1796. Had Mr. Reid consulted the Claus and Haldimand Papers in the Public Archives of Canada, he would have discovered that far from dropping out of the pages of history after fleeing to Niagara, she entered into them, as I shall attempt to indicate in this paper.

The established facts of Molly Brant's life up to the death of Sir William Johnson, July 11, 1774, are disappointingly meagre. The year of her birth may be fairly accurately determined as 1736[4] but her place of birth and her parentage remain in doubt. Among the Kirby Papers in the Provincial Archives of Ontario is a letter from Mr. Lyman C. Draper, the American antiquarian, to William Kirby of Niagara, dated September 1, 1889, in which he says: "I beg you will inform me more fully about the tradition of Molly Brant being a Cayuga and only an adopted sister of Joseph Brant. It is one of those things that should not be adopted without investigation. You say you 'have it from the family'—some of the Brant family—or Molly's—perhaps from the Hills." He goes on to say that he strongly suspects this alleged "tradition" to be wholly erroneous. Kirby's reply has not been preserved.

The Rev. John Strachan, writing from Kingston in 1819, was the first to allege that Joseph, and by presumption his sister, who was six years his senior, were Brants only by adoption, their father having died

---

(1) W. L. Stone, *The Life and Times of Sir William Johnson, Bart.* 2 vol. Albany, 1865. A. C. Buell, The Family of Sir William Johnson, N.Y., 1903; Arthur Pound, *Johnson of the Mohawks*, N.Y., 1930; F. W. Seymour, *Lords of the Valley*: *Sir William Johnson and his Mohawk Brothers*, N.Y., 1930.
(2) *Cf.* Harvey Chalmers, *West to the Setting Sun*, Toronto, 1943; John J. Vrooman, *Clarissa Putman of Tribes Hill*, Johnstown, N.Y., 1950; Margaret Widdemer, *Lady of the Mohawk*, N.Y., 1951.
(3) W. Max Reid, *The Story of Old Fort Johnson*, N.Y., 1906, pp. 21-22.
(4) In a Return of Loyalists at Carleton Island, Nov. 26, 1738, her age is given as 47. Haldimand Papers, B. 127, p. 338.

Ontario History, Vol. xlv (1953), No. 3.

on the Ohio when they were small children.[5] This same information has been given to me by Chief.Amos Brant of the Tyendinaga Indian Reserve. Other authorities,[6] however, assert that Joseph and Molly were the children of Nickus Brant who owned a substantial frame house and cultivated a prosperous farm at Canajoharie, where he "lived and dressed altogether after the fashion of white men".[7] His father was one of the five Indian Kings who visited Queen Anne in 1710.

Augustus C. Buell, a descendant of Sir William Johnson through Caroline Hendrick, states without citing any authority that Molly was "educated in the common English branches in the manor school at Canajoharie."[8] Whether true or not, extant letters of Molly Brant in the Dominion Archives show her command of English and her superior penmanship.

As a child, she probably visited Fort Johnson after the death of Sir William's first wife, Catherine Weisenberg, when he took as his mistress and housekeeper Caroline Hendrick, daughter of Sachem Abraham and aunt of Molly and Joseph. According to a romantic legend, first recounted by Stone, Johnson fell in love with Molly after Caroline's death about 1752 at a military muster held on his estate. In response to a dare by a mounted ensign, Molly is said to have leaped to the crupper behind him, and with eyes flashing, Indian blanket and braided hair streaming in the wind, capered about the field to Johnson's huge delight. "Becoming enamoured of her person", says Stone, "[the Colonel] brought her to his house."[9]

Various references to a marriage between Sir William and Molly have been tracked down by Mr. Justice Riddell and all declared spurious.[10] Catherine Weisenberg was his only legal wife, although Caroline Hendrick and Molly Brant were in all probability united to him according to Mohawk marriage rites.

As chatelaine of Fort Johnson, the fine stone house still standing near Amsterdam, New York, and later of Johnson Hall, the larger baronial manor which Sir William build in 1762 at Johnstown, Molly held a position of respect and responsibility. Negro slaves cultivated the lands and did the menial chores; a governess looked after Sir William's three legitimate children, and Molly had her personal servants to care for her own growing family, of whom eight, two boys and six girls, survived childhood and were amply provided for in Sir William's will.[11]

In her *Memoirs of an American Lady*, Anne Grant speaks of the lavish entertainment at Johnson Hall, where Sir William "lived like a

---

(5) *Christian Register*, vol. 1, No. 3, Kingston, Upper Canada, 1819.
(6) J. W. Lydekker, *The Faithful Mohawks*, Appendix B, "Pedigree of 'King' Henrick and Joseph Brant", Cambridge, 1938; A. C. Buell, *Sir William Johnson*, N.Y., 1903.
(7) *Ibid.* p. 57.
(8) *Ibid.*
(9) Stone, *Op. Cit.* Vol. I, n. pp. 327-8.
(10) Hon. W. R. Riddell, "Was Molly Brant Married?", OHS *Papers and Records*, vol. xix (1922), pp. 147-57.
(11) Stone, *op. cit.* Appendix.

little sovereign" with his consort, Miss Molly, "an Indian maiden, daughter to a sachem, who possessed an uncommonly agreeable person, and
good understanding . . . and contrived to live with him in great union
and affection all his life".[12] During the month of June, 1765, the actor
William O'Brien and his wife Lady Susan, eldest daughter of the Earl
of the Earl of Ilchester, were guests of Sir William and Molly. In her
correspondence, quoted by Stone, Lady Susan spoke of Miss Molly as a
" 'well bred and pleasant lady' who in many a ramble . . . proved a delightful companion".[13]

All the extant references to Molly during the twenty odd years she
lived with Sir William attest to her personal charm, her competence, the
good terms on which she lived with her English and Dutch neighbours
and with the people of her own race. A contemporary traveller who
saw her in Kingston shortly before her death, says of her earlier life
with Sir William: "When treaties and purchases were about to be made
at Johnson Hall, she often persuaded the obstinate chiefs into compliance
with the proposals."[14]

Upon the death of Sir William in 1774 on the eve of the Revolution,
Molly must have had many forebodings. His last words were to her
brother: "Joseph, control your people". His own people, too, were getting
beyond control as the Continental Congress met to discuss grievances.
Sir William's legal heir, Sir John, and his two brothers-in-law, Col. Guy
Johnson and Col. Daniel Claus, were, all three, ardent royalists who,
before long, joined Haldimand in Canada. Their houses and estates were
promptly confiscated. Molly, whose son, Peter Warren was a Lieutenant
in the British forces at Long Island,[15] and whose two eldest daughters
were at boarding school, moved probably to the Mohawk settlement at
Canajoharie. Here she would be in a favourable position to supply intelligence to the British forces on Long Island or in the north. "Every
endeavour", her son-in-law later stated, "was made use of by the people
in power in the State of New York to prevent her from sacrificing all
her possessions in that country to her attachment to His Majesty, as
they well knew her influence over the Indians."[16] Molly's course was clear,
however, - unswerving allegiance to the ideals of Sir William, Indian
alliance with the British, and unquestioned loyalty to the Crown.

Her first recorded assistance to the British was in 1777 when St.
Leger was attempting a diversionary raid against Fort Stanwix in conjunction with Sir John Johnson, Claus, Butler and Joseph Brant. The
Americans, learning of this expedition through an Oneida spy, rushed
troops north under General Herkimer to surprise the British and their

(12)   Mrs. Anne Grant, *Memoirs of an American Lady, with Sketches of Manners
and Scenes in America as they Existed Previous to the Revolution*, 2 vol., N.Y., 1901,
v. 2, p. 16.
    (13)   Stone, *op. cit.* v. 2, p, 244.
    (14)   Quoted by Canon Starr, *Old St. George's*, Kingston, 1913, p.
    (15)   Killed in action, August 27, 1776.
    (16)

Indian allies. Molly immediately sent a Mohawk runner to St. Leger who was thus able to prepare an ambush eight miles before Fort Stanwix at the Oriskany. General Herkimer was mortally wounded, some 400 of his men killed, and the rest put to flight.

Suspected as the informant, Molly was harried out of the country with her seven children aged four to sixteen, and took refuge with the Five Nations at Onandaga.

Two years later, in Montreal, she gave an account of her experiences to Daniel Claus, who, in his breathless German style, recorded the conversation for the benefit of General Haldimand as follows:

> As soon as Molly Brant heard of my arrival she paid me a visit and gave me a Full Detail of her Adventures and Misfortunes since the Rebellion began, but in particular in Full 1777, after our Retreat from Fort Stanwix when she was insulted and robbed of everything she had in the World by the Rebels and their Indians, which they said she deserved for giving us Intelligence of their Motions which occasioned their being surprized and defeated when she was obliged to leave her home and flee for her and children's safety to the Five Nations wherein she was happily assisted by her brother Joseph & other Indians after their return from Genl Burgoyne's Army and proceeded to Onondaga where she was most kindly received & askd to stay but Cayuga being more centrical and having some distant Relations there, she fixed herself & family at the principal Chiefs home. Upon the news of General Burgoyne's disaster she found the five Nations very wavering and unstable and even the head Man of the Senecas Cayengwaraghton, with whom she had a pointed conversation in Publick Council at Canadasegey, reminding him of the former great Friendship & attachment which sussisted between him and the late Sr Wm Johnson, whose memory she never mentions but with Tears in her Eyes, which affects Indians greatly, and to whom continued she, he so often declared and promised to live and die a firm Friend and Ally to the King of England and his Friends with other striking Arguments and reasonings, which had such an Effect upon that Chief and the rest of the 5 Nations present that they promised her faithfully to stick up strictly to the Engagements of her late worthy Friend, and for his sake and her sake espouse the Kings Cause vigourously and steadily avenge her Wrongs & Injuries for she is in every respect considered & esteemed by them as Sr Wms Relict and one word from her is more taken Notice of by the Five Nations than a thousand from my White Man without Exception."

Col. Claus goes on to say that as soon as Major Butler learned that Molly was at Cayuga, he "sent her repeated and very pressing and encouraging messages to come & reside at Niagara". At first she was reluctant in case her going would offend her hosts, but at length she managed to part with them on friendly terms. Her flight to Niagara was thus by military entreaty, if not command.

She arrived late in the fall of 1777, and appears to have made her home with Joseph for the winter. By summer she had her own establishment and had obtained clothing and other supplies from Col. Claus in

---

(17) Haldimand Papers. B 114, p. 63 ff.

Montreal. One of her extant letters in the Public Archives is the acknowl-
edgement she sent to Claus.

Niagara 23d. June 1778.

Dear Sir

I have been favor'd with yours and the Trunk of Presents by
Mr. Streit, everything mentioned in the Invoice you sent me has come
safe except the pair of gold ear-rings which I have not been able to
find.

We have a report of Joseph having had a brush with the Rebels,
but do not know at what place. A Cauyga Chief is said to be wounded,
one Schohary Indian (Jacob) killed, and one missing since when its
reported that Col. Butler & Joseph have joined. Every hour we look
for a confirmation of this news.

I am much obliged to you for the care and attention in sending
me up those very necessary articles. I should be very glad if you
have any accounts from New York that you would let me know
them as well as of the health of George and Peggy whom I hope
are agreeably settled. My children are all in good health & desire
their loves to you, Mr. Claus, Lady & Sir John Johnson. I hope the
time is very near when we shall all return to our habitations on the
Mohawk River.

I am Dr Sir ever
Affectionately yours,
Mary Brandt[18]

Joseph gave her £30,[19] Haldimand sent her £25,[20] and in the fall another trunk was dispatched by Col. Claus. To the latter she sent a message
of thanks through the traders Taylor and Duffin, explaining that "the
manner she lives here is pretty expensive to her: being obliged to keep,
in a manner, open house for all those Indians that have any weight in
the 6 Nations Confederacy. We have told her" they write, "we will not
see her in want." Joseph is still on the frontier and "Miss Molly says
he now has thoughts of penetrating through to the army in New York . . .
Miss Molly, however, thinks the risk is too great". Instead, he may go
to Quebec to confer with Claus and Haldimand. As for Molly, "if it
were not for the service she thinks she can be of here : in advising and
conversg with the Indians; she wou'd go down to Canada with her
Family".[21]

A letter from Molly written in Mohawk to Chief Deserotyon at
Lachine is quoted by him in writing to Claus, December 23, 1778. She
tells him that a raiding party of 500 left Niagara for Cherry Valley on
October 28, led not by Joseph but by a Senecan chief. The letter is quoted
by Kirby in his *Annals of Niagara* in the original Mohawk and in translation.[22] One point of interest is that it supplies Molly's Indian name,
"Degonwadonti".

(18) Claus Papers, MG 29 (2) p. 29.
(19) Ibid. p. 43.
(20) Haldimand Papers, B 114, pp. 10-12.
(21) Ibid.
(22) William Kirby, *Annals of Niagara*, (Ed. Lorne Pierce), Toronto, 1927, pp.
63-64.

Six months later, Col. Bolton, the Commandant at Niagara, wrote to Haldimand, suggesting that Molly and her family be transferred to Montreal. The problem of providing for so many refugees and Indians in addition to the garrison was becoming acute.[23] The Governor approved and asked Claus to write to Joseph while he directed a personal invitation to Miss Molly. On July 16, Bolton wrote: "Miss Molly & Family have accepted your Excellency's Invitation and will leave this place to-morrow."[24] It was a few weeks later when Claus met her and was told the story of her flight from the Mohawk Valley. In the same memorandum to Haldimand he continues:

> She says her leaving Niagara now is merely owing to your Excellency's kind and friendly Invitation for it at first seemed very hard for her to leave her old Mother & other Indn Relatives & live in a Country she was an entire Stranger in, besides her absence would be regretted by the generality of the five Nations, she having been their Confident in every Matter of Importance & was consulted thereupon, and prevented many an unbecoming and extravagant proposal to the Commanding Officer at Niagara . . . She says [she] expected to see your Excelleny before now at this place & should that not soon be the Case, would be glad to have your Directions about her Situation.[25]

Haldimand promised to see Miss Molly shortly and to do what he could to "make her situation as easy as possible."[26]

Meanwhile the carefully planned Sullivan campaign of 1779 was well under way, destroying crops and villages of the Five Nations, and threatening an assault on Niagara.[27] After settling two of her daughters in a Montreal boarding school, Molly was in great haste to return to Niagara, explaining to Claus that "her staying away at this critical time may prove very injurious to her character hereafter, being at the head of a Society of Six Nations Matrons who have a great deal to say among the young men in particular in time of war".[28] Haldimand immediately informed Claus that "if she thinks her presence necessary she must be suffered to depart";[29] and to Col. Guy Johnson he wrote: "I have acquainted Colonel Claus that Miss Molly is to Act as she thinks best, whether remaining in this province or returning to the Seneca country, and that you or Col. Claus will give her such Presents as you may think necessary, and if she goes provide for her journey as it seems to be a Political one . . ."[30] "I believe," replied Johnson, "she will be of great use to the King's Service at this time."[31]

---

(23) Haldimand Papers, B 104, p. 24.
(24) Ibid. 203.
(25) Claus, op. cit.
(26) Ibid.
(27) Howard Swiggett, War Out of Niagara, N.Y., 1933, p. 185.
(28) Haldimand Papers, B 114, p. 68.
(29) Ibid. p. 70.
(30) B 107, p. 35.
(31) Ibid. p. 36.

The Secretary of State, Lord Germaine, was kept fully informed by Haldimand about the service of Joseph and Miss Molly. On September 13, 1779, he wrote to His Lordship:

His [Joseph's] sister who lived many years with Sir Wm Johnson by whom he had many children and to whose influence he was much indebted in his successful management of the Six Nations, was driven from her home and with her family took refuge at Niagara two years ago. Her situation there not being as comfortable as could be wished, she brought her family down to Montreal by my desire, where I settled her to her satisfaction, but upon hearing of the Rebels advancing into the Indian country, thinking she might be of use in encouraging the Indians to preserve their Fidelity, she returned to Niagara.[32]

In point of fact, Molly got only as far as Carleton Island, which had been established the previous fall and winter as a forwarding post for the upper forts.[33] She arrived on September 29 with five of her children and her two negro maid servants, Jenny and Juba,[34] all of whom were quartered in the Barracks. Every vessel leaving for Niagara was commandeered for troops, Indians and supplies.

As early as the preceding June, the Indian Chiefs had urged that aid should be sent at once under their 'son' Sir John Johnson. But Haldimand, fearing an invasion of Quebec, had been forced to procrastinate. Supply ships had been delayed and there was a desperate shortage of provisions and ammunition.[35] In August, after Butler's Rangers and Indians had been forced to retreat from Chemung to Niagara, demands for a relief force became so insistent that Haldimand ordered a detachment sent from Lachine under Sir John Johnson, whose batteaux must have passed Miss Molly's party on their way to Carleton Island. From near Oswegatchie, Sir John wrote, September 23, "I have pressed forward with the utmost Dispatch, going night and day when it could be done with safety."[36] He arrived at Carleton on the 26th, three days before Molly. Together they must have talked over the situation. At all events, Molly agreed to remain on the island where she could be of immediate service to Captain Fraser, the Commandant, in keeping the remaining Indians from getting out of hand.

It was a fortunate decision. A month later the relief expedition had to turn back, for, as Sir John reported, "owing to the lateness of the season, nothing could be accomplished."[37] Hundreds of disgruntled Indians were thus forced to winter on Carleton Island.

A few months earlier, the Indians there had been reported to Haldimand as "exceedingly troublesome";[38] now, denied the opportunity of

(32) B 54 p. 155.
(33) N. H. Casler, *Cape Vincent and Its History*, Watertown, N.Y., 1906, pp. 33-43.
(34) Haldimand Papers, B 127, p. 338.
(35) *See* E. A. Cruikshank, "The King's Royal Regiment of New York," IV. OHS. *Papers and Records*, vol. 27, pp. 219-226.
(36) *Ibid.* p. 225.
(37) *Ibid.* p. 226.
(38) Casler, op. cit. p. 66.

avenging Sullivan's scorched earth tactics, they were in a mood to turn on their allies. Owing largely to Molly's firm authority, however, no incidents took place during the winter. Captain Fraser praised her services to Haldimand, March 21, 1780: " . . . their [the Indians'] uncommon good behaviour is in a great measure to be ascribed to Miss Molly Brants influence over them, which is far superior to that of all their Chiefs put together and she has in the course of the winter done everything in her power to maintain them strongly in the King's interest . . . "[39]

At about the same time Captain Gilbert Tice wrote to Col. Claus from Carleton Island: "I enclose you Sir a letter from Miss Molly Brant who has shown her usual zeal for Gov't by her constant endeavour to maintain the Indians in His Majesty's Interest—I wish you would find an occasion of putting His Excellency in mind of her numerous family—I have wrote the General to acquaint him of the assistance she gave in keeping the Indians orderly and well disposed and I have done all that lay in my power to make their quarters agreable to Her and her family."[40]

On June 21, 1780, Molly took the opportunity of leaving the island with Col. Butler who was en route to Montreal. This independent action considerably upset the Commandant who wrote an oddly inconsistent letter to the Governor suggesting that Molly was probably going to make unreasonable demands for herself and her family and "will probably wish to change her place of Residence and may want to go to Niagara". Worse still, "she may by the violence of her temper be led to create mischief". With the greatest altruism he advises that she be kept at Carleton Island where he could have a house built for her "as it would be more comfortable for her family than living in barracks".[41] His alarm is transparent lest her valuable assistance, temper or no temper, be denied to him. Haldimand calmed his fears by informing him, through Captain Mathews, that Miss Molly's "inclination fortunately leads her to settle at Carleton Island, rather than return to Niagara" Fraser is directed to have built for her "a House as will lodge Her and Family comfortably, chusing a favorable Situation within a few hundred Yards of the Fort".[42]

The winter of 1780-81 was not particularly eventful at Carleton Island. Molly passed on to Haldimand information which she had obtained about rebel activities from another Indian woman, Mary Aaron, who had been General Schuyler's mistress but had deserted him to join the loyalists during one of Sir John Johnson's raids on the Mohawk valley.[43]

When Captain Fraser was relieved as Commandant by Major Ross, he reported to Haldimand: "I gave particular directions regarding Miss Molly, she has got into her new house, and seemed better satisfyed with her situation than I have ever known her before."[44]

(39)   Claus Papers, MG 29 (2) p. 177.
(40)   Ibid. p. 173.
(41)   Haldimand Papers, B 110, p. 111.
(42)   Ibid. B 128, p. 72.
(43)   B 114, p. 153.
(44)   B 127, p. 214.

In April, Molly was in deep concern over a report that Joseph had been "almost murdered" by certain officers of Col. Guy Johnson at Niagara, on his return from a scout. "I entreat His Excellency General Haldimand," she wrote to Claus, "to use His authority and settle this matter, it is hard for me to have an only Bror whom I dearly love, to see him thus treated, but what I am most concerned about is that it may affect the King's Indn Interest".[45] The report was apparently false, but Haldimand wrote to General Powell at Niagara, instructing him to "see that Colonel Johnson gives that support to Joseph which his services & attachment to Government really merit".[46]

In July 1781, Molly went to Montreal to bring back three of her children who had been attending school, and asked Claus to express her gratitude to the Governor for his assistance. Mathews replied that "His Excellency is pleased to find his Intuition in the Education of Miss Molly's Children has so well succeeded and that she appears sensible of the Benefit they have Received".[47]

For two more years Molly remained on Carleton Island, although henceforth she is seldom mentioned in the official correspondence. When it became obvious that peace would have to be concluded, Haldimand, fearing the Indian reaction, wrote to Major Ross instructing him to represent to the Indians "the destructive consequences of being perpetually at war".[48] Molly's authority was no doubt again at the service of the Commandant. She must have shared Joseph's resentment when the terms of peace ignored the Indian alliance, but there were no uprisings on Carleton Island.

The frontier forts were not to be immediately evacuated, but Haldimand in the summer of 1783 decided upon Cataraqui as a military post. Ross reported that it would be "as capacious for both troops and stores . . . as Carleton Island ever was". Three houses had already been moved to the mainland. "On my arrival here", he continues, "I received the enclosed letter from Miss Molly, and if the General approves of a house being built for her it can soon be done".[49] Replying for Haldimand, Mathews wrote: "His Excellency has perused Miss Molly's letter and has no objection to your complying with Her Request".[50]

A month later Joseph visited Cataraqui but found no sign of the promised house for his sister. His displeasure brought a prompt note from Ross to Headquarters. "I hear that Joseph is exceedinly Surprised that no house is as yet built for Miss Molly I will write to him by the first opportunity that it shall be done as soon as possible".[51] To keep

(45)   B 114, p. 169.
(46)   B 104, p. 214.
(47)   B 114, p. 195.
(48)   B 124, p. 78.
(49)   B 126, p. 24 (Molly's letter is not preserved).
(50)   *Ibid.*   p. 40.
(51)   B 126, p. 62.

Joseph in good humour, the Governor proposed that Ross have a second house built. "As it is natural that Joseph Brant would wish to have a Home contiguous to His Sister for the purpose of leaving His Family under Her protection when Called abroad by War, or Business, I would have a comfortable House Built for him as near as possible (but distinct from) to Molly's—it will give them both Satisfaction . . . "[52]

On February 17, 1784, Major Ross wrote: "Capt. Brant who is the bearer of this letter seems highly pleased with the favor shown him by His Excellency in Causing a house to be built for him at Cataraqui which together with Miss Mollys is in great forwardness and to flatter him Still more Some little alteration has been made agreeable to his wishes".[53] An inventory of "work completed and in hand during the winter" dated June 14, 1784 includes: "Captain Brant's House 40 foot in front by 30 in depth and one storey and a half complete. Miss Molly Brant's House nearly complete".[54]

The site of the two houses was near the Cataraqui on land now occupied by Anglin's Lumber Yard. Both have long since been torn down and not even the foundation stones remain to mark their place.[55]

Of Miss Molly's life in Cataraqui, soon to be re-christened Kingston, little information remains. In 1785, while Joseph was in England, she paid a last visit to her beloved Mohawk Valley. We know this from a land petition of her son-in-law, John Ferguson, in which he states "that in the year 1785 she, Mary Brant, went to Schenectady at which time great offers were made to Her by the same people [the Americans] if she and Her family would return to that country and about three years ago, they offered to Her and to such of Her children as would return a sum of money equal to the sum their lands were sold for by the Commission of Confiscation . . . that these offers altho' very great were rejected with the utmost contempt".[56]

The events that must have meant most to Molly Brant in her latter years were the successive marriages of five daughters into the upper society of the new province. Possibly before she left Carleton Island, her eldest daughter, Elizabeth, married Dr. Robert Kerr of Niagara; Magdalen, in 1791 married John Ferguson of Kingston who became a member of the legislature of Upper Canada. Margaret became the wife of Captain George Farley of the 60th Regiment; Susannah, wife of Ensign Henry Lamoine of the 24th Regiment. Anne (or Nancy) married a naval officer, Captain Hugh Earl, for whom Earl Street in Kingston is named.

---

(52) *Ibid.* p. 85.
(53) Ibid. p. 99.
(54) Cruikshank, *op. cit.* p. 312.
(55) Katherine Hale in *Historic Houses of Canada* (Toronto, 1952) p. 75, repeats the misinformation given in two of her earlier books that Molly Brant's house is still standing.
(56) Upper Canada Land Petitions, F³ No. 41, 1797.

Mary alone remained single. George, the only surviving son, married and became a farmer.[57]

Molly is twice mentioned in Mrs. Simcoe's *Diary*. On September 13, 1794, they sailed together on the *Mississaga* from Niagara to Kingston. The Governor had ordered, for the greater comfort of his wife, that all passengers be excluded, "but I relented," writes Mrs. Simcoe, "in favour of Brant's sister who was ill and very desirous to go. She speaks English well and is a civil and very sensible old woman."[58] Next year, Molly did a good turn for the Simcoes. The Governor was ill in Kingston without a medical attendant and wracked by a cough which prevented him from sleeping. Mrs. Simcoe was at her wit's end until "Capt. Brant's sister prescribed a root . . . which really relieved his cough in a very short time."[59]

An anonymous traveller who visited Upper Canada in the seventeen nineties gives us our last glimpse of Miss Molly. "In the Church at Kingston," he says, "we saw an Indian woman who sat in an honourable place among the English. She appeared very devout during Divine Service and very attentive to the Sermon. She was the relict of the late Sir William Johnson, Superintendent of Indian Affairs in the province of New York, and mother of several children by him, who are married to Englishmen and provided for by the Crown . . . When Indian embassies arrived she was sent for, dined at Governor Simcoe's, and was treated with respect by himself and his lady . . . During the life of Sir William, she was attended with spendor and respect, and since the war receives a pension and compensation for losses for herself and her children.[60]

On April 16, 1796, in her sixty-first year, Molly Brant died and was buried in St. George's churchyard (now St. Paul's) by the Rev. Dr. John Stuart, whose appointment, twenty-six year earlier, to the Indian mission at Fort Hunter, he owed to Sir William Johnson. No record remains of the funeral save Dr. Stuart's inscription of her name and the date under "Burials" in the Parish Records.[61] Some years ago, Lieut. Col. C. E. Long located a number of tomb stones and memorials under St. Paul's parish hall. "He regrets he did not find Molly Brant's grave or a stone to her memory".[62]

(57) E. M. Chadwick, *Ontarian Families*, Toronto, 1894, v. 1, p. 67; *The Parish Register of Kingston, Upper Canada, 1785-1811*, Ed. A. H. Young, Kingston, 1921 (Introduction, p. 60, states erroneously that Mrs. Kerr was Molly's niece); Mrs. Celia B. File, "Descendants of Molly Brant and Sir William Johnson" (Typescript in Ontario Department of Public Records and Archives).
(58) *The Diary of Mrs. John Graves Simcoe*, Ed. J. Ross Robertson, Toronto, 1911, p. 247.
(59) *Diary, op. cit.* pp. 274-5.
(60) Quoted by G. L. Starr, *Old St. George's*, Kingston, 1913, pp. 29-30.
(61) *Parish Register, op. cit.* p. 156.
(62) C. E. Long, *A Sketchy History of St. Paul's Church, Kingston, Ontario* . . . Kingston, 1937, p. 12.

We have tried to piece together an account of Molly Brant from various scraps of information largely disconnected except for the decade 1774-84 when her activities can be fairly closely documented. What deductions can we make about Miss Molly? What manner of woman was this Mohawk matron who commanded the attention and respect of savages, soldiers, ordinary citizens, aristocrats, generals, governors, and even the British Secretary of State? What she *did* we now know, at least in part; what she *was* we can judge partly from her own actions, partly from the testimony of those who knew her. No portrait, drawing, or any other likeness of Molly Brant has been preserved, so far as I can discover. If she resembled her brother Joseph, whose portraits are well known, we may picture her as being of medium height, with fine features, the jet black hair and high cheek-bones of her race, but probably a lighter complexion owing to her civilized mode of life. Isaac Weld, who wrote an account of his travels in North America during the years 1795 to 1797, says of the Iroquois women: " . . . when young their faces and persons are really pleasing, not to say sometimes captivating". He points out, however, that they age very rapidly and soon lose their youthful attractiveness. "I never saw an Indian woman of the age of thirty but what her eyes were sunk, her forhead wrinkled, her skin loose and shrivelled, and her whole person in short forbidding."[63] Miss Molly, we may fairly assume, in large measure escaped this common metamorphosis, attended as she was at Johnson Hall with "spendor and respect".

A woman of extraordinary competence, her mind was always active and alert as suggested by her bold and cursive handwriting, and the "striking arguments and reasonings" with which she supported her council in public debate. She assumed an authority which she was wont to exercise in adversity as in prosperity; indeed, there was a personal magnetism about her which captivated redmen and white men of high or low degree. A titled Englishwoman who spent a month as her guest considered her "well-bred"; the clergy respected her no less than the rough woodsmen. She was a woman of high principles not to be set aside for private gain. When the war was over she could have returned to the Mohawk Valley to live in affluence at the price of renouncing her British connection; but this proposal she "rejected with contempt".

Posterity has done scant justice to this remarkable woman—a threefold loyalist, to Sir William, to the Mohawks, and to the Crown.

---

(63) Isaac Weld, Jr., *Travels through the States of North America and the Provinces of Upper and Lower Canada during the Years 1795, 1796, and 1797.* London, 4th ed. 1800, p.452.

EARLY WOMEN PRINTERS OF AMERICA

Ellen M. Oldham

Early Women Printers of America

By ELLEN M. OLDHAM

THE annals of printing in America before the Revolution have preserved the names of eleven women who supported themselves by this profession. Seven colonies and ten towns knew their presence; five did official printing for the government; all but one carried on the constant care of a weekly newspaper. For a short time there may have been four women operating in different parts of the country, a remarkable fact in the days before the emancipation of women. It is well worth making a brief study of these ladies. What did they have in common? What were their backgrounds, and what the trials they had to face? Many important details will probably remain unknown, but much useful material can be located through the journals of the legislatures and the pages of their own newspapers.

The earliest member of the group was Dinah Nuthead, who worked in Maryland about 1696; the latest was Mary Katharine Goddard who, beginning her career before the Revolution, continued on to the middle of the next decade, also in Maryland. Three, at least, were immigrants; one died in England. All but one were married, the mothers of numerous children. Each was in her late thirties when she took up her trade; one may have been little more than forty when she died, while one lived to ninety. The extent of their active careers varies from the twenty-three years of Ann Franklin at Newport, Rhode Island, to the one year and one month of Clementina Rind, at Williamsburg, Virginia. The one uniting factor was the necessity of supporting themselves, and in most cases their children, upon the death of their husbands, good printers all! The only exceptions were Sarah and Mary Katharine Goddard, mother and sister of the printer William Goddard.

Six of the women had sons who also became printers, in most cases completing their apprenticeship under their mother's supervision. As they came of age, the boys would take a more or less important part in the firm, but in several instances the mother definitely considered herself the head and continued so for some time. All eleven women must hāve had unusual forcefulness of character. Benjamin Franklin preferred the accounting of Elizabeth Timothy to that of her husband, and he spoke highly of her abilities in his *Autobiography;* Anne Catherine Green of Annapolis seems to have been a bit disdainful of her husband's "lenity and backwardness in collecting his just debts," and one gets the impression that *she* had no intention of standing for such nonsense.

Many of the problems and much of the daily life of these women were shared, of course, by all printers of the time, and for that reason will be discussed briefly here. A standard stock-in-trade of almost all printers in these early days was the blank form. These included all types of legal documents used in the indenture of apprentices, the sale of slaves or real estate, drawing up of wills and letters of administration, ships' bills of lading, and so forth. Though the twentieth-century form executed in quintuplicate was not prevalent, there was a tremendous amount of paper work, and the advent of a printer in the community was a great boon to the local lawyers and officials. This bread-and-butter sort of work bore no imprint and is hard to identify.

In his office the printer usually had for sale not only these blanks and copies of his own publications, but a selection of other books and often a wide variety of miscellaneous merchandise. Although the only true store was that of Cornelia Bradford in Philadelphia, with a complete line of stationery supplies, it was a common occurrence for a printer to receive payment in kind for a newspaper subscription or a bit of job-printing; he in turn would dispose of the goods through his office. Thus Mrs. Zenger in New York offered "very good Canary wine" and Mrs. Crouch at Salem could provide "a few bolts of English Duck." The office served as an accommodation address for many of the newspaper's advertisers who might live some distance away. It was a frequent procedure for a notice to read "wanted, a wet nurse" or "for information about a good negroe servant inquire at the Printing Office."

The output of these presses varied, but none ranked high in quantity. An almanac, a few broadsides, a pamphlet or two were the extent of a year's publication. For some, printing the records of the government sessions was a task recurring annually or even quarterly. But the newspaper was the principal occupation of the staff. It had its own problems, chief among them being the difficulty of getting news regularly and promptly. This is not the place for a discussion of provincial newspapers; it will be sufficient to note a few of the apologies offered by the lady publishers. Mrs. Rind had to announce, in February 1774, "no mail from the Northward this week"; and Mrs. Crouch, founding the *Salem Gazette* in wintertime, admitted that news would be hard to come by for awhile. The latter was troubled as well by the failure of her paper supply, and was forced "to make use of an inferior quality" on several occasions.

But while lack of news or paper might be humiliating, it was lack of money that really hurt. The tremendous growth of consumer credit is a notable phenomenon of our time, but certainly in those days few people paid cash in advance, at least to the printer. The minimum number of subscribers to make a weekly paper a financial possibility was about three hundred; unfortunately, many subscribers let their bills pile up for years. It was a source of constant distress to printers everywhere, and the pages of their newspapers were filled with pleas to settle up and threats of retribution. Mrs. Zenger was forced to request, "All persons in arrear for this paper, are desired to pay off the arrearage, to enable the Printer to keep the press going"; and Mrs. Timothy of Charleston, South Carolina, warned that "Persons will be employ'd" to collect from subscribers who "owe from three to eight years."

As to the actual part the ladies played in their printing offices, there is little information. Isaiah Thomas, the great printer-publisher and historian of American printing, reported that the daughters of Ann Franklin were "correct and quick compositors"; and undoubtedly in many instances the female as well as the male proprietor had to be prepared to take over such work in an emergency. Editorial work and the handling of accounts were more likely their accustomed occupations; yet even here one notes that at one time or another most of the women had partners.

Dinah Nuthead, Ann Franklin, and Cornelia Bradford

THE story of Dinah Nuthead has been told by Lawrence Wroth in as full detail as it is likely to be known; only a brief summary is needed here.[1] Her husband, William Nuthead, set up his printing plant — the second of the colonies — in Jamestown, Virginia, in 1682. However, the authorities were against the enterprise and he shortly moved to Maryland, where he acted as public printer for the Province and had also a flourishing business in all sorts of printed forms. What else he produced is hard to tell, since only a single broadside of his remains.

Dinah Nuthead — her maiden name, as well as the date of her marriage, is unknown — was a woman of little education since she seems never to have learned to write. Her husband died early in 1695, without leaving a will. The inventory of his property shows that, besides the printing press and type which were appraised at only five pounds, his principal legacy was that of uncollected debts. There were at least sixty accounts outstanding, with the amount owed ranging from thirty to three thousands pounds of tobacco (the medium of currency), with a total value of nearly one hundred pounds sterling.

Shortly before his death William had signed a petition against the removal of Maryland's capital from St. Mary's City, his home, to the new town of Annapolis. But in spite of the many protests, the government did move and with them went Widow Nuthead and her two children, William and Susannah. She applied for and obtained permission to print, two of her former neighbors in St. Mary's posting a hundred pound bond for her good behavior. The government however stipulated that Mrs. Nuthead only use the press for the printing of "blank bills, bonds, writts, warrants of attorney, letters of administration, and other like blanks," unless a special license was obtained from the Governor.

Until 1930 no remnants of Dinah's printing were known. In that year a number of printed forms were found in the Maryland Land Office which proved, because King William III's name alone was used in the legal formulas, to be attributable only to her. These poor fragments are not lovely; short though they are, they are full of errors of spelling. Yet they are the earliest output of an American woman's press.

Dinah Nuthead carried on her husband's business for a short time; soon she remarried, her second husband being Manus Devoran. After the latter's death in 1700, she was married once more, to a German by the name of Sebastian Oley, whom she also survived.

Ann Franklin, sister-in-law of Benjamin Franklin, wife of a printer and mother of another, was the first woman in the colonies whose imprint appeared on a book as publisher. She was also the first American woman to act as printer to a legislative body. The daughter of Samuel and Anna Smith, she was born in Boston on October 2, 1696, and married James Franklin in 1723. For a few years the couple remained in Boston where James had his printing shop, but in 1727 they moved to Newport, Rhode Island.

Early in 1735 Mrs. Franklin was left a widow·with three young daughters and a son. She immediately set herself to carrying on the work of the press and soon issued a hundred and fifty page volume, *A Brief Essay on the Number Seven* . . . The next fall she upheld an age-old printers' tradition by publishing an almanac, prepared by Joseph Stafford. Two years later, when Stafford's work was turned over to a Boston firm, she was forced to prepare her own, thus becoming also one of the first woman almanac writers. The series, utilizing her husband's pseudonym of "Poor Robin," continued for three years. After that she depended upon Benjamin Franklin to supply her shop with almanacs.

In October, 1736, the General Assembly of the colony had voted to issue a supplement to the public laws, appointing a committee to "treat with the Widow Franklin about printing said acts, and inquire into her ability for that purpose; and if it appears to them that she is qualified for the same, and they can agree with her upon reasonable terms, that she be employed to do the same as conveniently as may be." Ann Franklin was duly adjudged "qualified," and the parties agreed to the "reasonable terms" of ten pounds.

Early in 1744 a complete revision of the *Acts and Laws* was

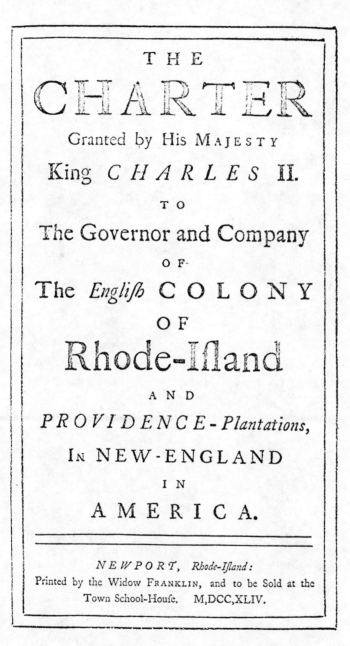

THE
CHARTER
Granted by His MAJESTY
King *CHARLES* II.

TO

The Governor and Company

OF

The *English* COLONY

OF

Rhode-Island

AND

PROVIDENCE - *Plantations,*

IN NEW-ENGLAND

IN

AMERICA.

NEWPORT, *Rhode-Island:*
Printed by the Widow FRANKLIN, and to be Sold at the
Town School-House.   M,DCC,XLIV.

Facsimiles of Title-Page-Reduced

voted to be printed in an edition of five hundred copies and bound in marble paper. The Committee of the Assembly provided the paper, and John Callender, one of its members, was paid thirty pounds "for correcting the press." Mrs. Franklin, however, printed a number of law books for herself, "over and above what she was employed to print for the colony." She was disciplined for her breach of the contract by being forbidden to sell any of her extra books for one year, upon penalty of five pounds per book sold. (Since the price for the copies in the hands of the General Treasurer was only thirty shillings, there was little incentive for her to disobey.) Yet when the Assembly decided in 1747 that the record of their sessions should be printed regularly — rather than transcribed by hand for each town — it was specifically authorized "that the printer shall have liberty to make as many more copies as he or she shall think fit, and dispose of the same for his or her private profit or advantage." From then on the Franklin firm was responsible for printing the so-called Schedules.[2]

In the summer of 1748 James Franklin Jr. became a partner with his mother. Next year he issued the first book with his name alone in the imprint, William Penn's *Some Fruits of Solitude*. His mother, however, was by no means ready to retire, especially where money was concerned. For ten more years bills submitted for government work were made out in the joint names of Ann and James Franklin.

In 1758 James Franklin started a weekly newspaper, the *Newport Mercury*. It got him into trouble with the legislature because of his delay in printing the record of the sessions. He admitted his fault, but, "having procur'd an assistant," he promised to do better in the future. Yet without his mother's efficient hand in the printing office, things continued to go wrong. James mislaid a whole batch of finished sheets one year, to the disgust of the Secretary. In fact, this "high, mighty, indolent gentleman" so incensed the Assembly that the law requiring the printing of the sessions to be done by the Newport printer was repealed and at least twice in 1759 the work was sent to Boston. However, the following year the task was returned to James Franklin's office.

After the death of her son in April 1762, Ann Franklin, at

the age of sixty-five, emerged from her retirement to carry on the business once more. For a year, with the help of Samuel Hall she continued the *Newport Mercury,* and printed the Schedules and individual Acts for the government. On April 19, 1763, she died, having outlived all her children. The obituary in her newspaper paid her high tribute:

> . . . She was a woman of great integrity and uprightness in her station and conversation, and was well beloved in the town. She was a faithful friend, and a compassionate benefactor to the poor . . . and often relieved them in the extremity of winter. And, she was a constant and seasonable attendant on public worship, and would not suffer herself to be detained by trivial family-concerns: herein she excell'd most of her sex . . .[3]

*

Cornelia Smith Bradford, of a well-to-do New York family, was the second wife of Andrew Bradford, the son of William Bradford and for some years the only printer in Philadelphia. Andrew died there in November of 1742, two years after his marriage. Besides his personal effects, he bequeathed his widow his share in the Durham Iron Works and five hundred acres of land in lower Dublin Pennsylvania. The real estate in Philadelphia and the printing press and its appurtenances were left for Cornelia's use in her lifetime.[4]

Even more than the usual delays were attendant upon the settling of the estate, for while the first notice to pay debts and present accounts appeared on March 24, 1743, a year and a half later Cornelia was forced to threaten the debtors "to put that in execution against them, which if possible, she would by all means avoid." Three years later she was still pleading for settlement.

A week after Andrew Bradford's death the *American Weekly Mercury,* which he had founded in 1718, re-appeared, with heavy black lines on every page. The new publisher, "the Widow Bradford," apologized for the omission of the previous issue and notified her customers that "all persons who have any printing work to do, or have any occasion for stationary ware, shall be thankfully serv'd at the lowest prices." For a while she had as editor and manager Isaiah Warner, a "young Beginner" he called himself, who had served his apprenticeship in the Bradford shop. But in the fall of 1744 he went out on his own, and for the next two years, till the paper ceased publication, Mrs. Bradford's name alone appeared in the imprint.

Philadelphians must have been avid users of almanacs, for from November 1 to December 31, 1743, the firm of Bradford and Warner printed no less than five: those of William Ball, William Birkett, John Jerman, Titan Leed, and Jacob Taylor. This first year, however, marks the highpoint of Cornelia's output. By 1746 she was publishing only Birkett. There is no evidence for any production from her press in the following two years, but then for three consecutive years she again published an almanac.

Mrs. Bradford had another important source of income in the family store which sold stationery supplies of all types as well as many books. "Good English glue" could be bought both wholesale and retail, while lamp-black was made and sold. Book-binding was a regular service; customers however were apt to forget to return for their orders, forcing Cornelia to announce that all books not called for would be sold to pay for the binding. The Bradford company had been advertised from the beginning as "at the sign of the Bible," and the widow carried on the tradition by stocking "folio, octavo and duodecimo Bibles, Testaments of several prices, large & small Common-Prayer-Books, Tate & Brady's Psalms." She had both serious and lighter works for sale, as well as children's primers; the most popular author was Daniel Defoe with four of his books on the list — one of them being *Moll Flanders*.

Cornelia Bradford died in August 1755. Her will is an interesting document, giving much information about her family and possessions. Her property was to be divided among her two nephews and two nieces; indeed, three of the legatees were already occupying houses on their land. Her two negro servants were given their freedom, with the added provision of three pounds a year if either of them should become incapable of earning a living. Her will was signed with an "X," which, unless the result of temporary physical inability, indicates that, in spite of her years of association with books, Mrs. Bradford, like Dinah Nuthead, was illiterate.[5]

Elizabeth Timothy, Printer of South Carolina

ELIZABETH TIMOTHY, for eight years printer of the Colony of South Carolina, was born in the first years of the eighteenth century in Holland. She married there, about 1723, a young Huguenot refugee, Louis Timothée, who took up printing as a trade. In 1731 the couple, together with their four children, emigrated to America. Landing in Philadelphia, Timothée attempted to support his family as a teacher. In the *Philadelphia Gazette* for October 14, 1731, his advertisement first appeared:

> This is to give notice, that Mr. Louis Timothee, master of the French tongue, hath settled himself with his family in this city, in order to keep a publick French school; he will also, if required, teach the said language to any young Gentlemen or Ladies, at their lodgings.
> He dwelleth in Front-street, next door to Dr. Kearsley.

About this time Timothée became acquainted with young Benjamin Franklin, and in June of the following year the two joined in promoting a bi-weekly German newspaper, to be known as the *Philadelphische Zeitung*. Timothée was described as "language master," responsible for translating any advertisements. The venture was not a success, yet Franklin's association with the family was to continue for more than forty years. Timothée became a journeyman in his establishment, and for some time served as the first librarian of the Philadelphia Library Company. At the time he lived in a house in Jones Alley (now Church Street), one room of which was set aside for the Library.[6]

In the fall of 1733 Timothée entered into a six-year contract with Franklin to go to Charleston, South Carolina, and take over the printing office of the late Thomas Whitmarsh who, himself financed by Franklin, had gone there in answer to an appeal by the Governor and House of Assembly. Elizabeth stayed in Philadelphia at least through the following March to settle their affairs. Franklin's ledger and journal show that she paid him, on her departure, some sixteen pounds, of which fourteen were for rent which he had advanced. In the meantime her husband had re-established Whitmarsh's paper, the

South-Carolina Gazette, and shortly thereafter anglicized his name to Lewis Timothy.

During the next few years Mrs. Timothy was doubtless kept busy with her growing family. The southern town was congenial, for it had a large Huguenot population, most of which, like the Timothys themselves, turned to a more socially "correct" church, the Timothys joining St. Philip's Episcopal Church. Lewis became a founder of the South Carolina Society, a social and charitable organization of Franco-Americans, and in 1736 obtained a land grant of six hundred acres and a town lot in Charleston. This period of calm prosperity was broken in the summer of 1738 by a smallpox epidemic which took the life of his youngest boy. In October Timothy apologized for a delay in his paper "by reason of sickness, myself and son having been visited with this feaver that reigns at present." By the end of the year he was dead, although it seems by accident.

On January 4, 1739, Mrs. Timothy announced her resolution to carry on the paper as usual, hoping "by the assistance of my friends, to make it as entertaining and correct as may be reasonably expected," and requesting her husband's subscribers and benefactors "to continue their favours and good offices to his poor afflicted Widow and six small children and another hourly is expected." As the contract with Franklin had not yet run its course, it was continued with Mrs. Timothy, and at the end of the year she was able to buy up the press and equipment for herself. From the first, it was the name of her eldest boy Peter, about fourteen, that alone appeared in the imprint both of the newspaper and of the books they published. Yet the business and financial end of things she kept firmly in her own hands.

Although as early as the end of January 1739 the Timothys advertised two books (both continuations of the smallpox-inoculation controversy, which had been going on for some time) as "being in the press," neither one appeared until the middle of May, and little other work was done that year except for the *Gazette.* Mrs. Timothy explained in November when, as administrator of the estate, she requested a prompt settlement of all debts, that "she hath been much retarded by sickness, as well of herself as her family." During the preceding fall she had lost two more sons.

At this same time the House of Commons paid to her, as administrator, the sum of £173, which it owed to her husband toward the printing of the Session Laws for the previous year. From then, at least till the middle of 1746, there is a full account of her relations with that body as public printer for the colony.[7] Her first big problem arose in connection with these same laws, for, presumably because of sickness and the difficulty of getting proper help, their printing was greatly delayed. She presented a petition to the legislature early in 1741, pointing out that, although several sheets had been printed by her husband before his death, she "was left, with a large family of seven small children, greatly involved in debt, on account of printing the said laws, and unable to go on with the printing them, till in a few months past." The work was to have been paid for in large measure by subscriptions, and she went on to say that, because of the delay, "many of the subscribed either died, or had departed this province; most of whom having received part of the said laws, had left the remaining-part in the hands of the petitioner unpaid for." There was still another problem: the General Assembly had agreed to allow Timothy a gratuity of five pounds per sheet for this, but

the petitioner had been obliged to send for a workman to help finish the said laws; to whom the petitioner paid the sum of £4 and 10s per week besides his board. Since which it appeared to the petitioner, labouring under the disadvantages afore-mentioned, that the said £5:00:00 per sheet was greatly insufficient to enable the petitioner to go on with the printing the said laws.

Upon due deliberation, the House agreed to increase the allowance to six pounds per sheet, "in consideration of the petitioner's delivering fifty-five copies of the printed laws," one for each of the members of His Majesty's Council and the members of the House of Commons.

In the meantime the Timothy firm had been printing various Acts and Reports for the legislators, both separately and in the pages of the *Gazette*. But after a bill of £56:15 had been presented, largely for printing proclamations and abstracts of laws in the newspaper, the House voted to make no further provision for paying such charges, "it being the opinion of this House that those articles may be inserted in that paper instead of news." They had reasons also for dissatisfaction with the execution of the work. On November 24, 1742, they decided to look for another printer:

Whereas the printer in this Province hath not printed the Laws and other public business with that accuracy and dispatch which was necessary, it is therefore resolved, that any capable printer who shall come over to this Province from England to settle here shall (during his good behaviour) have the printing of the Laws and all other public business.

Poor Mrs. Timothy! A considerable portion of her income came from official work, and its elimination would have been a severe blow. Fortunately, nothing more was heard of this resolution in the Journals, and the relations between legislature and printer continued more or less amicably.

Benjamin Franklin testified to Mrs. Timothy's capable business sense, which apparently included a habit of padding her accounts. On several occasions the Committee on Petitions and Accounts was forced to take her to task. In February 1743 they found an over-charge of some £35 out of a total bill of £1,135, and shortly after they were emphatic:

We think her account is exorbitant, as to the charge of printing the Report on the Augustine expedition, and recommend it to be reconsidered. We observe that she hath charged £20 per sheet for the report, and £25 per sheet for the Appendix, whereas in the same account she hath charged only £10 per sheet for printing some laws, which, upon examination are found to contain in the same type more words in a line, and more lines in a page, than the said Report doth; and therefore we think there can be no reason for allowing more for the Report or Appendix than for the Laws, but rather the contrary, as she was so dilatory and negligent in printing the Report.

The upshot was a new resolution that two hundred pounds be deducted out of the sum allowed the printer "and that the matter be further enquired into next year."

On another occasion, however, Elizabeth came off victoriously. The Committee "observed an over-charge of sundry articles, amounting to twenty-nine pounds" in one account, but when referred to the House it appeared that "an article of twenty-five pounds charged in the said account, and disallowed by the committee, was done by the order of his Majesty's Honourable Council." The latest volume of the House of Commons Journals, published only in 1956, ends in the middle of 1746, at which time it is likely that Mrs. Timothy ceased from active participation in the firm. In the seven and a half years preceding, as the records show, at least twenty-eight hundred pounds had been paid to her for government work.

Although the legislators criticized the Timothy firm for dilatoriness, the presses were far from idle. Besides the official printing and the weekly paper, there was a steady stream of other works, the majority of a religious nature. The local preachers had many of their sermons printed, and before the end of 1746 at least five volumes had appeared by or relating to George Whitefield. Among the more interesting products are a *Historical Narrative of the Colony of Georgia,* published in 1741 by subscription; *A Black Joak Blazing, or The secret History of Caesar & Dianna, a poem humbly inscribed to Mrs. Bald-Joak* (1741); and the translation of a French work by James de la Chappelle on the culture and manufacture of indigo (1746).

Mrs. Timothy continued her good relations with Benjamin Franklin, and his account books show that he kept her supplied, among other things, with almanacs, since the Timothys at no time seem to have issued one of their own. He had previously helped her husband in the same way. There is no indication of any orders for the years 1739 (just after Lewis's death) or 1740, but for the next eight years the little volumes arrived regularly, usually averaging two or three hundred copies. On January 5, 1745, Franklin billed her for one thousand, the largest single order recorded from the firm. In February 1741 Mrs. Timothy published *The Querists* (a pamphlet in the Whitefield controversy); and as the edition apparently sold out, she purchased two and a half dozen copies from Franklin's edition. Occasionally Franklin acted as agent for various types of merchandise, shipping her a box of candles and barrels of beer, tallow, and flour, and once half a gallon of varnish.[8]

Peter Timothy seems to have attained his majority about the middle of 1746, and at that time Elizabeth turned the business completely over to him. In that year she made it known that she planned "to depart this Province," and requested all those still indebted either to the estate of Lewis Timothy or to herself for the *Gazette* and other things to pay off their debts at once. Yet in June Benjamin Franklin had sent her "sundry books" to the amount of £12:18, and in December she was operating a small book and stationery store. The next March she was to receive a further shipment, books of a religious turn, the largest quantity of a single item being two dozen "Scotch Psalters."

Soon afterwards she really left Charleston. Between 1748, when her attorney advertised in her absence for a prompt settling of her affairs, and July 1756, when she was back in Charleston, her whereabouts is unknown. It is possible that she had returned to Philadelphia. She died sometime in April 1757, and her will shows how well her business abilities had served her. To her son Peter, successfully carrying on the family firm, she left "all my Books of Account . . . and whatsoever may be due upon said Books." She left in his custody also "a silver watch which did belong to my late husband," with the provision that it should go eventually to her grandson. Of her three daughters, two were married and one a widow; to each she left a house and two or three slaves, as well as other bequests.[9]

Peter Timothy, as he reached middle age, became increasingly involved in politics and thought seriously of giving up the business in favor of "getting a post."[10] Fortunately for his wife, Ann Donavan, he never realized his ambition; and, when in 1782 he and two of their married daughters were shipwrecked and drowned, his widow was able to carry on the family tradition and take over the press herself until her death ten years later. The child of their old age, Benjamin Franklin Timothy, continued the paper into the nineteenth century.

The Widow of John Peter Zenger

WITH the exception of Benjamin Franklin, the Zengers of New York, because of their outstanding position in the history of the freedom of the press, have had greater popular appeal than any other early American printers. Within recent years biographies have appeared both about John Peter Zenger and his wife.[11]

On September 11, 1722, Anna Catharine Maul or Maulin was married in the old Dutch Reformed Church of New York to John Peter Zenger, a young widower of twenty-five. They belonged to those refugee families from the Palatinate who had fled first to the Netherlands then to England, from where they were shipped to America. They may well have first met as youngsters of thirteen when, in 1710, they reached this country, each accompanying a widowed mother and several brothers and sisters. Zenger was apprenticed to William Bradford of New York, and moved afterwards to Maryland, where he was appointed printer to the Assembly. His years in Maryland are obscure, since no imprints of his remain and the documents of his naturalization indicate that his press was in Kent County near Chesterton, rather than at the capital city of Annapolis. On his way to the south, in Philadelphia he married Mary White, who died shortly thereafter. Returning to New York, in the first few years of his marriage to Anna Catharine, he worked for Bradford as a journeyman. In 1725 the two formed a partnership long enough to publish a book in Dutch.

The next year he moved to Smith Street and set up his own shop. For his wife the time must have passed much as it did for other housewives, with births, marriages, and deaths occupying a large part of her life. Zenger became a citizen of New York, and earned some extra money as organ blower and later as organist in the Dutch Church. In November 1733 a major change came into his life. On the fifth of that month he published the first issue of the *New York Weekly Journal,* a newspaper opposed to Bradford's *New York Gazette,* an organ of the government, which was strongly disliked by many prominent men.

The articles which filled the *Journal's* pages so incensed the Governor and Council that in the fall of 1734 an order was issued to burn certain numbers. Zenger himself was arrested on charges of libel. His bail was set far beyond his ability to pay, and for ten months he languished in prison. During this period Catharine Zenger won the distinction of being the first woman

in the colonies to publish a newspaper, for, except for one issue, the *Journal* appeared regularly under her guidance. Her
husband's name continued in the imprint, and she undoubtedly
conferred with him as well as with their backers. One would
like to accept her biographer's theory that she was the moving
force behind the entire enterprise, and that hers was even the
anonymous pen that, used in the name of freedom, so vexed
the Governor. Unfortunately, there is no evidence for this.

After the trial, which brought a verdict of not guilty, thanks'
to the brilliant defence of Andrew Hamilton, the printing for·
the colony of New York was placed in Zenger's hands, and the·
following year he succeeded to the same position also in New.
Jersey. All these facts are widely known. What is past over
in the popular accounts is, that he soon lost both offices, owing
to his being "an indifferent printer and very ignorant of the
English language." On July 28, 1746, he died intestate, with·
his widow appointed administrator.

When she had to take over the press, Mrs. Zenger had some
experience, to say nothing of a houseful of boys whom she
could impress for help. The earliest issue of the *New York
Weekly Journal* with her name in the imprint dates from September 1, 1746. One finds the usual notice of intention to carry
on the paper and the hope that "the gentlemen who have been
the deceasd's kind benefactors will still continue to be such in
encouraging the said paper as before." The most interesting
item in the first number was an advertisement of *The Book of
the Chronicles of the Duke of Cumberland,* by J. Anderson. The
notice read: "Just published, and are to be sold by John Zenger,
Junior at the Widow Zenger's . . . ," seemingly indicating a
partnership of some sort, Junior perhaps running the book-
store. But in the next extant issue the same advertisement
appeared as "Just published and to be sold by the Widow Zenger . . ."[12] Young John Zenger's name did not appear again
until the paper was transferred to him in 1748.

John Zenger Jr. was evidently John Peter's eldest son;
Isaiah Thomas's suggestion, however, that he was still a minor
at his father's death, seems erroneous, as he was by then
twenty-three years old.[13] Some writers contend that he was
the son of the first Mrs. Zenger, but this theory is weakened by

the fact that in August 1736 the Mayoralty Court of New York recommended to Alexander Malcolm, the Public Schoolmaster of the city, that Johan Zenger, son of John Peter Zenger, printer "be taught the Latin Tongue and Mathematicks, according to the Directions of the Act of Assembly";[14] and it is far more likely that such an opportunity would be given a lad of thirteen (which he would have been if the son of Catharine) than one of seventeen (which he would have been if the son of the first Mrs. Zenger). In 1741 the boy married Anneke Lynssen and it is possible that, like his father before him, wanderlust drove him away from New York for a few years. Peter, twenty-one years old, and Nicolas, nineteen, would still remain to help their mother, as well as the two younger boys.

Mrs. Zenger's career as printer, publisher, and general business woman is thoroughly typical. She seems to have had a good sense of journalism, often leaving the last column of her newspaper for late news, rather than filling it up with the ads which could be set ahead of time. When necessary, "stop press" flashes were added by a single line of italics running vertically along the edge of the page. But besides the weekly paper, she found time to publish several small volumes, including the yearly Almanack prepared by John Nathan. Early in April 1747 she printed two pamphlets, *A Genuine and Authentick Account of the Behaviour and Dying Words of the Lord Balmorine, and the Earl of Kilmarnock* . . . and *The Lives, Parentage, and last Dying Speech of the Rebel Lords aforesaid* . . . These gentlemen were beheaded in the Tower of London as Jacobites in 1746. Apparently they created considerable interest in America, for James Foster's account of Lord Kilmarnock was reprinted in Boston, New York, and Philadelphia. Four months later appeared *An Answer to the Council of Proprietors* . . . , and in December *The Country Man's Help and Traders Friend.* From 1748 date *The Cries of the Oppressed* . . . *at the Taking of Bergen op Zoom by the French* and *The Congress of the Beasts,* the latter translated from High Dutch.

In her shop Catharine Zenger must have sold also other books but the only ones she advertised were *The Charter of the City of New York* (printed by her husband in 1735) and some "curious High Dutch Almanacks," *Der Hoch-Deutsch Ameri-*

canishe Calender published in Philadelphia by Christopher Saur. The miscellanies of the store included "very good Bonnet Papers" which were regularly carried in stock and a choice parcel of China Ware. Book-binding for the firm was done by John Hinshaw, succeeding Henry De Foreest when the latter set up his own press. Naturally Mrs. Zenger was prepared with all sorts of blanks for her customers — bonds, indentures, bills of lading, etc. But in the late summer of 1747 she must have had a period of discouragement, as someone circulated the rumor that she had gone out of business. For the rest of the year she was forced to run an announcement in the *Journal* that "the said report is notoriously false, and that the said Widow still continues the printing business, where any person may have their work done reasonably, in a good manner, with expedition."

When in December of 1748 John Zenger Jr. at last took over the paper and Mrs. Zenger could retire, she continued to handle the book-store, still advertising the inexhaustible supply of *The Book of the Chronicles*. Some time later, probably in September 1750, she seems to have opened a small shop of her own, for the New York *Charter* was announced as for sale "by the Widow Catharine Zenger, near Hermanus Rutgers on Golden-Hill, also by the Printer hereof." On his death the following year, John left "no person qualified to carry on his business," for Mrs. Zenger no longer had the desire to return to the printing office and the other boys had gone on to other occupations. The press and types were sold.

There is one more notice of Catharine Zenger. Mary Crosbie of Jamaica, Queens County, who died in 1751, left her estate to the Reverend David Bostwick, pastor of the Presbyterian church in Jamaica, with the request that the money should be used for the reprinting of two small books of her own composition. Of the edition five pounds worth were bequeathed "to the widow of John Peter Zenger, of New York."[15] The indomitable widow may have been still selling books at that time.

(To be concluded)

Notes

1. L. C. Wroth, *A History of Printing in Colonial Maryland, 1686–1776* (Baltimore, 1922), 1–16; "The St. Mary's City Press, a New Chronology of American Printing," *The Colophon*, New Series, I, no. 3, 333–67.

2. J. R. Bartlett (ed.), *Records of the Colony of Rhode Island and Providence Plantations* (Providence, 1856–65, IV, 524–25; V, 67–125 *passim; Acts and Laws of His Majesty's Colony of Rhode-Island . . . anno 1745 to anno 1752* (Newport, 1752), 43–44.

3. Howard M. Chapin, "Ann Franklin of Newport, Printer, 1736–1763;" *Bibliographic Essays: A Tribute to Wilberforce Eames* (Cambridge, Mass., 1924), 337–344.

4. Anna J. DeArmond, *Andrew Bradford, Colonial Journalist* (Newark, Del., 1949), 243–44.

5. *Ibid.*, 245–46.

6. William Friedman, "The First Librarian of America," *Library Journal*, LVI (Nov. 1931), 902–03.

7. *The Journal of the Commons House of Assembly* (Columbia, S. C., 1951–56), Vol. II, IV, V, *passim*.

8. G. S. Eddy (ed.), *Account Books Kept by Benjamin Franklin Ledger "D" 1739–1747* (New York, 1929), 121.

9. Henig Cohen, *The South Carolina Gazette, 1732–1775* (Columbia, S. C., 1953), 241.

10. Albert H. Smyth (ed.), *The Writings of Benjamin Franklin* (New York, 1907), V, 446–47.

11. Tom Galt, *Peter Zenger, Fighter for Freedom* (New York, 1951); Kent Cooper, *Anna Zenger, Mother of Freedom* (New York, 1946).

12. Evans, in his *American Bibliography* (no. 5732), implies that *The Book of the Chronicles* was published by Catharine Zenger; unfortunately, earlier issues of the *Journal* advertise the book as "just published and to be sold" by her husband.

13. *The New York Genealogical and Biographical Record*, XIX (1888), 169. Here is listed the baptism in November, 1723, of Johannes, son of Anna Catharina and Johan Peter Zenger. By some oversight the Zenger name does not appear in the index of the volume, hence a casual search through these printed records of the New York Dutch Church might pass by this reference.

14. Richard B. Morris (ed.), *Select Cases of the Mayor's Court of New York City, 1674–1784* (Washington, D. C., 1935), 189.

15. *Collections of the New York Historical Society*, XXVIII (1895), 353.

Early Women Printers of America

(Continued from the January 1958 issue)

By ELLEN M. OLDHAM

A Great-Great-Aunt of Daniel B. Updike

SARAH UPDIKE GODDARD and later her daughter Mary Katharine were the only women who undertook to carry on a printing establishment for reasons other than the death of a printer-husband. Sarah Updike was one of the five daughters of Lodowick and Abigail (Newton) Updike, and on both her father's and mother's side — they were cousins — descended from prosperous early settlers. Her great-grandfather, Richard Smith, had bought thirty thousand acres from the Narragansett Indians, while her grandfather, Gysbert Opdyck, once owned what is now Coney Island. Sarah's older brother, Daniel, became an eminent lawyer and the Attorney General of Rhode Island Colony. One of his intimate friends was George Berkeley, the Irish Bishop and philosopher, author of the *Principles of Human Knowledge,* who spent three years (1728-31) in Rhode Island occupied with his cherished project of founding a college in the Bermudas. A descendant of Daniel Updike, Sarah's great-great-great nephew, was Daniel Berkeley Updike, founder of the Merrymount Press, one of the foremost American printers and writers on printing in the twentieth century.

The date of Sarah Updike's birth is not known, but it must have been in the early years of the eighteenth century. Brought up in Wickford, Rhode Island, and educated at home by a foreign tutor, she married Giles Goddard of New London, Connecticut, a physician and for many years postmaster in that town.[16]

Her husband dying in 1757, Mrs. Goddard was left with a seventeen-year-old son, William, and a daughter, Mary Katharine, but for once widowhood brought no financial problems. Her father had been a wealthy man and, even though he had seven children, her portion doubtless made her independent, even without her share in her mother's and husband's estates. Young William was already serving an apprenticeship under the printer James Parker in New Haven and New York, and shortly after his time was up he returned to Providence as the first printer in that city. His mother advanced him three hundred pounds to open an office in the summer of 1762 and probably moved to Rhode Island herself, to keep house for her son. In October of that year appeared the first issue of the *Providence Gazette and Country Journal,* a weekly newspaper which struggled along for two and a half years without acquiring nearly as many subscribers as Goddard had hoped for "in this flourishing and prosperous part of New England." One intimate detail is known from these years. On the afternoon of September 25, 1764, Mrs. Goddard held a party, a "petticoat frisk" it was called, for which William set up the invitations on his press. A copy of this broadside, probably unique, was presented to the Rhode Island Historical Society by Goddard's great-granddaughter.[17]

In May 1765 the prospect of heavy stamp duties became the final straw in William's struggle with the paper, and he announced its suspension for six months. He might still have continued, however, did not the running of the paper "immediately interfere with some other concerns in which he is about to be engaged, in order to establish himself on a more advantageous footing."[18] He went on to say that "the printing-business is still to be carried on in Providence as heretofor," but, since he himself went back to New York to work with James Parker and John Holt, this points to the earliest time in which his mother Sarah took over the firm.

She must have proved herself thoroughly capable, for in August when an "extraordinary" issue of the *Gazette* appeared it proclaimed that it was "printed by Sarah and William Goddard." Among the important local items in this number was the announcement of the completion of the new paper mill, and that of "an elegant printing house . . . in this town, which, with encouragement equal to the extensive undertaking, will equal any in America." Sarah and William Goddard offered "a variety of books for sale" and especially invited "traders and others in the several New-England colonies" to purchase their *New England Almanack* for 1766.[19]

When the "Proposals for Printing" the new and improved *Gazette* finally appeared the next March, the required number of subscribers was given as eight hundred, and the price as seven shillings a year, due to the "great disbursements" necessitated by the renovation of the printing equipment. While it was a common occurrence for the printer to be paid in kind, the Goddards are unusual in specifically allowing for such a practice — "Provisions, grain of any kind, wood, and other country produce, will be received in lieu of cash, from near dwellers if brought seasonably." One may note that it was as difficult to collect payment in kind as in cash, for Mrs. Goddard had to request "those of our good customers whose engagements have been to pay for their newspapers in wood . . . to consider the severity of the season, and send an immediate supply."[20] Rags of all kinds were requested for the use of the new paper mill and a definite price scale was printed. William must have had a good sense of humor. As an encouragement to the saving of linen rags he promised "to the unmarried ladies . . . that if they will be pleased to distinguish to him such pieces of the linen as were parts of their nether garments, he will cause it to be wrought into the finest paper, so that it may be returned to them in letters, from kind correspondents who are abroad."[21]

Sarah Goddard herself contributed a letter to the "Proposals" in which her own point of view was expressed. "Having been a means of bringing the printing-business into this town," she wrote, "and of furnishing a complete office, in which I purpose to take part for the future, with my son, from a desire of residing in my native colony, I am unwilling to give up the agreeable hopes I had formed, however lucrative a removal might be . . ."

The first issue of the revived *Gazette* did not appear until the August of 1766, when it was printed by "Sarah Goddard and Company, at the Printing Office near the Great Bridge," Mrs. Goddard's principal assistant being Samuel Inslee sent by William from New York. In the meantime the firm had produced several volumes, including a theological tract by Timothy Allen, which still acknowledged William Goddard as a partner.

The earliest imprint by "Sarah Goddard and Company" alone may have been a sermon delivered by David Rowland on June 4, 1766, and probably published shortly thereafter. The most ambitious undertaking by Mrs. Goddard, the two-hundred page edition of the *Letters* of Lady Montague, also dates from this year.[22]

When the time came to set up the customary *New-England Almanack* for 1767, prepared annually by Benjamin West, there was consternation at the discovery that a group of Boston publishers had advertised this same almanac as being printed in their city. Sarah protested in her paper that she had purchased the work which was even then in the press. She continued, "Charity bids [her] hope that those gentlemen have more virtue and honor, than to pursue under-handed measures to obtain the property of others and that Mr. West could not be deluded by *any consideration* to deviate from the paths of rectitude, and risque the loss of his credit by selling a second time what he had already disposed of."[23] Yet the New-England almanac *did* make its appearance in Boston as well as Providence! Still she continued to publish this staple product of the colonial printer in the succeeding years.

In the latter part of 1766, when William had gone to Philadelphia to begin those hectic years described in his *The Partnership*, Mrs. Goddard had to advertise for more help. She "wanted immediately, as an apprentice to the printing-business, an honest, sober, sprightly lad, who can read and write . . ." Sometime in the following months Samuel Inslee left her employ, and in the next year William sent to her aid John Carter, who had formerly worked for Benjamin Franklin, and on September 19 his name first appeared with hers in their imprint.[24] The printing office had been removed "to the house where the Post-Office is now kept, near the sign of the Golden Eagle, and opposite to Knight Dexter's Esq.," and the shop was advertised as "at the Sign of Shakespeare's Head," a symbol which had been used by William some years before.

Late in 1768 Sarah finally decided to leave her native colony, selling out the Providence business to John Carter and joining her son in Philadelphia. She spent her last years supporting him with money and good advice — which he did not take — in his conflict with his erst-while partners Joseph Galloway and Thomas Wharton, and died in Philadelphia on January 5, 1770. Her obituary in the *New York Gazette* paid her this tribute:

> Her conduct through all the changing, trying scenes of life, was not only unblamable but exemplary; a sincere piety and unaffected humility, an easy agreeable cheerfulness and affability, an entertaining, sensible and edifying conversation, and a prudent attention to all the duties of domestic life, endeared her to all of her acquaintances, especially in the relations of wife, parent, friend, and neighbour. The death of such a person is a public loss.[25]

Anne Green of Annapolis

IN 1738, after William Parks had left Maryland for Virginia, the vacant post of public printer was filled by Jonas Green, a young man from the famous New England printing family. Born in Boston, he learned his trade in New London, Connecticut, under his father Timothy Green, who moved there in 1714. Following a few years of work in Boston, Jonas moved on to Philadelphia where he was working, probably with Benjamin Franklin, in 1737, at the time that the Maryland legislature was forced to turn to that city for printing. It may have been thus that he became aware of the opening. Before leaving Philadelphia, he married Anne Catharine Hoof, whose family had emigrated from Holland when she was a child.[26]

For the next thirty years Anne Green was busy caring for her growing family. She bore fourteen children, six sons and eight daughters, although eight died within a year or two of birth. Her husband, meantime, was occupied not only with his printing but with many civic and social activities. He held the posts of alderman, vestryman of St. Anne's Parish, and postmaster; like other printers mentioned here, he was active in the Masonic Lodge, and among the gentlemen of the Tuesday Club he was known as "Poet, Printer, Punster, Purveyor and Punchmaker general."[27] His printing was confined at first to government business, but in 1745 he established the *Maryland Gazette*. Isaiah Thomas said, "His printing was correct, and few, if any, in the colonies exceeded him in the neatness of his work."[28] In 1747 he wrote to Franklin, "Our Assembly added this session five pounds in each county to my salary, but added to the work likewise, which I am well content with; they give me now two hundred and sixty pounds our currency a year . . ." And of his paper he added: "I have about 450 or 460 good customers for seal'd papers, and about 80 unseal'd."[29]

In 1767 Green died. In the next issue of the *Gazette* his widow made the usual plea for patronage, expressing her confidence that "with your kind indulgence and encouragement, MYSELF, and SON, will be enabled to continue in [the business of Provincial Printer] on the same footing."[30] Two of her sons, William, 20, and Frederick, 17, worked in the printing shop, and as soon as he reached his majority William was given the privilege of including his name in the imprint of the *Gazette*. The new firm immediately went to work to complete the *Acts of Assembly* and *Votes and Proceedings* for the preceding session of the legislature, completing the task by April 30. There was considerable delay before Anne Green could be sure that the Assembly would continue to entrust her with its business. On May 30, 1768, her petition came before the Upper and Lower Houses, and on June 18 the Governor signed into law the "Act for the Speedy and Effectual Publication of the Laws of this Province and for the Encouragement of Anne Catharine Green of the City of Annapolis Printer."[31] It will be noted that, as in the case of Elizabeth Timothy and Ann Franklin, the matriarch conducted all negotiations in her own name, even though her son was no longer a minor.

The terms of the Act (identical to those in her late husband's contract) are of some interest. Maryland was still on a "tobacco standard" and each county was assessed an amount of tobacco proportionate to its size and importance. The county of Baltimore, the largest, was expected to contribute 5,160 pounds towards the cost of the printer, and the total from the province was 44,044 pounds, at a conversion rate of twelve shillings and six pence per hundred pounds. In order to ensure a continuity of the office, Mrs. Green was allowed a somewhat lower salary even in a year in which the Assembly did not meet and there were, therefore, no laws to print. In return, she was required to reside at Annapolis during the continuance of the Act and "to print, stitch, cover with marble or blue paper, and deliver" a specified number of copies of the public laws within three months, and the *Votes and Proceedings* of the Lower

House within four months after the end of each session. The legislature realized that emergencies sometimes occurred and, accordingly, the printer would be excused a delay caused "by the death of her hands employed in the press or by sickness or the unavoidable accident of her press breaking." Mrs. Green was also allowed 320 pounds of tobacco a year by each county court for "printing and delivering a sufficient number of books, notes, and manifests for the inspectors of each inspection."[32] The Act was renewed for several years.

In the meantime, Anne Green was facing the old problem of settling the estate. In May 1767 she requested that "all persons having just claims against the estate of Jonas Green, late of this city, deceased" bring them in for adjustment and that "all those who are indebted, immediately to settle with Mr. John Clapham [her son-in-law], and pay off their balances, that I may thereby be enabled to pay off the claims, and compleat this business without loss of time."[33] There was no nonsense about Mrs. Green; six weeks later she gave notice that she had appointed local representatives in each county to collect the outstanding debts. Shortly thereafter she announced that no advertisements would be accepted, unless from subscribers, without cash in advance, in order to avoid this multiplicity of small accounts.[34]

Mrs. Green and her firm confined themselves almost entirely to the printing of the annual *Laws* and *Votes and Proceedings* and the weekly *Gazette*. However, she did issue the ubiquitous "almanack," and some dozen or more broadsides or single sheets on contemporary local affairs are known. In 1774 she published a pamphlet by the Reverend James Maury against the Anabaptists. The two most important volumes from her press, besides the government publications, were the Charter and Bye-laws of the city of Annapolis, and Elie Valette's *The Deputy Commissary's Guide*. The former has been described as "a beautifully printed little volume of fifty-two pages, which for typographical nicety could hardly have been surpassed by the best of her contemporaries in the colonies."[35] The second, published in May 1774, was a larger book of 260 pages. According to an advertisement, non-subscribers could be supplied "with a few remaining books, at the same price of 12s 6d, ready

bound." The advertisement was bolstered by a recommenda-
tion from the Commissary General himself, William Fitzhugh.
The *Guide* is noted as the only colonial Maryland imprint with
an engraved title-page. The artist was Thomas Sparrow, a
protegé, and possibly a ward, of Jonas Green. After an apprenticeship as goldsmith and jeweler in Philadelphia, he returned
to Annapolis in 1765 where he set up his own shop, assisting
the Greens with wood engravings for title-pages, tail-pieces,
and so forth. The *Guide* contains his one copper engraving.[36]

In 1770 Anne Green received $1,000 or £225 for printing
bills of credit to the amount of $318,000. The Act authorizing
this issue took great care to avoid fraud:

> The printer who shall be employed in printing and stamping the
> said bills of credit and all his apprentices and servants which he may
> employ in the said work shall before he or they begin or enter upon
> the same take before some justice of the provincial or county court
> the following oath to wit "I A.B. do swear that I will truly, faith-
> fully and honestly perform the duty of printer . . . and will not
> advisedly print or stamp any greater number of blank bills of credit
> than in that act mentioned or of other denominations than therein
> expressed except such sheets as may be blotted unfair or imperfect
> in the impressing or printing thereof that the same shall be unfit
> for use."

If the printer should be found guilty of breach of contract, he
would be fined £500, and any apprentice or servant "shall on
conviction in due course of law receive corporal punishment
by whipping not exceeding thirty-nine stripes."[37] Three years
later there was another issue of paper money, with the printer's
fee being $1,500.

William Green died in August 1770, and for awhile the
Gazette was again published in the name of Anne Catharine
Green alone. With the issue of January 2, 1772, the imprint
became "Anne Catharine and Son," the son being, of course,
Frederick, then twenty-two years old. Mrs. Green died March
23, 1775. "She was of a mild and benevolent disposition and
for conjugal affection, and parental tenderness, an example to
her sex," ran her obituary.[38] Frederick and his younger brother
Samuel were left to carry on the business. It is of interest to
note that the printing-office's equipment, assessed at the death
of Jonas as something over £90, had by then depreciated to

£53. Among other items in the inventory there were two presses, "one very old," and worth but two pounds, the other, with its furniture, valued at ten pounds.

Frederick and Samuel continued to print the *Gazette* until 1811, in which year both died. Samuel's son, Jonas, succeeded to the business carrying it on until the end of 1839.

Clementina Rind of Williamsburg

LITTLE is known of Clementina Rind's early days, save that she was born in Maryland. Her husband, William Rind, had been an apprentice and later a partner of Jonas Green at Annapolis. William carried on also a book store and circulating library. It was probably toward the end of this period (1758-1766) that he married Clementina, for in 1766 Thomas Jefferson and a group of his friends invited him to move to Virginia and set up a press which would offer competition to that of William Parks, the only one then in the colony and considered to be too subservient to the Governor.[39]

The new establishment was set up in Williamsburg and on May 16, 1766, appeared the first issue of *Rind's Virginia Gazette,* later known simply as the *Virginia Gazette* — although there was a rival paper of that name. Backed by his sponsors, Rind soon became the public printer, the November session of the *Journal* of the House of Burgesses appearing under his imprint. His annual salary in time grew to £450, and his official work, together with his newspaper, job printing, and almanacs, etc. provided a living for his family which now included two small boys, William Alexander and John. At some point in the next few years, John Pinkney, a young relative, joined the firm, probably as an apprentice.[40]

In 1773, "after a lingering illness," William Rind died at the age of forty-nine and was buried with full Masonic honors. The notice in the Rinds' paper was short, the "afflicted family" gratefully acknowledging "the kind attention and concern expressed by each individual."[41] Burial took place at the church of the parish of Bruton; the Reverend John Dixon, a Mason and professor of divinity in William and Mary College, read the office "and a solemn dirge, suitable to the occasion, was performed on the organ by Mr. Peter Pelham, a brother likewise."[42]

In the next issue of the paper Clementina Rind expressed the hope that she might carry on the business successfully and asked for the support — financial as well as moral — of her readers:

The ardent desire I have of rendering this paper as useful and entertaining as possible urges the necessity of attending to this request; as it must be obvious to every one that business of so extensive a nature cannot be carried on with that spirit which is necessary, without a sufficient fund to support it; mine, in great measure, depends on the punctuality of those who favor me with their commands . . . An unaffected desire to please, an indefatigable attention to my business, and the assistance of persons whose abilities and attachment I can rely on, will, I hope, make me not entirely unworthy of encouragement from the public in general, and from the Honourable House of Burgesses in particular; whose favour I once more take the liberty to solicit, and in whose generous breasts it lies to bestow happiness and plenty on my orphan family; if they find me capable of being their servant.[43]

In order to settle her husband's estate, Clementina was obliged to sell at public auction all the personal possessions of the little family, "consisting of Household and Kitchen Furniture, &c." The inventory and appraisal drawn up in preparation for the sale by Alexander Purdie, John Dixon, Robert Prentis, and John Pinkney show these objects in minute detail. Here are the sheets and pillow cases, the warming pan and fish kettle, four silver tea spoons and fourteen bushels of coal. The total worth of the estate was £272-5-6, the most valuable objects being those in the printing office. The two presses were estimated at £25 and the fonts of Long Primer and English at £31-5-0 each. There was also a "cutting press and other materials for binding." These tools of course were not to be auctioned, but one wonders what happened to the two cows and the "Negro man Dick" who was valued at £30.[44]

The impending loss of all her intimate belongings was not the only problem with which Mrs. Rind had to contend. The same day on which the sheriff's notice appeared in the *Gazette,* there was advertised for sale three "tenements in the city of Williamsburg which . . . are now held by William Lee, Esq. of

the city of London" — one of them being "the brick house on
the Main St., where Mrs. Rind lives."[45]   There is no evidence
that the new owner dispossessed his tenants, since her imprint
in the *Gazette* remained "at the New Printing-Office on the Main
Street," but there must have been many an anxious moment
for the young mother.

Even the appointment as public printer, on which she pinned
her hopes for security, was by no means a foregone conclusion.
When the House of Burgesses took up the matter the following
May, there were three applicants, for Alexander Purdie and
John Dixon had each submitted his own petition.   But on May
24 it was resolved that the Printer to the Public should be
chosen by secret ballot and Mrs. Rind was elected by a large
majority, receiving sixty out of the eighty-seven votes cast.[46]
The Assembly was prorogued two days later, not to meet again
until June 1, 1775; fortunately, the matter of payment to the
Printer had been decided a year earlier when William Rind had
requested that his salary, about to expire, be continued through
the 1774 session.   Thus the £450 was assured, the terms under
which Clementina carried on her duties being similar to those
in effect elsewhere.

Even before the outcome of her petition was known, Clementina was ambitiously ordering "an elegant set of types from
London, of a smaller size than those used at present, together
with all other materials relating to the printing business."   The
old bugbear of delinquent payments was with her, however,
and while boasting of "having lately considerably enlarged her
paper . . . and being extremely desirous of supporting the dignity of her gazette, and keeping it at a fixed standard," she
begged especially those who had placed advertisements or purchased blanks, etc. "either to send cash, or settle at the next
general court."[47]

As the break with England drew inevitably closer, Clementina faithfully carried out the motto of the paper, "Open to all
parties, but influenced by none."   Her philosophy as editor is
well given in one of her columns:

At a time when the liberties of the colonies are daringly in-
fringed, and despotism is exerting her baneful influence in the
minds of those who wish not well to the just privileges of America,

it certainly behooves every well-wisher to her rights, and more particularly a publisher of intelligence who has her cause sincerely at heart, to lay openly those matters which may, in any respect, tend to the discovery of arbitrary or illegal measures, threatened by the mother country towards us. Under this head, the printer of this paper conceives herself obligated to convey to the public the late despotic proceedings of the H—e of C—s in the most ample manner, and to brand with infamy those unprecedented resolves which they have so precipitately entered into . . .[48]

With the public business assured and her new types in use, the future seemed promising. On the first anniversary of her husband's death she wrote:

The printer would by no means be understood to boast a *superiority* in the conduct of a vehicle of this nature; she only advances, that it shall be her particular endeavour to amuse and instruct, and, at the same time, her firm determination, ever to preserve the *dignity* of her paper . . .

A general correspondence with all the printers of this continent, as also with many of the printers and others with whom it is convenient to carry on a correspondence of this sort, in many of the principal towns and cities of Great Britain, is established, which will of course, be materially interesting and useful to us, by affording means to supply our readers with the latest intelligence from those different quarters . . .[49]

The article appeared on September 8, 1774. Two weeks later she died.

Besides the 1774 *Journal* of the House of Burgesses, two broadside proclamations and the two-page *Association* . . . *signed by 89 members of the late House* . . . *May 27, 1774*, only one pamphlet is attributed to Mrs. Rind's press, *A Summary View of the Rights of British America* . . . by Thomas Jefferson. The exact date of the publication of this last piece is not known, but it was definitely in print by the end of August. However, like her fellow-craftsmen elsewhere, Clementina added to her income by the sale of books. She had, of course, the Virginia almanack for 1774 "by the celebrated Mr. Rittenhouse," the last item prepared for the press by her husband. In May she offered as "just published" and "to be sold at both printing houses" the Reverend Samuel Henley's *Candid Refutation of the Heresy* . . . and a sermon of his preached at the Parish church of Bruton. Most likely they were printed by Purdie and Dixon.

In August Mrs. Rind received a small shipment of books from John Sparhawk of Philadelphia — "a few copies" of Josiah Quincy Jr.'s *Observations on the Boston Port Bill,* James Murray's *[New] Sermons to Asses,* and *The History of Juliet Grenville* by Henry Brooke.

In order to stretch the family income further, she even took in boarders. On July 7, B. Dandridge, an attorney, advertised to his clients that he would "attend at his lodgings, at Mrs. Rind's, in Williamsburg, the day before the courts . . . and in all public times, to receive the commands of those that will employ him." And that at other times, "his clients letters left there will be forwarded to him in New Kent by a careful hand . . ."

Clementina Rind's obituary appeared in the September 29, 1774, *Gazette,* which was published by John Pinkney "for the benefit of Clementina Rind's Estate":

It ill beseems the printer, he apprehends, as being a relation, to pretend to characterize her. The public, who must in general have been acquainted with her, know her qualifications. It shall, however, be his most ardent study to protect her children, for which purpose, he hopes those who have hitherto favoured this office, will not now discontinue their kindness.

Pinkney seems to have been as good as his word, for his two imprints, the *Virginia Almanack* for 1775 and Francis Hopkinson's *A Pretty Story* . . . as well as the *Gazette* for six months, were printed by him "for the benefit of Clementina Rind's children." In February he announced the appointment of Jacob Bruce to collect the debts due to the estate. And in April Bruce himself ran an advertisement requesting all those still owing any money to bring or send it by the next meeting of the merchants, adding that "the amount of Mrs. Rind's paper, from the first to her death, is 13 shillings and 6 pence."

There was again competition for the post of public printer, with Alexander Purdie and the firm of Dixon and Hunter applying, as well as Pinkney. Purdie won by a margin of five votes.[50] The Rinds' friends doubtless would have liked to help out, but the choice now was between man and man, and Purdie was older and better established as a printer; then, too, John's father Jonathan was known to be a Loyalist, a fact which may well have swung some votes. Purdie, however, showed himself to be a true gentleman, by presenting a petition to the House "to be allowed for printing the proceedings of the convention at Richmond in March last; and that such allowance be for the benefit of the orphans of Mrs. Rind." The motion was denied; at the same time, the burgesses voted the sum of £347-10-0 to be paid John Pinkney "for performing the duty of public Printer, since the death of Mrs. Rind."[51] Pinkney found himself ever deeper in debt, until early in 1776 the *Gazette* was suspended. He grasped eagerly at an invitation to go to Halifax, capital of North Carolina, to take the place of James Davis, who had fallen into disfavor politically. In order to satisfy his creditors, he was forced to borrow four hundred pounds from one of his new sponsors. Unfortunately, the new enterprise did not work out very well, and within a year he was dead.[52]

With their cousin's departure the two children, William and John, were left alone. But the Masonic brethren came to the rescue and for several years the account books of the Williamsburg Lodge showed regular payments for board, schooling, and clothing for the "orphans of Mr. Wm. Rind."[53] The older boy was apprenticed in the family trade and, after publishing the *Virginia Federalist* at Richmond, became the first printer in the District of Columbia.

(To be concluded)

Notes

16. Charles W. Opdyke, *The Op Dyck Genealogy* (New York, 1889), 87–93.

17. [Bradford F. Swan], "A Petticoat Frisk," *Rhode Island History* for October 1945, 117.

18. *Providence Gazette*, May 4, 1765.

19. *Ibid.*, "Extraordinary issue," August 24, 1765.

20. *Ibid.*, January 3, 1767.

21. *Proposals for Printing the Providence Gazette* (Providence, March 12, 1766).

22. For Sarah Goddard's imprints, see John E. Alden, *Rhode Island Imprints, 1727–1800* (New York, 1949).

23. *Providence Gazette*, October 15, 1766.

24. John Carter Brown, the famous book-collector and benefactor of Brown University, was this printer's grandson.

25. Opdyke, *op. cit.*, 93.
26. Wroth, *op. cit.*, 76.
27. *Ibid.*, 80–81.
28. Isaiah Thomas, *The History of Printing in America* (2d ed.: Albany, 1874), I, 321.
29. Quoted in Wroth, *op. cit.*, 82–83.
30. *Maryland Gazette*, April 16, 1767.
31. *Archives of Maryland*, Vol. LXI (Maryland Historical Society, 1944), 287, 343, 314.
32. *Ibid.*, 455–58.
33. *Maryland Gazette*, May 7, 1767.
34. *Ibid.*, July 9, 1767.
35. Wroth, *op. cit.*, 91.
36. *Ibid.*, 87–89.
37. *Archives of Maryland*, Vol. LXII (Maryland Historical Society, 1945), 134–35.
38. *Maryland Gazette*, March 30, 1775.
39. Douglas C. McMurtrie, *A History of Printing in the United States*, Vol. II, *Middle & South Atlantic States* (New York, 1936), 116.
40. The exact relation of William Rind and John Pinkney is uncertain, but Jonathan Pinkney, an immigrant to Annapolis, Maryland, from England, married successively Margaret Rind and her sister Ann. William was probably a brother of these girls and John his nephew. Cf. *Dictionary of American Biography sub* William Pinkney.
41. *Virginia Gazette* (Rind), August 26, 1773.
42. *Virginia Gazette* (Purdie and Dixon), August 26, 1773.
43. *Virginia Gazette* (Rind), September 23, 1773.
44. *William and Mary College Quarterly* (1937), 53–55.
45. *Virginia Gazette* (Rind), September 23, 1773.
46. *Journals of the House of Burgesses of Virginia*, 1773–1776 (Richmond, 1905), I, 77, 124–25. (May 7, May 24, 1773.)
47. *Virginia Gazette* (Rind), April 14, 1774.
48. *Ibid.*, May 19, 1774.
49. *Ibid.*, September 8, 1774.
50. *Journals* (June 16, 1775), 195.
51. *Ibid.* (June 19, 20, 1775), 264. 270.
52. McMurtrie, *op. cit.*, 291.
53. *Wm. & Mary Coll. Quar.*, July 1892, 13–14.

Early Women Printers of America

(*Continued from the January and April 1958 issues*)

By ELLEN M. OLDHAM

Margaret Draper, the Loyalist

OF the four women printers who were at work at the outbreak of the American Revolution, only one was a Loyalist — Margaret Draper. Born in May 1727 in Boston, she was married in May 1750 to Richard, son of John Draper and grandson of Bartholomew Green. The latter was the son of Samuel Green, Stephen Day's successor at the Cambridge press and founder of the famous Green family of printers. Margaret Draper may have been a grand-daughter of Bartholomew Green also and thus a cousin of her husband. Richard Draper had learned printing under his father, working with the latter until his death in 1762, and afterwards carried on the family firm.

Richard Draper was official printer to the Governor and Council of Massachusetts Bay and remained loyal to the British cause till his death in 1774. Perhaps the most important of his enterprises was the famous *Massachusetts Gazette and Boston News Letter,* established in 1704 and throughout its long history intimately connected with the Green-Draper family, for Bartholomew Green had been printer of the paper from its inception, taking over as editor and publisher in 1723.

Massachusetts, home of the earliest colonial press, was far better equipped than many other sites to support printers; and, in spite of much competition, Richard Draper was apparently a well-to-do man, erecting, as Isaiah Thomas relates, "a handsome brick house on a convenient spot in front of the old printing house in Newbury Street, in which he resided."[54] The Drapers were childless; however, probably after 1766, they adopted Margaret's niece, Margaret Collier. They also took into their home, as an apprentice and later as journeyman printer, Edward Draper, son of Richard's uncle, Samuel Draper. In 1765 the Drapers were admitted to full communion in the West Church of Boston. She was deeply attached to Dr. Jonathan

Mayhew, their pastor, and there are still extant two of her letters to her cousin James Green of Providence, one apparently describing the death of the Doctor's only son and the other on the last illness of the minister himself. The first begins, "I haveing a Leasure hour and I think it cant be spent more to my Sattersfaction then in Writing to you. You know I promist it last week to inform you how our Doct behaved at the Death of his only Son and let me tel you it was with all the composure of a Christon. The Sabbath after he pretched from those words . . ." Margaret's spelling was based entirely upon her own system of phonetics. It is obvious that she never had to set type.

Richard Draper is said to have been sickly throughout his life; certainly his health was poor in his later years. On May 5, 1774, he was forced to announce in his paper: "The Publisher and Printer of this paper being in a very low state of health, prevents his making such collection of intelligence and speculation, as his customers must have expected to be given them . . . A Printer that understands collecting news, and carrying on a news paper, by applying to the Printer hereof, may be concerned on very advantagious terms." The partner selected, and announced one week later, was John Boyle, associated in printing and binding for the firm since 1769.[55] In less than a month Richard's disease proved fatal, and on June 5, 1774, his "innocent, exemplary and useful life . . . was terminated by a lingering consumptive disorder."

His widow announced that she would continue to carry on the paper with the assistance of John Boyle. "Those who have hitherto been customers to this paper will be continued as usual; and the utmost endeavors will be taken to maintain the character it has had for upwards of seventy years past."[56] Edward Draper continued to work at the press and there were, besides, two apprentices. With the issue of August 4, however, the partnership with John Boyle was dissolved. Although no reason was given for the separation save that of "mutual consent," Mrs. Draper later testified that Boyle left her employ because of the frustration of his desire to "make her newspaper subservient to the party of rebellion."[57] In her public announcement the following week, she informed her readers that she was to continue the paper herself, hoping that she "shall meet with such assistance as may enable her to keep up the credit which the paper had for a long time sustained in the days of her deceased husband."[58] For the next year, therefore, the heading of the paper continued as simply *Draper's.*

During these months Mrs. Draper was endeavoring to settle her husband's estate. By the terms of his will, his entire property was left to her, including the reversion of the house and land currently occupied by his step-mother, Elizabeth Draper, and Mr. John Loring.[59] At the end of October she advertised for sale "for the sterling cost and charges" a large new font of pica and one of Great Primer "as neat as was ever imported from England." These types had been purchased from the Caslon firm of London by Richard Draper shortly before his death, at the request of Governor Hutchinson, for printing a new law book. Probably because of the unsettled conditions of the time, there were no purchasers in Boston, and eventually the types were resold to Caslon for £20, a loss of £46-9-4. When Margaret presented her inventory of the estate in December, 1774, the total was valued at £973-4-8. The largest items included:

Printing Press and letters and utensils in printing office £105–5–2
Revenue of a house in Cornhill   200 – –
The mansion house, printing office, and other buildings 500 – –[60]

Mrs. Draper issued several pamphlets on contemporary affairs, such as General Charles Lee's *Letter to General Burgoyne* and *The Interest of the Merchants and Manufacturers of Great Britain . . . Considered.* The largest work from her press was William Windham's *A Plan of Exercise for the Militia,* a volume of over one hundred pages. She also continued to print broadsides for the Governor. Like her husband, she emphasized in the *Gazette* the British point of view. Since the other newspapers were more sympathetic to the colonists, she found herself on several occasions attacked by her competitors. In her replies she showed herself to be of a restrained nature and, according to her lights, a firm upholder of the freedom of the press.

In January 1775 Isaiah Thomas, in the *Massachusetts Spy,* accused her of publishing a false report of a recent Barnstable town meeting. She did not feel she could ignore his intimations "lest our customers should therefrom be induced to think that we are so attached to a party, as to insert any intelligence which we know to be false for the sake of gratifying that party." She went on to explain that her information had come from a usually well-informed source, and trusted that the present report of a later town-meeting

will appear much more forceable for the truth of [the proceedings] than the bare assertions of these paragraph writers to the contrary, and their unmanly attacks upon a woman. And our customers may be assured that when intelligence of any kind is to be communicated, it shall be done with that fairness and impartiality which hath always distinguished the Massachusetts-Gazette.[61]

It was not only the local publishers who looked askance at the Loyalist slant of the *Massachusetts Gazette*. Just two days later than Mr. Thomas's criticism, the Convention of Committees for the county of Worcester passed a resolution condemning a number of printers, including Draper of Boston, for assisting "the enemies of these united colonies," and recommending a boycott of such newspapers. Mrs. Draper's reply is worth quoting here:

The Printers of this paper are at a loss how to reconcile this resolve of the Committees of the County of Worcester, with the Declaration of the Continental Congress, who in their address to the Canadians say, that the Liberty of the Press is one of those "Rights without which a people cannot be free and happy, and under the protecting and encouraging influence of which, these colonies have hitherto so amazingly flourished and increased." This glorious privilege which every one has a right to enjoy, and which has been productive of such inestimable blessings, is in a most glaring instance struck at in this resolve, and the printers pointed out as inimical to their country who have not conformed so far to the dogmas of a party, as to refuse to insert lucubrations of those, whose sentiments were unpopular, and who laboured under the disadvantage of being obliged to think different from the generality, with whose welfare their own was most intimately connected. And as every member of the community is interested in all the public measures which are adopted, and as communities as well as individuals, are liable to err. The printers of this paper have not refused to insert the performances of ANY, which were wrote with decency, and free from personal reflections, that so the sentiments of ALL being collected, the conductors of our public affairs might

be lead into those measures that would have a tendency to restore
this unhappy country to its former state of quietude and peace, for
the return of which, none more ardently wish than the publishers
of this Gazette . . .[62]

But the life of the *Massachusetts Gazette* and Margaret Draper's
days in Boston were drawing to a close. With the issue of
April 20, 1775, publication was interrupted; on May 18, however, the paper went to press once more, with a notice that con-
tinuation would be contingent on the assurance of three hundred subscribers. It was a modest aspiration, since formerly
as many as 1,500 copies were printed weekly.[63] It was pointed out
that due to the siege communication with the outside world
was nearly cut off, hence two folio pages were the most that
could be expected. Likewise, since there would be few customers at best, the price would be raised to eight shillings a
year. On October 13, 1775, the name of John Howe first appeared as printer, while that of Draper disappeared completely.
Howe had previously been an employee of Mrs. Draper, and it
may be that at this time he bought her out. Be that as it
may, the last known number was that of February 22, 1776, although a quotation in the March 4 issue of the *Boston Gazette*
shows that at least one more number appeared.[64]

When the British evacuated Boston, Mrs. Draper went with
them to Halifax. Her party included five persons—her adopted
daughter Margaret and presumably servants. Halifax was an
uncomfortable place at best, its facilities overcrowded by the
influx of refugees, and probably Mrs. Draper was glad to seize
the first chance to continue on to England. As an absentee
Loyalist her property in Boston was forfeit, and in April 1779
Richard Devens, Commissary General of Massachusetts, posted
bond, together with David Devens, a cooper and Jonathan Harris,
a baker, as agent for her property. When Devens filed his inventory nearly a year later, he valued the total at £13,210-12-00.
The Newbury Street house and land was appraised at £12,000,
the printing press at £400, two frames and the type at £378.
Other objects ranged from "one square mahogany table, £36"
and "two fire bucketts £6" to "a quantity of wastepaper &c. in
the office chamber & up Garrett £40." The courts functioned
slowly and it took two more years before the agent's account-

ing was presented, amounting to nearly forty pounds paid out for various legal and business fees, including replacement of a pane of glass.[65] Richard Devens himself bought the real estate.

At the same time in England, in accordance with an Act of Parliament, Mrs. Draper applied to obtain compensation for her losses from the Crown. She submitted a claim for £2,093, and finally was allowed £920.[66] Among the affidavits of loyalty on her behalf were those of General Gage, Colonel Nisbet Balfour, and Chief Justice Peter Oliver. The British government granted her a pension of one hundred pounds yearly, which her daughter endeavoured to have increased though without success.[67]

In England, Margaret settled in William Street, Pimlico, where her adopted daughter married James Hamilton. To their child, Margaret, Mrs. Draper willed all her effects and property, including her share of the house and land in Boston still occupied by John Loring (and apparently not appropriated by the Massachusetts government). The exact date of her death is not known; however, her pension ceased in 1804 by which time she was seventy-seven. Her will was admitted to probate in February 1807.[68]

Mary Crouch, Salem Printer

IN South Carolina flourished not only Elizabeth Timothy and her daughter-in-law Anne, but also, in the early years of the Revolution, Mrs. Mary Crouch. The latter seems to have been one of the most enterprising of the eleven women printers; certainly in later years she was the most traveled.

One of four children of David and Mary Wilkinson, she was born in Smithfield, Rhode Island, in 1740. At the age of twenty-two she married Charles Crouch in Providence, and there her daughter Anne was born. Mr. Crouch was a native of Charleston, South Carolina, but his parents were originally from Massachusetts. It is difficult to trace the Crouches in published records, but there was at least one other family of that name in the southern city, and it may have been the presence of relatives that caused Charles's parents to move there. The boy's apprenticeship was served under Peter Timothy —

though after his mother, Elizabeth, had given up active participation in the firm. Unfortunately for his master, Charles Crouch was not a docile assistant and on four different occasions was advertised for as a run-away. Finally in February 1754 Timothy gave up, as he informed Benjamin Franklin:

I discharged my villainous apprentice: gave him two years time, quitted all claims on him for monies received and gamed away, for loss of time, and charges for taking up, etc. etc. etc. A lad very capable of the business, and might have been of vast service to me but for three years has always pulled the contrary way; owing to an unhappy affection for drink, play, and scandalous company.[69]

It was perhaps a year after their marriage that the young Crouches left for Charleston. About this time Charles began his own printing shop, in competition with his former master. He seems to have made a success of the business and was engaged as well in the practice of law. In December of 1765, while the Timothy paper was suspended because of the Stamp Act, he began a newspaper, the *South-Carolina Gazeteer* or, as it was soon called, the *South-Carolina Gazette and Country Journal*. During these years there is little information to be found about the family. Two and possibly three sons were born, and little Anne died. But Mrs. Crouch, at least, never became completely acclimatized to Charleston. As her husband prospered, she found it possible nearly every summer to return to Rhode Island for a visit. Sometimes she went alone with the children; sometimes they appeared among the list of prominent passengers as "Mr. Charles Crouch printer & Lady."[70]

One wonders about the "Mr. Crouch, son of Mr. Charles Crouch" who arrived at Newport from Charleston in July of 1772. If this were the child of Mary, he would have been but eight years old at the most. However, the reference must be to the Charles Crouch who was among the exiles to Philadelphia in 1781, possibly a cousin of the printer. But the Charles Crouch who was buried at King's Church, Providence, in April 1774 may well have been Mary's son, dead on one of their visits north. The last journey undertaken by Charles Sr. was in August 1775, a proposed business trip to Philadelphia. As usual he went by boat, and on the way was drowned.

Crouch had announced the temporary suspension of his

paper before his departure; it did not appear again for three years. What did Mrs. Crouch do in the meantime? Did she return to her family in Rhode Island, or did she carry on her husband's business as best she could, concentrating on "job printing"? Although Evans in his *American Bibliography* indicates that Mrs. Crouch continued her husband's paper under its original title from the time of his death until she left South Carolina in 1780, the evidence as shown in Brigham's *History and Bibliography of American Newspapers, 1690-1820,* is against this. When, in the late summer of 1778, the publication was revived, it was with the title *Charlestown Gazette* and the imprint "Mary Crouch & Company." No other imprints of hers in South Carolina are known. For nearly a year and a half she made her living from the newspaper, but the siege of Charleston in 1780 put a halt to any attempt at publishing.

Faced with this disaster, Mrs. Crouch went north, all the way to Salem, Massachusetts. It is not known who suggested this distant town; her sponsors may have been Masons if Charles Crouch, like William Rind, was one of the fraternity. The "Proposals for printing" the *Salem Gazette and General Advertiser* were issued on December 6, 1780. Mrs. Crouch speaks of the "Invitation and encouragement of sundry gentlemen of reputation" to establish a printing office in Salem (which had been without one since the removal of Ezekiel Russell to Danvers in 1777). In instituting her new newspaper, she intended to give her readers "a weekly relation of the most remarkable and important occurrences, foreign and domestic, having a particular regard to such matters as shall intimately relate to the safety and welfare of the United States, to the liberty and independence of which the *Salem Gazette* will be ever sacredly devoted." Her pages would also be open to the usual advertisements, to "striking anecdotes, improvements in agriculture," as well as to "judicious remarks and political essays of the learned and ingenious" who are cordially requested to send in their contributions. Her price was fifty cents a quarter, with delivery to local residents; the minimum number of subscribers required would be three hundred.

The first issue of the paper appeared on January 2, 1781; in the meantime she carried out some job-printing for the Masons.

This included tickets of admission to their Hall, and blank notices for their meetings, the earliest of which in the Essex Institute is dated December 11, 1780. From this time, too, comes what appears to be the only separate publication of the press, *A Charge, Delivered at St. Peter's Church, in Salem . . . December 27th, 5780* by Joseph Hiller to the Masons, a pamphlet of eight pages.[71]

The time of year was not propitious for beginning a newspaper, for the winter with the resultant delays in mail made it difficult, as Mrs. Crouch pointed out to her readers, to collect "regular intelligence." Therefore the printers would, for the present, insert "such entertaining pieces, and the latest intelligence they can possibly obtain." For this reason, the lead article in the first number (occupying the entire front page) was a reprint from the November 1779 issue of the *London Magazine*, entitled "Edwin and Adela, a Tragick Story." Of the three bits of local news, one was the arrival of a ship, one a marriage account, and one the notice of a Masonic meeting. In succeeding issues Salem news was almost entirely confined to the arrival of ships, though there was an occasional mention of a wedding or a fire. Of the three death notices, two were of Masons, and in June she carried the announcement of a meeting of the Masonic Lodge in Marblehead.[72]

She frequently advertised for rags: "The highest prices in continental dollars will be given for clean linen or cotton rags at the Printing Office in Salem." Later appeared notices of "a few bolts of English Duck" for sale, followed by "a quantity of quart bottles, by the gross" to be obtained from the printers. The Crouches also were, of course, prepared with all the usual kinds of blanks, the emphasis being on those required by the shipping trade. There were a few books offered from time to time — Bickerstaff's almanac, the New England Primer, and Dilworth's "much approved spelling books" made up the lot.

One wonders just who composed the "Company" of "Mrs. Crouch and Company." Her oldest son may have been about fifteen, and doubtless took his part in the office as an apprentice; Abraham was only thirteen. In one of her earliest papers Mrs. Crouch advertised for "a likely Negro boy, about twelve or fourteen years old, to serve till he is twenty-one years of age."[73]

But the position for which he was required is not told, and the printer may have been simply an agent for someone else. Anxieties continually beset the firm. There were complaints from subscribers that the Tuesday Salem paper did not reach them till after the Boston papers published on Thursday; this was finally corrected in the spring by the initiation of a private post which, setting out from Salem at eight in the morning, planned to reach Newbury-Port post office by four in the afternoon, passing through Beverly, Wenham, Ipswich, etc.[74] There were also difficulties in obtaining paper, and finally, on July 3, she was forced to advertise for a journeyman printer, wanted "immediately."

Mary Crouch must have had high hopes for her venture, to induce her to take her family so far from friends and relatives. But the piling up of troubles eventually became too great. In her notice of September 4, 1781, announcing the imminent discontinuation of the paper, she singles out not only the "want of sufficient assistance" but also the "impossibility of procuring houseroom for herself and family to reside near her business." Apparently she left town as soon as she could find a buyer for her press and types — Samuel Hall, who had previously conducted the *Essex Gazette* in the town before moving on to Boston.[75] She asked those behind in their payments to pay up as soon as possible, Mr. Williams, the Postmaster, being appointed her deputy for the collections.[76]

The rest of Mary Crouch's life is obscure. She went back to Providence, probably living with relatives while the two boys were at school, for Abraham, at least, graduated from Brown University in 1787. Eventually all three returned to Charleston, South Carolina, and there Mrs. Crouch died in October 1818, at the age of seventy-eight. She had made a faithful attempt to carry on her husband's business, but probably her heart was never really in it to the extent found in some of her contemporary lady printers.

A Providence Woman in Baltimore

MARY KATHARINE GODDARD, a Maryland printer like

Dinah Nuthead, has been exhaustively studied by both Lawrence Wroth in his *History of Printing in Colonial Maryland, 1686-1776*, 1922, and Joseph Wheeler in *The Maryland Press, 1777-1790*, 1938. For this brief study one need only summarize their findings. Mary Katharine was born in 1736, four years before her brother William, to Sarah and Giles Goddard of New London, Connecticut. As has been seen, the family moved to Providence in 1762 when William set up the first printing press in that town. Isaiah Thomas remarked of her, as of Ann Franklin's daughters, that she was "an expert and correct compositor of types," and it is reasonable to suppose that, learning something of the trade from her brother, she was able to assist her mother when the latter ran the printing office.

In 1768 the two women joined William in Philadelphia, and there Mrs. Goddard died a short time later. Mary Katharine probably worked with her brother on the *Philadelphia Chronicle*, and apparently was left in charge when, in 1772, he continued south to Baltimore where he founded the *Maryland Journal*. The beginnings of this latter newspaper were impeded by William's recurrent illness, but by February 1774 it was a going enterprise. In that month Mary Katharine, having wound up the affairs of the *Chronicle*, advertised that she would conduct the Baltimore newspaper and printing business of her brother during his absence "on an affair interesting to the common liberties of all America."

The affair was the organization of the Constitutional Post Office, on which our present system is founded. Since he was still occupied by the organizational work a year later, his name was removed from the imprint of the *Journal*. At this period, 1775, Mary Katharine was herself appointed post-mistress of Baltimore, a task which she faithfully carried out for fourteen years.

Late in 1776 William Goddard returned at last to Baltimore, and while he remained in the background (his sister's name alone continued in their imprints), he took an important part in the editorial direction. Yet in June 1779 he formed a partnership with Eleazer Oswald to operate a printing, bookselling, and stationery business in the city, to be conducted "neither in opposition to or in conjunction with" Mary Katharine. Mr.

Wroth believes, however, that the two men continued to be employed by Miss Goddard on the *Journal,* since it is unlikely that their own business was sufficient to support them.

In 1783 William received a large legacy of land, with the proceeds of which he seems to have bought out his sister, for her name disappeared from the *Journal's* imprint after the single issue of January 2, 1784 announced that the paper would be published by "William and Mary Katharine Goddard." It was not until 1792 that Goddard, after a series of partners, finally relinquished the business and retired to a farm in Rhode Island.

Besides her work on the *Maryland Journal,* Mary Katharine did not issue much from her press, though doubtless she had a good trade in blank forms and job printing. Most of her existing imprints are broadsides on contemporary affairs, often relating to the War. She first printed an almanac in 1780, which she continued for several years. After the war, culture appears to have come to Baltimore in a big way, for in 1782 the Goddard firm printed at least seventy-four broadside playbills or theatrical notices. The New Theater opened on January 15 with *King Richard III* and closed December 31 with *Hamlet;* in between had been a wide variety of comedies, tragedies, farces, dances, etc. The last item issued by Mary Katharine was her almanac for 1785, published in deliberate competition with her brother's, after he had ungraciously if legitimately ousted her from the business.

Along with her work in the Post Office and at the printing shop, Miss Goddard had carried on for years a dry-goods and stationery store, to which she added a book-shop. Her later years may be followed to some extent in the Baltimore Directory, which lists her, in 1803, as a store keeper in Chatham Street. By this time she was nearing seventy, and shortly thereafter seems to have retired. She died in 1816, leaving her remaining property to a colored servant. "In the old burial ground of St. Paul's Parish in Baltimore," Mr. Wroth writes, "lies the body of this New England woman who served her adopted Maryland in a way and to a degree that no woman of the period served another American community."[77]

Notes

54. Thomas, *op. cit.*, I, 146.

55. E. Alfred Jones, *The Loyalists of Massachusetts* (London, 1930), 122.

56. *Massachusetts Gazette*, June 9, 1774.

57. *Ibid.*

58. *Massachusetts Gazette*, August 11, 1774.

59. Suffolk County Probate Records, LXXIII, 687.

60. *Ibid.*, LXXIV, 239.

61. *Massachusetts Gazette*, February 2, 1775.

62. *Ibid.*, February 16, 1775.

63. Jones, *op. cit.*, 121.

64. Clarence S. Brigham, *History and Bibliography of American Newspapers, 1690–1820* (American Antiquarian Society, 1947), I, 328.

65. Suffolk County Probate Records, LXXVIII, 683; LXXIX, 19; XCII, 349.

66. Any attempt to equate values of currency at this time is difficult, but if the 1783 Massachusetts pound can be considered roughly equivalent to the English, Mrs. Draper's allowance was not much lower than Devens's inventory as converted from the earlier inflated appraisal.

67. Jones, *op. cit.*, 122.

68. Suffolk County Probate Records, CV, 440–41.

69. Douglas C. McMurtrie, "The Correspondence of Peter Timothy, Printer of Charlestown, with Benjamin Franklin," *South Carolina Historical and Genealogical Magazine*, XXXV (Oct. 1934), 125.

70. *S. C. Hist. and Gen. Mag.*, XLI (1940), 45–57.

71. Harriet S. Tapley, *Salem Imprints, 1768–1825* (The Essex Institute, 1927), 336.

72. *Salem Gazette*, January 9, April 17, June 19, 1781.

73. *Ibid*, January 9, 1781.

74. *Ibid.*, March 27, April 10, 1781.

75. This was the same Samuel Hall who had been Ann Franklin's partner in 1762–63.

76. *Salem Gazette*, September 4, 1781.

77. L. C. Wroth, "William Goddard and Some of his Friends," *Rhode Island Historical Society Collections*, XVII (April 1924), 39.

PRUDENCE CRANDALL
CHAMPION OF NEGRO EDUCATION

Edwin W. Small
and
Miriam R. Small

PRUDENCE CRANDALL
CHAMPION OF NEGRO EDUCATION

EDWIN W. AND MIRIAM R. SMALL

A hundred and ten years ago, in the town of Canterbury, Connecticut, a Yankee schoolmistress was forced by local public opinion to give up the school for Negro girls which she had established there. The incident aroused much vigorous and indignant protest at the time; and fifty-odd years later the state legislature of Connecticut offered a partial restitution by granting her, then a resident of Kansas, a pension for the remainder of her life. Through an examination of the Canterbury town records, a collection of letters and manuscripts in the possession of Andrew Judson Clark of Canterbury, and advertisements and comments in Garrison's *Liberator* and other contemporary newspapers, it is possible today to get a clear understanding of the controversy and of the forces and feelings which animated it.

There is still standing in Canterbury, on the corner diagonally opposite the green, where a fine old church tops the rising slope, what is commonly referred to as the Prudence Crandall house—one of the fine low-pitched, hip-roofed houses of the semi-monitor type erected in eastern Connecticut early in the nineteenth century. With its distinctive entrance pavilion framed by two-story pilasters, it has been described as exhibiting "aristocratic assurance" and "sophisticated refinement."[1] Just across the road stood the residence of Andrew T. Judson, one of the most prominent and influential personages in the politics of the town and state.

It was this house which Miss Prudence Crandall purchased in 1831, when at the request of aristocratic residents of Canterbury she set up a select school for their daughters. She was

---

[1] The house is fully described by Richard T. Dana, in *An Architectural Monograph on Old Canterbury on the Quinebaug*, White Pine Series of Architectural Monographs, Volume IX, Number 6 (St. Paul, Minnesota, 1923).

then a young woman of twenty-seven, a graduate of the
Friends' Boarding School in Providence, and had been teaching "young ladies" in the town of Plainfield, near by, when
she received her invitation to Canterbury. As principal of the
Female·Boarding School there she was also successful, and her
school flourished until September of the following year.

Her attitude toward slavery and the Negroes may be
inferred from her having been brought up and educated as a
Quaker, but according to her own account[2] she was "entirely
unacquainted, save by reputation," with "the friends of color,
called 'abolitionists,' " at the time of her going to Canterbury.
There, however, she had "a nice colored girl" named Marcia
as "help" in her family,[3] whose intended husband, Charles
Harris, was son of William Harris, a local agent for William
Lloyd Garrison's *Liberator*. Marcia brought home copies of
the paper, which her mistress read with eager interest.

... In that [paper] the condition of the colored people, both
slaves and free, was truthfully portrayed, the double-dealing and
manifest deception of the Colonization Society were faithfully
expressed, and the question of Immediate Emancipation of the
millions of slaves in the United States was boldly advocated. Having been taught from early childhood the sin of slavery, my sympathies were greatly aroused.[4]

An earlier account describes her reactions thus:

My feelings began to awaken. I saw that the prejudice of the
whites against color was deep and inveterate. In my humble opinion it was the strongest, if not the only chain that bound those
heavy burdens on the wretched slaves, ... I contemplated for a
while, the manner in which I might best serve the people of color.

[2] A letter dated May 7, 8; printed in *The Liberator*, May 25, 1833.
[3] Letter dated May 15, 1869, from Elk Falls, Kansas to Miss E. D. Larned,
historian of Windham County, Connecticut, quoted in Wendell Phillips Garrison, "Connecticut in the Middle Ages," *Century Magazine*, xxx (September,
1885), 780.
[4] Garrison, "Connecticut in the Middle Ages," 780.

As wealth was not mine, I saw no other means of benefiting them, than by imparting to those of my own sex that were anxious to learn, all the instruction I might be able to give, however small the amount.[5]

Miss Crandall's first move to put her resolution into action has been differently narrated. In a letter written many years later, she wrote:

... Sarah Harris, a respectable young woman and a member of the church (now Mrs. Fairweather, and sister to the before-named intended husband), called often to see her friend Marcia, my family assistant. In some of her calls I ascertained that she wished to attend my school, and board at her own father's house at some little distance from the village. I allowed her to enter as one of my pupils.[6]

Earlier, at the height of the controversy, she had emphasized the girl's eagerness to join her school:

A colored girl of respectability—a professor of religion—and daughter of respectable parents, called on me some time during the month of September last, and said in a very earnest manner, "Miss Crandall, I want to get a little more learning, enough if possible to teach colored children, and if you will admit me to your school, I shall forever be under the greatest obligation to you. If you think it will be the means of injuring you, I will not insist on the favor."

I did not answer her immediately, as I thought perhaps, if I gave her permission some of my scholars might be disturbed. In further conversation with her, however, I found she had a great anxiety to improve in learning.

Her repeated solicitations were more than my feelings could resist, and I told her if I was injured on her account I would bear it—she might enter as one of my pupils.[7]

---

5 *The Liberator*, May 25, 1833.
6 Garrison, "Connecticut in the Middle Ages," 780.
7 *The Liberator*, May 25, 1833.

A version which contradicts Miss Crandall's receptive attitude was given by another girl, named Mary Barber, who was a servant in the household of Jedediah Shephard at the same time with Sarah Harris. This testimonial, in the form of a letter dated September 10, 1833, was read at Miss Crandall's trial. According to the girl, Sarah told her that Prudence

inquired of her what her education was, she said in reply that it was but poor. She said that Miss Crandall then invited her to come to her school, and become a scholar with her white schollars and she could instruct her so that in nine months or a year she could teach a school. She further added during the same conversation, that she should never have thought of going if Miss Crandall had not *proposed* it to her, and she had concluded to go.[8]

The exact truth probably lies somewhere between the zealous protestations of Miss Crandall and the misrepresentations of her opponents. In any event, the outcome was what she had perhaps anticipated:

The girl had not long been under my instruction, before I was informed by several persons, that she must be removed, or my school would be greatly injured.
This was unpleasant news for me to hear; but I still continued her in school.[9]

By this act, she said, "I gave great offense." Yet she stuck tenaciously to her guns.

... The wife of an Episcopal clergyman who lived in the village told me that if I continued that colored girl in my school, it could not be sustained. I replied to her *That it might sink, then, for I should not turn her out!*[10]

Confronted with the certainty that she would lose most, if not all, of her white pupils if Sarah Harris remained in the

---

[8] Letter in Clark family papers.
[9] *The Liberator*, May 25, 1833.
[10] Garrison, "Connecticut in the Middle Ages," 780.

school, Miss Crandall decided to accept the challenge of intolerance by excluding from her school not the colored girl but the white pupils. To the consternation of the villagers, she proceeded to convert the Canterbury Female Boarding School into an institution for the training of Negro girls who should themselves become teachers for the children of their race.

The decision was easy for Prudence Crandall to make, but how to go about the undertaking was another matter; and for advice she turned to the redoubtable editor of *The Liberator*, "to obtain his opinion respecting the propriety of establishing a school for colored females—and the prospect of success, should I attempt it." [11]

Three letters from Miss Crandall to Garrison during January and February, 1833, trace the evolution of the undertaking.[12] In the first, January 18, 1833, she introduced herself to Garrison and asked his advice about making her school one for young ladies of color: whether she would be able to get twenty or twenty-five pupils from the neighboring cities at $25 a quarter. On January 29, she was in Boston and consulted with him there. He apparently referred her to George Benson and others in Providence, whom she visited on her way home, getting the promise of at least six pupils from that city. On February 12, she was about to leave for New York, to see a colored minister, Mr. Miller; she asked Garrison to send to her there the information he had promised, if he had not already done so.

Thus Miss Crandall moved rapidly and effectively, in her visits to the three cities; and within three weeks she was able to "lay her subject before the public." *The Liberator* for March 2 carried the following advertisement:

Prudence Crandall, Principal of the Canterbury (Conn.) Female Boarding School, Returns her most sincere thanks to those who have patronized her School, and would give information that on

---

11 *The Liberator*, May 25, 1833.
12 Quoted in Garrison, "Connecticut in the Middle Ages."

the first Monday of April next, her School will be opened for the reception of Young Ladies and Little Misses of color. The branches taught are as follows:—Reading, Writing, Arithmetic, English Grammar, Geography, History, Natural and Moral Philosophy, Chemistry, Astronomy, Drawing and Painting, Music on the Piano, together with the French language.

*The terms, including *board, washing,* and tuition, are $25 per quarter, one half paid in advance.

* Books and Stationery will be furnished on the most reasonable terms.

For information respecting the School, reference may be made to the following gentlemen, viz: Arthur Tappan, Esq., Rev. Peter Williams, Rev. Theodore Raymond, Rev. Theodore Wright, Rev. Samuel C. Cornish, Rev. George Bourne, Rev. Mr. Hayborn, *New-York City;*—Mr. James Forten, Mr. Joseph Cassey, *Philadelphia, Pa.;*—Rev. S. J. May, *Brooklyn, Ct.;*—Rev. Mr. Beman, *Middletown, Ct.;*—Rev. S. S. Jocelyn, *New-Haven, Ct.;*—William Lloyd Garrison, Arnold Buffum, *Boston, Mass.;*—George Benson, *Providence, R. I.*

Canterbury, (Ct.), Feb. 25, 1833.

This advertisement was carried regularly in *The Liberator* until the notice of the abandonment of the school was inserted by Prudence's recently acquired husband, a year and a half later, in the number for September 20, 1834.

Another column on March 2, 1833, praised Miss Crandall's proposal and recommended her strongly

for her peculiar qualifications in conducting it, as for her untiring zeal for the improvement of those entrusted to her charge.

It also praises her courage and

great share of the excellent virtue, viz. *Philanthropy,* which has been provoked by the benevolent exertions of the day towards ameliorating the condition of the wretched suffering African, in this country.

Others, nearer home, also supported her plans, especially the Reverend Samuel May, then pastor of a Unitarian church in nearby Brooklyn, Connecticut. Meanwhile, the resentment of the village at the quick resourcefulness of Miss Crandall and her keeping her intentions secret is vividly presented in a statement by Richard Fenner, the Canterbury storekeeper, probably solicited for use against Miss Crandall in her second trial, since it is dated September 11, 1833.

This may certify that in the Month of January, 1833, the latter part of that month, or the fore part of February 1833, Prudence Crandal came into my store, and without any knowledge on my part that she was going to Boston, and without any request from me, or anyone else, she voluntarily told me that she was going to Boston to visit the infant schools and purchase an infant school apparatus, and asked me for a letter of introduction to some of my friends there. She made no mention of any other business she had there, except what is above stated, and this she did in such a manner as to preclude any belief that she had any other business. There was no allusion made to changing her school to a black one, and I had no suspicions of that kind until after her return from New York.

Richard Fenner

That her prospective change was soon known and deprecated by the residents of Canterbury we have evidence from a call made upon her in February by four prominent men of the town—Rufus Adams, Richard Fenner, Dr. Harris (whose wife was the daughter of General Moses Cleveland, founder of Cleveland, Ohio), and a Mr. Frost—to urge her to give up her idea of a colored school. Apparently Prudence took refuge in Scripture, answering, "Moses had a black wife."

One of the committee's chief concerns was lest Miss Crandall insist that her colored pupils attend the local church as her white ones had done. Apparently she did, as a protest by a committee of the parish in July indicates:

When the Committe visited you last February, stating their objections to your school, they understood from you, by your voluntary suggestions, that you should never desire and never would put your colored schollars into the meeting house—that you could have preaching at your own house, either black or white, and you also added, that the citizens of Canterbury need have no anxiety on that account, they might be assured no such request would ever be made. It appears now that you have departed from this voluntary declaration and put your colored schollars into pews ever occupied by the white females of the Parrish.

We wish you to inform us soon, by whose license you have thus taken possession of that part of the meeting house.

Canterbury July 26th 1833

Solomon Payne ⎫ Society
Andrew Harris ⎬
Isaiah Knight ⎭ Com^ee

Some of the irritation against the school arose from the fact that members of the community regarded themselves as the true friends of the Negro in their capacity as members of the Friends of Colonization in Africa. The insistence upon maintaining separation from people of color even in worship reflects the arguments against the amalgamation of the races voiced in letters continually printed in newspapers of the day, written usually by friends of the Cause of Colonization. This seemed the most hopeful solution to many persons, since it pointed toward a future when this country would be entirely free of the race problem. The Friends of Colonization, including many religious leaders, actively opposed any education for Negroes beyond training them to be leaders of their race in Africa, since any other efforts pointed to eventual equality, and the much-feared "amalgamation." This main charge Miss Crandall answered:

"In a word they hope to force the races to amalgamate." This is utterly false—*the object, and the sole object of this school, is to instruct the ignorant—and fit and prepare teachers for the people of color, that they may be elevated, and their intellectual and moral wants supplied.*[13]

---

[13] *The Liberator*, May 25, 1833.

At another visit on March first, the same committee of four represented "that by putting her design into execution she would bring disgrace upon them all." They "professed to feel a real regard for the colored people, and were perfectly willing they should be educated, provided it could be effected *in some other place.*" Feeling rose so rapidly in the town that on March fourth, Samuel May and George Benson, driving to Canterbury from the adjoining town of Brooklyn, were warned that the town was unfriendly to them and likely to show hostility, since they were known as Miss Crandall's friends. They saw that day a notice posted on the village green, calling a town meeting on the ninth of March to take action against the Negro school. The tense interest of northern abolitionists in the outcome of this meeting is shown by a letter written by William Lloyd Garrison to Benson of Brooklyn on the eighth of March:[14]

Although distracted with cares, I must seize my pen to express my admiration of your prompt and generous defense of Miss Crandall from her pitiful assailants. In view of their outrageous conduct, my indignation kindles intensely. What will be the result? If possible, Miss Crandall must be sustained at all hazards. If we suffer the school to be put down in Canterbury, other places will partake of the panic, and also prevent its introduction in their vicinity. We may as well, "first as last," meet this proscriptive spirit, *and conquer it.* We—i.e., all true friends of the cause—must make this a common concern. The New Haven excitement has furnished a bad precedent; a second must not be given, or I know not what we can do to raise up the colored population in a manner which their intellectual and moral necessities demand.

---

14 Quoted in Garrison, "Connecticut in the Middle Ages," 782–783. The "New Haven excitement" is a reference to the intention announced at the third convention for the Improvement of the Free People of Color, held in Philadelphia in 1830, to establish a manual labor college at New Haven. The officials of that city took prompt action. They met and decided that the founding of such a college was "an unwarrantable and dangerous undertaking," and that they would "resist the movement by every lawful means." Carter G. Woodson, *The Education of the Negro Prior to 1861* (New York, 1915), 290.

In Boston we are all excited at the Canterbury affair. Coloniza-
tionists are rejoicing, and abolitionists looking sternly.

The result of the meeting to be held in Canterbury tomorrow
will be waited for by us with great anxiety. Our brother May
deserves much credit for venturing to expostulate with the conspirators. If anyone can make them ashamed of their conduct,
he is the man. May the Lord give him courage, wisdom, and success!

The town meeting was held in the meeting house in Canterbury, almost across from Miss Crandall's house, on March
ninth, "to devise and adopt such measures as would effectually
avert the nuisance, or speedily abate it if it should be brought
into the village." The numbers of *The Liberator* for March
and April, 1833, devote many columns to Canterbury's treatment of her and her school. Accounts of the town meeting
are printed, and reprinted, from the local newspapers, giving
the views of both sides. Mr. May, Arnold Buffum, agent of
the New England Anti-Slavery Society, and George Benson
appeared to speak for Miss Crandall and to present on her
behalf an offer to move the school to a less conspicuous part
of the town if the citizens of Canterbury would take her house
off her hands; but these advocates, as "foreigners" and inter-
lopers, were given no opportunity to speak. Andrew Judson
rose and denounced the school at length, suggesting that there
were powerful conspirators plotting with Prudence Crandall,
and was followed by others. The only sympathetic words were
the offer of George S. White to assist in the purchase of the
house, but his proposal was interrupted and no attention was
paid to it. Disapprobation of the school was unanimously
voted and the town was pledged to oppose it at all hazards.
After the meeting was adjourned, May and Benson tried again
to speak, but to loud cries of "Out, out!" the trustees of the
church closed the meeting house, effectually preventing a
hearing of any defense of the school. Five days later the town
officers presented "Resolutions" to Prudence Crandall, giving
reasons why she should abandon her idea. Even her father,

Pardon Crandall, a Quaker and hence a peace-loving man, urged her to give it up.

Letters to the Norwich, Connecticut, *Republican* from Andrew Judson and other selectmen of the town charged that Miss Crandall wanted to give Negro misses fashionable airs, and to train them to be brides for white bachelors. Her most loyal and persuasive defender was the Reverend Samuel May, Bronson Alcott's brother-in-law, who inserted two letters in *The Liberator* of March 29 and April 6, entitled "The Right of Colored People to Education, Vindicated. Letters to Andrew T. Judson, Esq. and Others in Canterbury, Remonstrating with Them on their Unjust and Unjustifiable Procedure, relative to Miss Crandall and Her School for Colored Females." These and his other writings on the affair, giving the fullest account available, were printed in his *Recollections of Our Anti-Slavery Conflict.* Though Mr. May may not have won the staunch Connecticut Calvinists of his parish to Unitarianism, he did win their support for his many reform campaigns, including those for the Peace Society, temperance, the improvement of schools, and a village lyceum, besides his constant active interest in the anti-slavery movement.

Prudence Crandall cited his name to Garrison as one sure of esteem, when she wrote[15] appealing, Quaker-like, for mild treatment of her enemies after the names of five Canterbury offenders had been printed in *The Liberator* for March 16:

Permit me to entreat you to handle the prejudices of the people of Canterbury with all the *mildness* possible, as everything severe tends merely to heighten the flame of malignity amongst them. "Soft words turn away wrath, but grievous words stir up anger." Mr. May and many others of your warmhearted friends feel very much on this subject, and it is our opinion that you and the cause will gain many friends in this town and vicinity if you treat the matter with perfect mildness.

---

[15] Garrison, "Connecticut in the Middle Ages," 783.

On April 1, 1833, twenty colored girls arrived at Miss Crandall's school, largely through the enthusiastic support of Garrison and his friends. Opposition in Canterbury at once was shown by refusal of shopkeepers to sell food and by petty attacks. Since, however, as Garrison had told Benson, the Abolitionists were making the school a test case, *The Liberator* urged the negroes to send more pupils, and promised that Miss Crandall would continue her school "until the heathenish opposers repent of their barbarity."

Besides the local boycott, the irate Canterbury citizens invoked against her the Pauper and Vagrancy Law, one of the early "blue laws" of the Connecticut colony. This law required people not residents of a town to pay a fine of $1.67 a week; if the fine was not paid or the person gone in ten days, he was to be whipped on the naked body not exceeding ten stripes. Samuel May records that a warrant was issued against Eliza Ann Hammond, a Negro pupil of seventeen from Providence; and he was eager that she should endure the punishment, even to the stripes, since the treatment would rouse the country against her persecutors. A complaint and a warrant were issued against Ann Peterson, dated the third and fourth of May, but neither warrant was followed by action, probably because May soon got a bond of $10,000 from gentlemen in his parish to cover the fines.

In place of the obsolete Pauper and Vagrancy Law, a new law was enacted through Judson's influence by the Connecticut legislature on May 24, 1833, called the Black Law. At a second town meeting the citizens of Canterbury had condemned the school as a "rendezvous . . . designed by its projectors . . . to promulgate their disgusting doctrines of amalgamation and their pernicious sentiments of subverting the Union." The new law, stemming from that meeting, provided that no colored people from outside the State should be allowed instruction in any but the free public schools of Connecticut, unless the town gave special permission. The law carried severe penalties. Miss Crandall's first reaction to it was assuredly not one of peaceful submission. In *The Liberator* for June 15 appeared a letter from George Benson, dated June 11, which stated that Miss Crandall's school still continued despite the "blue law" of Connecticut, and urged other pupils to attend, for she had eighteen or twenty and could take eighteen or twenty more.

Part of a letter from one of Miss Crandall's girls, telling of the reception of the law in Canterbury, was published in *The Liberator* for June 22:

Canterbury, May 24th, 1833.

Mr. —

Sir—Agreeable to your request, I write you, knowing your anxiety for the school here. There are thirteen scholars now in the school. The Canterburians are *savage*—they will not sell Miss Crandall an article at their shops. My ride from Hartford to Brooklyn was very unpleasant, being made up of blackguards. I came on foot here from Brooklyn. But the happiness I enjoy here pays me for all. The place is delightful; all that is wanting to complete the scene is *civilized men*. Last evening the news reached us that the new Law had passed. The bell rang, and a cannon was fired for half an hour. Where is justice? In the midst of all this Miss Crandall is unmoved. When we walk out, horns are blown and pistols fired.

A long and rather elaborate address written by one of the pupils to the other scholars and published in *The Liberator* for July 6 mentions their dread of the law:

If the unrighteous law which has lately been made in this state compels us to be separated, let us submit to it, my dear associates, with no other feelings towards those that so dealt with us, than love and pity. Being an inhabitant of the state, I am not yet compelled to leave, but my feelings are inexpressible at the thought that you will be obliged to do so; and that too, just at the commencement of pleasure which showed itself in every apartment of our abode. Love and union seem to bind our little circle in the bonds of sisterly affection. I trust the means of knowledge will yet be ours, and if we are compelled to separate, let us,

adorned with virtue and modesty, earnestly and diligently pursue
everything that will bring respect to ourselves, and honor to our
friends who labor so much for our welfare.

Miss Larned, in her *History of Windham County*, gives an
account of one of the exhibition exercises or "gala days" at
Miss Crandall's school, a "Mental Feast," where four of the
youngest scholars, dressed in white, sang the story of their
trials composed by the teacher. In seven quatrains it recounted
their "complaints": for instance,

> Sometimes when we have walked the streets
> Saluted we have been,
> By guns, and drums, and cow-bells too,
> And horns of polished tin.
>
> With warnings, threats, and words severe
> They visit us at times,
> And gladly would they send us off
> To Afric's burning climes.

Some of the important men of Canterbury, perhaps influenced
by the example of Mr. May, ceased to molest Miss Crandall,
but they did not openly encourage the school.

The Liberator for July 6 also contains an account of a happy
Sunday spent by a minister at Prudence Crandall's school, now
with seventeen pupils but able to accommodate forty. The
writer urges that more girls be encouraged to join Miss Crandall and "her amiable and accomplished sister." He added,
however, that "Not content with the new instrument of
oppression put into their hands in the form of a law, about
thirty individuals have combined together, and resolved, I
presume under an oath, as did the Jews of old, not to sell
either Miss Crandall or her scholars the least article of food
or clothing."

The difficulties between Miss Crandall and the townsmen
came to a head when she was arrested in July and imprisoned
in the county jail. May relates that even the sheriff who

brought Miss Crandall to the county jail of Brooklyn urged him and Benson to give bail for her; but here, as with Eliza Ann Hammond, May saw the value of the publicity from the execution of the law, and, accident playing into his hands, shrewdly arranged for her to be put in the cell recently occupied by a criminal named Watkins, who had been hanged for murdering his wife. She was allowed to spend only one night in the jail; but that one night's incarceration, the murderer's cell, and the cause of her imprisonment were bruited about the country in many newspapers.

The Liberator used for its story the largest headlines used by the paper, usually reserved for the headings of departments:

Savage Barbarity! Miss Crandall Imprisoned!!! The persecutors of Miss Crandall have placed an indelible seal upon their infamy! *They have* cast her into prison! Yes, into the *very cell occupied* by WATKINS *the* MURDERER!! She was arrested on the 27th ult., and examined before Justices Adams and Bacon, leaders in the conspiracy, and by them committed to take her trial at the next session of the Supreme Court at Brooklyn, in August.[16]

Some idea of the nation-wide excitement roused by the incident may be gained from two letters received by Andrew Judson soon afterward. One, from distant Pittsburgh, is full of invective, with no regard for grammar or spelling, promising that if the writer does not himself come within three weeks and give Judson a beating, he will hire an Irishman to handle the "poor, dirty, mean, pitifull, dastardly, puppy." He signs only the initials G. P., since "I shall be in your little Hell." The author of the second letter, A. B. C. of New Bedford, Massachusetts, is more restrained and grammatical. His anger vents itself in satire as he submits a business proposal from one Yankee to another. Since Britain, France, and Germany, he says, are now interested in ideas of liberty and equal

---

[16] *The Liberator*, July 6, 1833.

rights, he offers to take Judson abroad on exhibition in a cage.
He guarantees good care and at least $5,000 a year for two and
a half years. He promises good food and no whipping or com-
pulsion unless absolutely necessary to make him allow examination of his "animal organization." He also promises that "a
coloured person shall every morning clean out your den, provide your food, and give you that attendance which is commonly given to that wise and elegant creature, which with
the exception of the tail most nearly resembles the human
form."

While the correspondents of *The Liberator* were indulging
in an emotional orgy over the martyrdom of Prudence Crandall, often adding the touch of her being ill the one night
spent in the jail cell, the number for July 20 reprinted from
the *Windham County Advertiser* one of the sanest letters
from Miss Crandall's opponents, with whose indignation at
the injury to the quiet village of Canterbury one often sympa-
thizes. He answers several charges lodged against the friends
of the Colonization cause, especially those of a Mr. Burleigh,
of the neighboring town of Plainfield; points out the false
reasoning of the abolitionists while he admits the perennial
appeal of the ideal of equality; and states concretely the lasting
problem of social acceptance of the Negro:

And here is the reason I oppose the negro school in Canterbury. I am not an inhabitant of that town, nor am I personally
interested in that particular institution. But I do oppose it as a
part or parcel of the abolition scheme. I oppose it as a gross vio-
lation of the rights of the people of Canterbury, who regard it as
a nuisance.

Let all things be done decently and in order. If such an institution is to be established, let it be done with ultimate reference
to the removal of the pupils to Africa. Here, and here only, can
they stand on the proud eminence of freedom and equality. But
whether they go or stay, such an institution ought to be located
in a neighborhood that is willing to receive it. If a whole community, with an unanimous voice, rises up and exclaims against

the location of such a school within its limits, it is the height of injustice to force it upon them. The white has his rights as well as the black.

...With Miss Crandall I have no personal controversy. As a woman, she ought to deserve the respect due to her sex. But in my judgement, in her reckless disregard of the rights and feelings of all her neighbors,—in her obstinate adherence to her plan in defiance of the entreaties of her friends and of the laws of the land—in her attempts to excite public sympathy, by ridiculously spending a night in prison without the smallest necessity of it—she has stepped out of the hallowed precincts of female propriety, and now stands on common ground, and must expect common treatment. With all her complaints of persecution, I suspect that she is pleased with the sudden notoriety she has gained. But it is not against such as her that we wage war. We oppose an unhappy system, and it is only as a voluntary instrument in the hands of others, to promote this system, that our attention is called for a moment to either her name or her school.

The same issue of *The Liberator* carries as "The Climax" the news that Andrew T. Judson has forbidden Pardon Crandall, his wife, or his daughter to go and see Prudence, under penalty of a fine of $100 or $200, the bond for which would be taken up as for burglary. As "Outrage on Outrage!" it gives more information in a letter from Canterbury:

Miss P. Crandall is now *sick*, probably in consequence of her late imprisonment. Her sister has charge of the scholars. Not many nights since, at about the hour of 10, a stone was thrown in the front parlor of Miss C.'s dwelling—dashing the glass over the room! Before morning a large heavy missile was thrown against some other portion of the building. Addled eggs have been profusely used by the enemies of the school, as a polite way of pouring forth their torrents of indignation; and fresh outrages are constantly occurring. Where will these things end?

The issue for August 3, under "Ladies' Department," contained an "Address Written by One of Miss Crandall's Scholars." Packed with quotations, chiefly Biblical, it urges all

Christian ladies to set aside a time of day to pray for Prudence
Crandall. The next number offers a rather stirring long poem
from F.H.W., Pomfret, Connecticut, July 14, 1833, who hails
Prudence as

> Heroic woman! Daring pioneer
> In the great cause of mental liberty!

who is to

> Go—battle with the tyranny of men,
> And meet his fierce assailings. Thou art based
> Upon a rock—the EVERLASTING TRUTH.

The poet ends on a note of hope:

> The cause is brightening—Afric's dawn is come.
> . . . .
> Be of good courage, then, and full of hope,
> And full of faith—for GOD IS ON THY SIDE!

The enthusiastic defences of Prudence Crandall in *The
Liberator* did not fully satisfy the eager mood of the reform-
ers; consequently on July 25, 1833, an abolitionist newspaper,
The Unionist, was started, at Brooklyn, Connecticut, for the
specific purpose of giving publicity to Miss Crandall's case.
It was financed by Arthur Tappan, of New York, whose help
had been enlisted, and edited by William H. Burleigh, of
Plainfield, son of the minister there and earlier editor of *The
Christian Monitor*.

The Crandall case came to trial in Brooklyn on August 23,
in the Windham County Court, with Judge Eaton presiding.[17]

---

[17] For Miss Crandall's trial, cf. *Remarks of Andrew T. Judson to the Jury
in the Case of the State v. Prudence Crandall before Superior Court, October
Term, 1833* (Hartford, 1833); *Report of the Case of Prudence Crandall vs.
State of Connecticut before Supreme Court of Errors* (Boston, 1834): *Report
of Trial of Prudence Crandall before County Court, August 1833* (Brooklyn,
Connecticut, 1833); and *Statement of Facts, Respecting the School for Colored
Females on Report of the Trial of Prudence Crandall* (Brooklyn, Connecticut,
1833).

Tappan gave May money to hire the best lawyers in the State;
and Calvin Goddard, Henry Strong, and W. W. Ellsworth
defended Miss Crandall, on the ground that the law was unconstitutional. Judson, Welch, and Bulkeley prosecuted, and
the result of the trial was that the jury three times failed to
agree. The case was transferred to the Supreme Court of the
State, where it was tried October 3 before Judge Daggett, a
strong supporter of the Black Law, with Judson and Cleveland prosecuting and the same three defending. The judge
gave a brilliant charge to the jury, urging conviction, and the
resulting verdict was against Miss Crandall. The case was,
however, appealed to the Court of Errors, where it came up
on July 22, 1834, and was quashed for lack of evidence.[18]

Before the legal attack on Prudence Crandall finally proved
unsuccessful, an attempt was made to involve her sister. A
complaint was lodged on September 26, 1833, from "Grand
Juror Nicholas Emsworth to Rufus Ames, Justice of the Peace
for County of Windham, that Almira Crandall did aid and
assist in instructing colored persons in a school in Canterbury,
not inhabitants of the state, since 1st July to 24th September,
1833; with force and arms, school had been set up." The
sheriff was enjoined to "arrest the body of Almira Crandall
of Canterbury and bring before Rufus Ames at the house of
Chauncey Bacon. As she is under 21, also to summon Pardon
Crandall, parent and natural guardian of said Almira to
appear and attend inquiry then and there to be made." Since
The Liberator, which burst into hue and cry over each fresh
attack on Miss Crandall and her school, contains no mention
of such an arrest, it seems likely that no action was taken.

Despite these legal attempts to stop her, Miss Crandall's
school continued throughout the rest of 1833 and most of
1834, but evidences of popular resentment must have made
life rather miserable for her and her sister. In September her
well was filled with manure from the barnyard, and since the

---

[18] Possibly as a result of these unsuccessful trials and a quieting of the
excitement, the Black Law was repealed within five years.

neighbors refused her their water, a quantity had to be hauled daily by her father from his farm, a distance of two miles.[19] A minister, Theodore Freylinghausen, was not allowed to preach in the Canterbury church because he had visited the school. The physician, summoned to attend a sick girl, warned Miss Crandall not to send for him again; the druggist refused to sell her medicines; and local miscreants threatened to demolish the house whenever the word should be given.[20] Fires were started in the building on January 28 and in August, leaving charred timbers, still visible in the attic. Windows were broken at times, and in June young Mr. Burleigh, temporarily serving as a teacher in the school, was pelted with addled eggs.[21] For his part in abetting Miss Crandall and reporting her persecutions, Garrison was served with papers instituting a suit for libel by five citizens of Canterbury: Andrew T. Judson, Rufus Adams, Solomon Paine, Captain Richard Fenner, and Dr. Adams.[22]

Meanwhile, Miss Crandall's courage and persistency were winning rewards also. In April, 1834, on a visit to Boston, she was entertained at banquets by abolitionist leaders and colored societies; and her portrait, now owned by Cornell University, was painted by the artist Francis Alexander.[23] Letters of approval and gifts poured in from Canada and from London, Bath, Glasgow, and Edinburgh.[24] She had the satisfaction of seeing her most active opponent, Squire Judson, defeated in his contest for the legislature in the spring of 1834,[25] though he was elected to Congress later in that year. The New England Anti-Slavery Convention at Boston on May 26, S. T. May, President, voted a resolution that "Miss Prudence and Miss Almira Crandall merit the warmest approbation of all

[19] *The Liberator*, September 21 and 28, 1834.
[20] *The Liberator*, November 2, 1834.
[21] *The Liberator*, June 14, 1834.
[22] *The Liberator*, November 2, 1833.
[23] *The Liberator*, April 5, 1834.
[24] *The Liberator*, November 25, 1833, September 13, and November 8, 1834.
[25] *The Liberator*, April 19, 1834.

friends of the colored race, for their persevering and untiring exertions to educate colored females, under a most bitter and unchristian persecution." [26] Best of all, the interest aroused in eastern Connecticut by her experiences produced a Female Anti-Slavery Society there in the summer of 1836, which was addressed by May and Garrison.[27]

In September, 1834, however, occurred two events which were more effective than fire and law in bringing Miss Crandall's school to a close. The first was her marriage in Brooklyn, Connecticut, probably on September 4, to the Reverend Calvin Philleo of Ithaca, New York, a Baptist preacher, who, judging from the evidence, was far more prudent than Prudence.[28] Only a few days afterward, on September 9, there occurred a final display of violence at Canterbury, which occasioned the rapid and final decision the next day, September 10, to close the school. The notices in *The Liberator* for September 20 give an account of the events and furnish grounds for the conclusion that the Reverend Calvin Philleo had less of the heroic martyr in him than did his wife. About midnight on September 9, five downstairs windows were smashed by men carrying iron bars or heavy clubs. The two front rooms were rendered uninhabitable. Mr. Philleo and Prudence were unwilling to go to the expense of repair, since there was no assurance that the attack would not be repeated and no one in town would help protect them against such attacks. The twenty Connecticut girls still remaining in the school were told by Mr. May, who hurried down from Brooklyn the next day, that they must return to their homes and that the school was abandoned. Philleo offered a reward of fifty dollars for the apprehension of the ruffians and advertised the house for sale.

Thus came summarily to a conclusion Prudence Crandall's attempt to carry on a school for Negro girls in Canterbury.

---

26 *The Liberator*, May 26, 1834.

27 *The Liberator*, July 5 and August 16, 1834.

28 An article on the marriage in the New York *Transcript* puns after a current journalistic custom upon the names "Prudence" and "Love."

The Liberator contains no further reference to her except in the form of an advertisement, continued through March of the next year, recommending *The Oasis,* by Mrs. Child, because it includes a likeness and an account of Miss Crandall. It is assumed that Mr. Philleo took his wife home to Ithaca, New York, where in Prudence Risley Hall of Cornell University her portrait hangs today. It came rather naturally, one may surmise, into the possession of Samuel May, who gave it on the day before his death to President Andrew D. White of Cornell.[29] From Ithaca the Philleos went on to Illinois, and later, accompanied by Prudence's brother Hezekiah, to Elk Falls, Kansas. Mr. Philleo died in Illinois in 1874, but Prudence lived on in Elk Falls until her death on January 28. 1890.[30]

Prudence Crandall's name appeared again in newspapers and magazines in 1885–1886, this time in recognition of her courageous pioneering. The shifting emphases of time are clearly shown by the fact that the petition to the Connecticut legislature to grant her a pension was started in Canterbury, and that Andrew Clark, Andrew T. Judson's nephew, was the chief promoter. In April, 1886, after the Committee on Appropriations had failed to approve the grant, the Connecticut legislature voted her an annuity of $400.

Several letters from Mrs. Philleo in connection with the movement to make reparations, not only for the loss of property but also for the loss of a profitable school, show that in 1886, at the age of eighty-two, she was alert and vivid, and still cared more for causes than for profits. She did not want the house given back to her, with an annuity of $500, as had been suggested, since she was happy and well in her "little pioneer box house of three rooms." Nor did she want charity, since she would rather dig than beg. But she would be grateful for

---

29 Garrison, "Connecticut in the Middle Ages," 780.
30 A brief account of her life by John C. Kimball was privately printed in 1886. Some inaccuracies in Kimball's work are corrected in the foregoing pages.

a yearly sum as payment for the "just debt" owed her by the State for destroying her "hopes and prospects . . . by an unjust and unconstitutional law." On April 5 she wrote to the gentleman who had telegraphed her the news, expressing gratitude for "the change that has been wrought in the views and feelings of the mass of the people." Hopefully she contrasted it with the joy evinced by the citizens of Canterbury, ringing the church bell and firing a cannon thirteen times, when the Black Law was passed. She named gratefully the particular men who had advocated her cause with the Legislature, including Mark Twain, "the man who offered to reinstate me in my old home in Canterbury."

The journalist George B. Thayer, who visited Mrs. Philleo in 1886,[31] found "a host of good books" in her house, and was rather startled to discover that she was conversant with the subjects of the day and eager to talk of them. Her talk he found "clear, connected, enlightened." She was reading William Denton's *Is Darwin Right?* at the time of his arrival. The testimony he reports from her then is worthy of quoting, since it etches sharply for us a woman who, before Margaret Fuller, dared to express new and liberal ideas publicly, and who had kept her mind active and unembittered through a trying and often lonely course.

My whole life has been one of opposition. I never could find anyone near me to agree with me. Even my husband opposed me, more than anyone. He would not let me read the books that he himself read, but I did read them. I read all sides, and searched for the truth whether it was in science, religion, or humanity. I sometimes think I would like to live somewhere else. Here, in Elk Falls, there is nothing for my soul to feed upon. Nothing,

---

31 Thayer began a bicycle trip across the country in April, 1886, writing a series of letters about his trip for the Hartford *Evening Post*, which letters later formed the book *Pedal and Path* (Hartford, 1888). Three letters (209–215) describe Thayer's visit to Prudence Crandall Philleo in Elk Falls. She showed him an appreciative letter from Mark Twain, then a resident in Connecticut, offering to send her a complete set of his books. She added regretfully that he had never sent them.

unless it comes from abroad in the shape of books, newspapers, and so on. There is no public library, and there are but one or two persons in the place that I can converse with profitably for any length of time. No one visits me, and I begin to think they are afraid of me. I think the ministers are afraid I shall upset their religious beliefs, and advise the members of their congregation not to call on me, but I don't care. I speak on spiritualism sometimes, but more on temperance, and am a self-appointed member of the International Arbitration League. I don't want to die yet. I want to live long enough to see some of these reforms consummated.

JANE GREY SWISSHELM: AGITATOR

Lester Burrell Shippee

JANE GREY SWISSHELM: AGITATOR

Into this world of sorrow are born some who can never be content to leave things as they find them; the seers, the prophets, the reformers, all of them discover in their souls something which is out of tune with the particular portion of the universe in which their lot is cast, and strive all their mortal days to bring to the exact degree of tautness the jangling string. Some of them pass into the beyond with the sickening sense that their efforts have been vain; others, perhaps more fortunate, survive to behold their ideas taken up and carried to a certain fruition. But they, in turn, may perceive the ever-renewing breed of the restless seeking to overturn and to reshape even those factors which have escaped the desecrating hand of earlier readjusters. Others, again, are never satisfied with the accomplishment of one change, but turn, impelled by the urge within, to newer fields of contest and perhaps conquest. These stormy petrels of society have a function to perform. To change the figure, they are the gadflies which sting their fellows from their self-content and their easily satisfied desires, prod them till, from very disgust at the importunity, they sluggishly and unwillingly allow themselves to deviate into new and untrodden paths.

Such a soul of revolt was born into the then frontier town of Pittsburgh in 1815. Jane Grey Cannon,[1] daughter of Scotch-Irish Presbyterians who treasured the legends of covenanter

---

[1] In 1880 Mrs. Swisshelm published the story of her life down to the close of the civil war under the title *Half a century* (Chicago). She states in this work that she wrote from memory, having destroyed all letters and papers lest they be used for some evil purpose. Sketches of her life are found in *Appletons' cyclopædia of American biography*, edited by James G. Wilson and John Fiske (New York, 1887-1889); in William B. Mitchell, *History of Stearns county* (Chicago, 1915), 2: 1080, 1404-1406; in Daniel S. B. Johnston, "Minnesota journalism in the territorial period," in *Minnesota historical collections*, 10 (part 1): 346-347; and in *A history of the republican party from its organization to the present time to which is added a political history of Minnesota from a republican point of view and biographical sketches of leading Minnesota republicans*, published by E. V. Smalley (St. Paul, 1896), 309-311. In the preparation of the present sketch *Half a century* has been much used.

days, was brought up in an atmosphere saturated with the ozone of service and poisoned with the mephitic exhalations of self-immolation and self-repression. Not even the love with which the mother enveloped the household could dissipate all the baleful influences of the less attractive side of Calvinism. Nothing but New England puritanism or covenanter severity can account for a two-year-old conscience ''tortured'' by the vanity of wearing new red shoes and white stockings ''beautifully clocked'' at services in a Presbyterian meetinghouse where the sanctuary was never profaned by the singing of ''human compositions, but resounded only to the cadence of Rouse's version of David's psalms.'' Nor otherwise could come easily the morbidity which would force an infant under six years of age to crouch at night by the side of an open grave where lay the body of a woman, three years buried yet in a ''wonderful state of preservation,'' and gaze at the still face in the opened coffin with confident expectation of beholding a supernatural apparition. Years afterwards the experience was described as ''inexpressibly grand, solemn and sad. . ... Earth was far away and heaven near at hand, but no ghost came, and I went home disappointed.''

Bereft of the head of the house when Jane was seven years old, the Cannon family, back in Pittsburgh, after a few years in the ''new village'' of Wilkinsburg, had a somewhat difficult time to make an adequate living. To eke out an income Jane was taught lace-making, an art which she, seated on the ample lap of an attentive pupil, passed on to women of the neighborhood. At this mature age she began painting and made a profit by selling the pictures which she produced, once receiving the munificent sum of five dollars from one who was willing to become her patron and finance her education in art. Later, after her marriage, while again dabbling in colors Jane was seized with the conviction that following this avocation was inconsistent with her duties as a wife, and she gave up what she believed was really her calling in life—for writing, wherein she did achieve at least notoriety, never impressed her as a true and satisfying outlet for her soul's expression.

Of course, joining the church was expected of the child, but a suggestion from her mother that she should do so threw her into a panic of doubt and soul-searching. All the torment which an adolescent could experience was hers, and after a descent into hell she arose "as one from a grave" with the conviction that her petition that "God should write his name upon my forehead, and give me a 'new name' which should mark me as his; and bring William [*her brother who had run away from home, and who subsequently died at New Orleans*] into the fold, and do with me as he would," had been favorably received. She was convinced that she had been chosen — was one of the elect — and this assurance remained with her to her death.

It was while journeying to a private school, a few miles from Pittsburgh, where she spent a few weeks earning her own keep and tuition by teaching the younger children, that she met the man whom she later married, just before she attained the age of twenty-one. James Swisshelm was the son of an old revolutionary soldier. His family was Methodist; his mother was one who "'lived without sin,' prayed aloud and shouted in meeting," and incidentally dominated her family, even trying to make her new daughter-in-law conform. An alliance between a covenanter Presbyterian and such a man was believed by Jane's mother to be productive of no good, a sound belief, as the years demonstrated. Nevertheless, despite religious incompatibility, the marriage took place and the young couple went to Swisshelm's home to live, for his services were needed there; at least such was his own and the opinion of his mother.

So long as the two families remained together there was little peace. Jane was convinced that mere marriage did not connote absolute self-abnegation. Her husband, strongly supported by his mother, could not see why his wife would not put aside her prejudices and strive to make him happy by doing as he wished. An early conflict grew out of Swisshelm's unquestioned admiration of his wife's abilities: he wanted her to exercise her undoubted talents by preaching in public, as Wesley ordained. "It was a very earnest discussion, and the Bible was on both sides; but I followed the lead of my church, which taught me to be silent. He quoted his preachers, who were in league with him, to get me to give myself to the Lord, help them save souls, by calling on men everywhere to repent; but I was obstinate. I would not get religion, would not preach, would not live with his mother, and stayed with my own." As Mrs. Swisshelm willingly admitted, their conflicts were all spiritual; "There never was a time when my husband's strong right arm would not be tempered to infantile gentleness to tend me in illness, or when he hesitated to throw himself between me and danger."

The irreconcilable incompatibility of the two is illustrated by a trivial affair following a sojourn in Louisville, and after Mrs. Swisshelm had returned to Pennsylvania. James sold out an unfortunate commercial enterprise for "a panther, two bears, and a roll of 'wild-cat money.'" He delighted in his domination over the panther, while his wife lived in mortal terror of the animal; and yet it was not until her life, as well as the lives of others, had been narrowly threatened by this beast more than once that he was induced to part with it. Apparently he was utterly at a loss to understand his wife's timidity.

The stay in Louisville impressed an indelible stamp upon the after career of Mrs. Swisshelm. There she saw slavery in some of its worst aspects — saw it as it is depicted in works of the type of Harriet Beecher Stowe's *Uncle Tom's cabin*. A hatred of the institution had been implanted in her by a clergyman in early days, but it was not until after her first-hand experience in a state where slaveholding was legal that she became a white-hot torch of abolition. It was then that she was impressed by the slaveholder as the beast she delighted to picture in the scathing denunciations which appeared in her later writings. In Kentucky she found the "advance guard of a great army of woman-whippers, which stretched away back to the Atlantic and around the shores of the Gulf of Mexico, and that they were on duty as a staring brigade, whose business it was to insult every woman who ventured on the street without a male protector, by a stare so lascivious as could not be imagined on American soil. I learned that they all lived, in whole or in part, by the sale of their own children and the labor of the mothers extorted by the lash. . . . I learned that none of the shapely hands displayed on the black vests had ever used other implement of toil than a pistol, bowie-knife or slave-whip; that any other tool would ruin the reputation of the owner of the taper digits; but they did not lose caste by horse-whipping the old mammies from whose bosoms they had drawn life in infancy."

Jane Swisshelm apparently never knew that there was another

type of slaveholder—the man who did not love the institution for itself but who was unable to see how southern society could exist with a large negro population in its midst in other than a state of bondage. She never believed that there was a man who owned slaves and at the same time was considerate of them and of his fellow men of a lighter hue; who ruled his estate as a patriarch of old and, when he died, went to his grave lamented alike by bond and free. The unquestioned softer side of southern life never came beneath her gaze, and it is much to be doubted whether she could have seen anything there which did not fit into the picture she had drawn for herself in those unhappy days in Louisville, had she been allowed to have a wider experience. Pursuit and capture of fugitive slaves on the soil of free states, both before and after the enactment of the law of 1850, but confirmed her in her fixed idea.

It was after Mrs. Swisshelm's return to Pittsburgh, occasioned by the fatal illness of her mother, that she first appeared in print, anonymously, in an attack upon capital punishment. Two years later, in 1842, after she and her husband had returned to the farm in Pennsylvania, she began writing stories and poems, over the name "Jennie Deans," for *The Dollar Newspaper* and *Neal's Saturday Gazette*. Abolition articles and thoughts on woman's rights were published in Fleeson's *Spirit of Liberty*, of Pittsburgh. Here again the inability of Mrs. Swisshelm and her husband to see eye to eye is evidenced, for he was wroth that she concealed her identity: If she were not ashamed of her production, why did she not sign her name?

Nevertheless, at this time things were in the way of progressing smoothly between Jane and her husband, when Swisshelm's mother went to live with the young people; and thereafter it was a case of constant friction, the principal cause of which seems to have been jealousy on the part of the elder woman, who resented the influence Mrs. Swisshelm exercised over her husband and others. Twice did things arrive at such a pass that Jane left Swisshelm, determined never to return, but in each case a reconciliation was effected.

The Mexican war came and went, affording additional texts for the nearly weekly essays and sermons which Mrs. Swisshelm wrote in the intervals between teaching school and attending to household duties. During this time she emerged from anonymity when there appeared in the *Pittsburgh Gazette* a "hexameter rhyme half a column long" flaying the Methodist preachers who lent adhesion to the "Black Gag" rule adopted by a conference of their church in 1840, which forbade "colored members of the church to give testimony in church-trials against white members, in any state where they were forbidden to testify in courts."

Like most of the abolitionist papers, the *Spirit of Liberty* did not live many years; but after its decease the Pittsburgh *Commercial Journal*, edited by Robert M. Riddle, served as an avenue through which Mrs. Swisshelm could find her public after it had printed a letter of hers, with, however, an editorial disclaimer. The editor, a whig, had antislavery proclivities, and so the more willingly gave a place to diatribes against the war, slavery, and kindred subjects. "My style," Mrs. Swisshelm later wrote of these, "I caught from my crude, rural surroundings, and was familiar to the unlearned, and I was not surprised to find the letters eagerly read. The *Journal* announced them the day before publication, the newsboys cried them, and papers called attention to them, some by daring to endorse, but more by abusing Mr. Riddle for publishing such unpatriotic and 'incendiary rant.'"

Out of her own difficulties in securing for herself and from her husband certain property left her by her mother came a series of letters on married woman's right to hold property. After discoursing on general principles she seized upon a flagrant case which stirred the community and so held up existing laws to public scorn that she was in part instrumental in securing a change in the statutes of Pennsylvania, making it possible for a woman to acquire and hold property in her own name. It was this campaign which brought Mrs. Swisshelm an acquaintance with Edwin M. Stanton, then a young Pittsburgh lawyer.

An abolitionist paper, however, was needed. The *Albatross*, started in Pittsburgh in the fall of 1847, was going on the rocks, and its demise would leave the liberty party without an organ in western Pennsylvania, a calamity tantamount to the disintegration of the organization in that region. A sudden and unconsidered suggestion from Mrs. Swisshelm that she might start a paper of her own met with approval and the *Pittsburgh Sat-*

urday Visiter (Mrs. Swisshelm insisted on the *e*) was the result. For several years this sheet was issued, bearing the impress of its editor from heading to last column, with much of its news and practically all its editorial material from her pen. From first to last it was an organ for the denunciation of slavery and occasionally a mouthpiece for the advocacy of woman's rights. It flung its blows right and left, not unconsidered, but with the intention of hitting every head which appeared. Its circulation grew until it was one of the best known of the abolitionist newspapers. Like Garrison with his *Liberator*, Mrs. Swisshelm was not content in reaching only those who relished its pungent paragraphs, but she placed on its mailing list editors and prominent people all over the country. It penetrated the south and stung to fury those who saw themselves and their institutions attacked, so often without justice. Its influence was wider than its circulation, for it was quoted extensively either to praise or to condemn. A woman was publishing a newspaper and that added to the anger of many.

"A woman has started a political paper! A woman! Could he [*an editor*] believe his eyes? A woman! Instantly he sprang to his feet and clutched his pantaloons, shouted to the assistant editor, when he, too, read and grasped frantically at his cassimeres, called to the reporters and pressmen and typos and devils, who all rushed in, heard the news, seized their nether garments and joined the general chorus, 'My breeches! Oh, my breeches!' "

One of the bold men who ventured a somewhat pointed remonstrance and, in the course of a two-thirds-column article stated that Mrs. Swisshelm was "a man all but the pantaloons," was answered in a rime which turned the laugh upon him. This man, George D. Prentice, editor of the *Louisville Journal*, had many a tilt with his female opponent, of which a little interchange in 1859, when Mrs. Swisshelm was editing the *St. Cloud Democrat*, is a sample. One or two opening passes brought from Prentice this invitation:

> "My pretty Jane, my dearest Jane,
>   Ah, never look so shy,
> But meet me in the sanctum, Jane,
>   When the flagon's filled with rye;"

and from Mrs. Swisshelm, this acceptance:

> "Will darling Georgy, norgy, porgy —
> My sweety, chicky chaw —
> He two 'pooneys in him's flagon
> Or two roundy bits of straw;
> Or dip him's brighty beak in
> And eat him's ryey raw?

In plain prose: Will that rye be made into mush? If so, couldn't you add a little 'lasses? or into coffee, when, as you have no cups, we would want two straws, or are we going to take our rye hen-fashion and whole?"[2]

Among the earliest results of the *Visiter's* tactics was a threatened libel suit growing out of an attack upon a federal district judge for his conduct of a case wherein a man was charged with harboring a fugitive slave. A week or so after the trial Mrs. Swisshelm stated that she had been long seeking a great legal luminary of the Pennsylvania heavens which had suddenly disappeared; after looking for it diligently through the best telescopes obtainable, she suddenly bethought herself of Paddy's gun barrel which he had twisted so that he might shoot around corners. "Paddy's idea was so excellent that I adopted it and made a crooked telescope, by which I found that luminary almost sixty degrees below our moral horizon." The anger of the good judge brought forth an "Apology," in which she stated that she would gladly be sent to Mount Airy, the county jail, because its elevation would make it an admirable observatory where she could use her telescope to better advantage. Judge Grier did not prosecute the suit for libel, and no longer played with fire, as is evidenced by a reputed remark of a lawyer engaged to defend another harborer of fugitive slaves. When it was suggested to him that Mrs. Swisshelm should be brought as a witness, he is alleged to have said: "Oh bring her by all

---

[2] A week or so later Mrs. Swisshelm closed the interchange of amenities with the following: "GEORGE D. PRENTICE. — This gentlemen and ourself have been having an 'old hen' confab; and we should have been glad to continue it *ad infinitum*, had he been pleased to be either witty or severe; but he has got into a barrell of 'treacle,' and is all sticky, and soft, and smeary and disgusting, Bah! He surely did not know we were subject to sever [sic] attacks of Nuralgia [sic] of the stomach, or he would not have run the risk of throwing us into vomiting which no medical skill could arrest." *St. Cloud Democrat,* October 27, 1859.

means. No matter what she knows, or whether she knows anything; bring her into court and I'll win the case for you. Grier is more afraid of her than the devil.''

While editing the *Visiter*, Mrs. Swisshelm wished to go to Washington at the time the question of the disposition of the territories taken from Mexico was uppermost in the country. An inquiry addressed to Horace Greeley brought her an offer of five dollars a column for Washington letters for his *Tribune*, so that the financial side of the pilgrimage was attended to. At the national capital she was brought in contact with many of the great personages of the day; she won the privilege of a seat in the reporters' gallery of the senate chamber, hitherto reserved for the exclusive use of masculine scribblers; and she brought gladness to the hearts of the thousands of readers of Greeley's "Bible" with her spicy letters describing persons and events, and commenting upon life in general.

No better illustration of the obsession regarding slavery which dominated Mrs. Swisshelm is found than in her poisoned view of every notable individual connected with the great struggle of 1850. Tales which passed current among many of the more hopeless type of abolitionists she seized upon as examples of the depravity of the whole tribe of slaveholders: that of President Tyler's selling a daughter into slavery because she tried to run away with and marry the man she loved; that of the profligacy of Henry Clay; and that of fleeing slaves seeking death in the Potomac rather than suffer capture and return to servitude. She smacked her lips over the yarn that President Taylor was put out of the way because he opposed the new fugitive-slave law: "He ate a plate of strawberries, just as President Harrison had done when he stood in the way of Southern policy, and like his great predecessor Taylor died opportunely, when Mr. Filmore became President, and signed the bill.''

But of all the examples of depravity the case which interested her most was a "family of eight mulattoes, bearing the image and superscription of the great New England statesman, who paid the rent and grocery bills of their mother as regularly as he did those of his wife.'' After much hesitation she decided to show to New Englanders the "true" picture of their idol, Daniel Webster, and wrote the yarn in a letter to the *Tribune* which that paper published but for which it later apologized. This exposé, she was convinced, was the real cause of Webster's defeat for the whig nomination in 1852, and she stated that Henry Wilson, a senator from Massachusetts and the author of *The history of the rise and fall of slave power in America*, assured her, on the occasion of the free democratic convention of that year, that her letter, rather than the "seventh of March" speech, or the Ashburton treaty of 1842, was the real reason for Webster's rejection.

About 1852 the *Visiter* was amalgamated with the weekly *Journal*, making a combination, under the name *Family Journal and Visiter*, with which Mrs. Swisshelm continued her editorial connection until March, 1857. Not long after this she took the step on which she had long been pondering. Her marriage had been a failure, "productive of mutual injury." For her it had meant twenty years "without the legal right to be alone one hour—to have the exclusive use of one foot of space—to receive an unopened letter, or to preserve a line of manuscript

'From sharp and sly inspection.' "

For her husband it had been a deprivation, since it had prevented his having a wife "who could pad the matrimonial fetters with those devices by which husbands are managed." To a formal separation Swisshelm would not listen. Plain desertion was then the only recourse. Accordingly, after a sharp struggle to secure her personal and separate property, Mrs. Swisshelm took her infant daughter and set out for St. Paul in May, 1857, intending to take up life anew near St. Cloud on land secured through her brother-in-law who, with her sister, had some time since gone to live in that new village of Minnesota.

The idyllic existence to which she looked forward could not be, since danger of Indian attacks made it madness to attempt to live beyond the protection of the settlement: "My cabin perished in a night, like Jonah's gourd—perished that liberty might be crushed in Kansas; for without a garrison at Fort Ripley, my project was utterly insane."

In St. Cloud itself, then, Mrs. Swisshelm settled, but not to bury in the past the struggle against slavery which she had been waging for years; for slavery, negro slavery, she found

in Minnesota. Even then the agreeable summers of this northern region tempted men of means to come from the southland
with retinues of domestic servants to avoid discomfort and
pestilence with which every returning hot season scourged plantation and town in the lower Mississippi valley. In Minneapolis
and St. Anthony, on the shores of Lake Minnetonka, southern
families summered as regularly as the seasons revolved.

In St. Cloud Mrs. Swisshelm found not merely transient visitors, but a permanent resident, "General" Sylvanus B. Lowry,
son of a Tennesseean who had been missionary, agent, and finally superintendent of manual-labor schools among the Winne-
bago. The "general," whose title was derived from the fact
that he had once been attorney-general of the territory, was the
democratic boss of northern Minnesota. He "lived in a semi-
barbaric splendor, in an imposing house on the bank of the Mississippi, where he kept slaves, bringing them from and returning them to his Tennessee estate, at his convenience, and no man
saying him nay." His sway was well-nigh despotic: "Republicans on their arrival in his dominion, were converted to the
Democratic faith, fast as sinners to Christianity in a Maffitt
meeting, and those on whom the spirit fell not, kept very quiet.
People had gone there to make homes, not to fight the Southern
tiger, and any attempt against such overwhelming odds seemed
madness, for Lowry's dominion was largely legitimate. He
was one of those who are born to command — of splendid physique and dignified bearing, superior intellect and mesmeric
fascination." With Jane Grey Swisshelm and General Lowry
in one town there were bound to be happenings of interest.

The opportunity for a clash was not slow in arriving. De-
prived of her dream of a farm home, Mrs. Swisshelm accepted
an invitation to take charge of a newly established paper and
"take town lots for a salary." She changed the name of the
paper to the *St. Cloud Visiter*, appealed through its columns
and personally to all the leading personages of the town for
support, and was assured of the backing of the community, even
to General Lowry himself, who responded by writing, "I myself will give the *St. Cloud Visiter* a support second to no paper
in the territory, if it will support Buchanan's administration."
To the astonishment of all who learned of it, Mrs. Swisshelm

agreed to the terms. Her brother-in-law, when told that the rumor was true, "said bad words, rushed from the room and slammed the door."

Soon an issue of the *Visiter* showed Lowry how his bargain was to work.[3] Stating that the paper would support Buchanan's administration, the leading editorial of three and one-half columns went on to tell what that administration stood for — the establishment of slavery in every state and territory, making good Toombs' boast that he would call the roll of his slaves at the foot of Bunker hill. Northern "mudsills" were talking of voting themselves farms, but they would much better vote themselves kind masters, such as southern laborers had, and Buchanan and the *Visiter* were working together to that end. Lowry was probably grieved; unquestionably he was angry. He sent word that such things must cease or the consequences would be fatal. The next issue of the *Visiter* traced the course by which it had become a supporter of the administration and of a policy long opposed by the editor: General Lowry, accustomed to buying lands and people, had bought her and she proposed to earn the support which he promised by being Mr. Buchanan's most enthusiastic supporter, "indeed . . . his only honest supporter"; for while some pretended otherwise, the sole object of his administration was the perpetuation and spread of slavery, and this object the *Visiter* would support with the best arguments in its power.

Then action became perceptibly accelerated. A speech by Lowry's lawyer, Shepley, on the place of woman; an editorial praising the lecture but calling attention to the omission in his classification of types of the gambling woman not unknown even in Minnesota in the fifties; the lawyer's pretense that this was an allusion to his wife; General Lowry's rush to the defense of an abused lady; and a decision to mob the paper and its editor, all came in rapid succession. St. Cloud, however, would stand for no such method of breaking up a fair fight. Nevertheless, by night, three men broke into the printing establishment, smashed the press, scattered the type, some in the river and some on the road, and so sought to put an end to the whole

[3] The issue of February 18, 1858, contains the mock defense of Buchanan and the explanation of the *Visiter's* position.

issue.[4] This aroused the indignation of the portion of the populace inclining to Mrs. Swisshelm's way of thinking; a public meeting, where she gave an account of the whole affair, produced resolutions of support; subscriptions were taken, a company was formed to reëstablish the paper, and new equipment was rushed from Chicago.

When the *Visiter* was reëstablished in the middle of May, 1858, there was no pretense of supporting Buchanan, for the paper came out as a republican organ of the abolitionist school. A printed story of the act of vandalism brought a libel suit. Thereupon Mrs. Swisshelm persuaded the backers of her sheet, much against their will,' to yield and give bond in the sum of $10,000 to retract the statement and promise never to use the *Visiter* as a political organ. One more issue, got out by the boys in the office, appeared, and the *Visiter* was no more. The next week brought no paper on the regular day of publication and great was the rejoicing of the forces who thought the discordant element had been removed from their tranquil settlement. But on the following day the *St. Cloud Democrat*, with Mrs. Swisshelm its sole owner and editor, made its bow to an astounded public.[5]

From 1858 until early in 1863 Mrs. Swisshelm scolded, praised, and generally guided St. Cloud, Minnesota, and the nation generally in the way they should go. Slavery, with its evils, was by far the most important issue displayed for condemnation, but it would be wearisome to go into the details of this fight. The paper generally supported the republican party, but it was not partisan in the strict sense of the word. Whenever the leaders of that new organization showed signs of yielding to expediency for political ends, they might have felt the lash of a mordant tongue as keenly as the most rabid southern democrat. Lincoln's nomination by the Chicago convention was greeted with no enthusiasm. Indeed, it was not till late and never with

[4] The *Visiter* for May 13, 1859, contains the story of the raid.

[5] This is an epitome of the somewhat dramatic presentation given in *Half a century*. Actually the chronology is slightly different. The last issue before the raid was on April 1; publication was resumed on May 13; the number for June 24, still bearing the old name, contained the announcement of the change of ownership and half a column of defiance to Mrs. Swisshelm's enemies. The issue got out by the boys was dated July 22, there having been none for about a month. The first number of the *Democrat* was dated August 5.

full approbation that Mrs. Swisshelm could lend her pen to support what she was pleased to call that president's truckling dealing with the crisis he was called to face. For a long time she was convinced that he was dominated by the proslavery border-state element. She poured the vials of her wrath upon his head when he took the ground that union forces were not to be used to assist negro slaves to escape from their masters. She condemned his reversing of Frémont's proclamation in Missouri. For what was the war being fought if not to put an end to slavery?

Late in 1861 her comments on Lincoln's first annual show her stand: "Our readers will regret, with us that while the world has been moving at railroad speed, for the past year, our good President has been fast anchored to that blessed, old, slave-catching Inaugural! No matter that slave-holders have been, all that time, using our armies to catch and return their slaves while the slaves have been used as the indispensable means of defeating our armies and destroying our government, Mr. Lincoln once recognized, and enlarged upon his presidential and constitutional duty of nigger-catching, as the one thing needful, and let the world wag as it will, or jog on if it likes Mr. Lincoln is going to be consistent with Mr. Lincoln, now! 'that's so.' No matter if the world moves to Jerico, he is going to stay and catch those niggers — 'he is, certain.'" While the recognition of Haiti was some advance, on the whole "all else is contemptible in matter and manner. It is more like the production of a provincial lawyer, than the Commander-in-chief of the armies of a great nation, at war for existence."[6]

When slavery was abolished in the District of Columbia, in the spring of 1862, Mrs. Swisshelm began to feel that Abe Lincoln and not Kentucky was in the saddle. But such approval as that might bring was tempered soon by Lincoln's abrogation of General Hunter's proclamation abolishing slavery in his district. The discharge of McClellan as a "stick-in-the-mud" was applauded; yet a few days later she summed up the record of the administration for its first twenty months by stating:

True, he has discharged Mr. McClellan, that arch traitor who for sixteen months has fought the battles of the Confederacy

[6] *St. Cloud Democrat*, December 12, 1861.

within the Union lines but he did it a full twelve months after he must have known him to be at least incompetent. He has issued his proclamation of Emancipation, to take effect sixteen months after he turned back the tide of popular sentiment by revoking that of General Frémont; and if he is thus to be always a year or more behind the flood tide of time he might as well remain stationary.

He is now in a position which eighteen months ago would have saved the nation but there is no assurance that his action is not too late; and there are but two things he could do either of which would give us confidence in the future of our Government — Resign or Die.[7]

When secession was actually in progress, Mrs. Swisshelm went with Greeley in saying, not sadly as did the bearded prophet of the *Tribune,* but blithely, "Let the erring sisters depart in peace."[8] From this position she swung to the ground that the south was too cowardly to fight; it could whip negro women, but could not stand up to men. Then, when the war was actually in progress, she was, true to her nature, all for action; one after another of the union military leaders fell under her disapprobation; either they were cowardly, or, more probably, they were poisoned with the virus of southern sympathy.

It should not be thought that, in the general national crisis, smaller issues were forgotten. General Lowry was for a long time an object of Mrs. Swisshelm's attention, particularly when in 1859 he was run by the Minnesota democrats for lieutenant governor against Ignatius Donnelly on the republican ticket.[9]

[7] *St. Cloud Democrat,* November 20, 1862.

[8] "The idea of getting up a civil war in order to compel the weaker States to remain in the Union, appears to us, horrible in the last degree. Threats of force are wicked and monstrous, as tending to exasperate a set of men little better than maniacs now. Let the North show a prompt willingness to make a fair and equitable settlement with the seceding States, and set them at rest about arming the States to repel Northern coercion and we shall have comparative quiet. We can see no good reason why the two confederacies should not live in as much harmony, at least, as that which has existed for some time past or is likely to do in the future, as members of the same nation." *Ibid.,* November 11, 1860.

[9] In 1862, when Donnelly was running for congress, Mrs. Swisshelm wrote him the following letter, the original of which is among the Donnelly manuscripts, owned by the Minnesota historical society. The letter is dated August 13.
Hon Ignacius Donnelly
    Dear Sir
    I write to say, privately, what it is not politic to urge in public viz. that I think your friends make a great mistake in taking your election as a foregone conclusion.

But in 1862, when the general became insane, she publicly announced that had people known his true condition, large allowance would have been made; for a man "struggling with the demon of hereditary insanity" there should have been nothing but "deep commiseration." Had his affliction been realized all would have felt the necessity of helping him, and would have borne with his weakness. "We recognize now," she continued, "the secret of that strange mesmeric influence he has exercised over those with whom he came in personal contact. It was

There is much dissatisfaction with the course of the National Administration — it so utterly fails to touch the heart of the people, that the masses are seized with apathy. You have to contend against the glaring fact that those who worked hardest to secure the election of your predecessor, and that administration, have been gen[er]ally overlooked in the press of the battle, and the Govnt patronage bestowed upon open enemies or doubtful friends, & against the strained efforts of the revived democracy, backed by the Volunteer system which draws off loyal men and leaves the rogues. If you are elected it will be after one of the hardest campaigns you have ever been through, or so it appears to me. If I could heartily support your opponent I should, in any event, expect some patronage, for the democrats reward their friends, the Republicans, their enemies. Major Cullen has large local interests here, & neutral people feel that to oppose him is to oppose our own local interests. He is one of my most liberal patrons & has been for years. I have disregarded my own pecuniary interests in time past, have served the Republican Party without money and without price, because there was a principle involved; but, as the present contest is, in reality for the U. S. Senatorship & that contest is between Rice and Aldrich & I should have to toss up a copper to choose between them I shall not oppose my patrons & and deprive my child of the means of education. I think you are much better qualified for Congress than Cullen & that Rice would make a better senator than Aldrich. So you are crossed, your platform is weak, Cullen's is wicked; but he gives me reason to believe he does not stand on it but agrees with Rice. You need the DEMOCRAT. To it you owe most of your popularity in this region, for it has persistently kept you before the people. I shall stop working sixteen hours a day to win office for people who give all their patronage to enemies. But Will Mitchell [*Mrs. Swisshelm's nephew*] is young and green (?), and wants badly to tear Cullen's platform to splinters. He would buy me out if he were able. I will take $1000 dollars [*sic*], half on delivery & the other on time. Or, I will do the best I can to [*illegible*] your election, *if you pay me fair living wages* or guarantee me in case you are elected some sufficient remuneration in the form of such public printing as I am justly entitled to, I shall place your name at the heads of my columns at any rate. It was forgotten last week in the rush of late news by the mail the night before; but more than this I cannot do in justice to those in my employ, unless you and your party help to sustain the paper. Kindest respects to Mrs Donnelly & in any case I am

Your Friend and Wellwisher

JANE G. SWISSHELM

On the back of the letter Donnelly made this indorsement: "Ans if elected would be glad to do anything in my power. Poor, or would do something at once."

the fitful self-assertion of a large, generous, genial soul, which has gone haltingly through this life, crippled by its clay fetters; but which will as certainly reach the object of its creation — the influence and happiness it was made to enjoy, as it is certain that even in the material economy of nature, nothing is ever suffered to go to waste." It was while she was on sick leave from Washington, in September, 1863, that she last saw the general. He was then enjoying one of the moments of lucidity which occasionally came to him, and in the course of the conversation he said to her:

I am the only person who ever understood you. People now think that you go into the hospitals from a sense of duty; from benevolence, like those good people who expect to get to heaven by doing disagreeable things on earth; but I know you go because you must; go for your own pleasure; you do not care for heaven or anything but yourself. . . .

You take care of the sick and wounded, go into all those dreadful places just as I used to drink brandy — for sake of the exhileration it brings you.

And who will say that the general did not hit at least a portion of the truth, not alone in the case of this restless woman, but in that of many another agitator who seeks to redirect in some degree the progress of society?

All was grist that came to Mrs. Swisshelm's mill: sickness and its proper treatment; the conduct of schools; woman's dress; social diversion. On one point, at any rate, the bringing-up of this woman had not been hedged about by puritanical narrowness, and this was with respect to dancing. She believed it a wholesome and harmless amusement, not merely to be tolerated but to be extolled as a positive good. Once she was taken to task by a good sister who, in a letter which was printed in the *Democrat*, rebuked the "sister" who not long before had been "speaking words of the most solemn import at a dying bed," for lending the approval of her presence at a dancing party. What wonder that God was visiting his people with sore afflictions when the dance hall was frequented "not only by the young and thoughtless, but by those who form public opinion, and profess to believe in Religion!"

"The business of dying," came the rejoinder, "will be time enough when it comes. . . . We have never met an instance of a person whom we could think dancing had unfitted for dying: have nothing in our experience to show that it takes us further away from the contemplation of sacred things than does singing or sailing, running or laughing.''[10]

She contrasted dancing with the ''plays'' with which godly people were wont to solace their lighter moments: ''The clergy and church members generally have a special aversion to dancing, that is, to men and women, or boys and girls dancing together, provided the amusement end in dancing. But they may go through any number of dancing figures and motions to the sound of music and it is all right, provided it be topped off with promiscuous kissing . . . what led us to propose dancing in St. Cloud as an evening amusement was to have it take the place of those kissing rough and tumbles out of which a lady was fortunate if she came with whole clothes; and it has, in a great measure superseded them; but still the children of our extra pious people meet at an evening party, the scenes of the baboon's wedding are reënacted.''[11]

Editorial duties were occasionally relieved by a lecture tour extending through the towns of Minnesota and even into the adjoining states. Woman's rights were ordinarily the subject of her talks, although slavery was not entirely overlooked. Wherever she went a good audience was assured,[12] and the people of

[10] *St. Cloud Democrat*, December 27, 1860.

[11] *Ibid.*, April 4, 1861. The good sister's biblical reference in the earlier issue was not allowed to pass without attention: ''We are gravely asked what we should think of an account of one of the Apostles whirling Mary Magdalene around a room in a waltz. Well what would we all think of a description of Peter kneeling on one knee in the center of a room half full of people and taking Mary Magdalene on the other knee and kissing her twenty times to pay a forfeit and redeem his pocket knife? What should we think of the whole possy of them going through the march quardrille to the tune of 'Dear Sister Phoebe,' while Mary the mother of James went around the room and kissed every man in it by way of amusing the company?''

[12] After a lecture in St. Paul on women's, particularly married women's, rights, the local critic cast his comments in the form of a breakfast chat with Mrs. Critic. The latter resented his likening Mrs. Swisshelm to Shylock, whereupon he said: ''As I anticipated, my dear, you are thinking of Shylock's inhumanity to Antonio in the celebrated trial scene. Now mind, I am not making Shylock immaculate — he unquestionably had human nature on his own eloquent showing, and unregenerate of course. I am only bound to show, before the toast gets cold, that you, as the sympathizer and friend of Mrs. Swisshelm, ought not to object to a comparison with the grand central figure of Shakspear's tale. And right here — in this trial scene —

St. Cloud were sure to find in their weekly paper animated accounts of what she saw and heard — everything from political gossip to accounts of the hotels where she stopped and descriptions of the dress and household management of women who entertained her.[13]

When the civil war was in progress Minnesota politics and small-town doings ceased to afford sufficient outlet for the pent-up energy of Jane Swisshelm's active mind and hand, and so she sold her paper and betook herself to Washington. There, after casting about for something to do, and incidentally meeting again her friend Stanton, the president, and particularly Mrs. Lincoln, with whom there sprang up a close friendship which lasted to her death, she found employment in nursing the wounded. Here, at least, was a chance to do and do again. Overcoming the disadvantage of being a woman and of being unconnected with some regular organization, she became a free lance and sought and found the worst hospitals, the most severe cases, and the most desperate need. For Miss Dorothea Dix, that woman's rights champion and organizer of a considerable portion of the sick-and-wounded relief of the war, she had small regard. Miss Dix was cold and unsympathetic, all for organization, order, and neatness, let the results be what they might. It is, indeed, a quite different picture than we are accustomed to find of the philanthropist who was instrumental in improving the conditions in prisons, insane asylums, and poorhouses, that Mrs. Swisshelm presents to us. Position meant nothing to her, unless

the analogy between the performances in the Venitian court chamber and Ingersoll Hall, strikes me most forcibly. Shylock would cut his pound of flesh — it was his own, his right, his revenge. Now think of Mrs. Swisshelm's plea for the justifiable homicide of husbands — the suppressed and terrible energy with which she reached the climax when she would 'tranfix her tyrant.' Now all that I say is, that Judge Palmer would be puzzled to settle accounts between the wronged Hebrew in the play, and the wronged wife of Mrs. Swisshelm's portraiture from real life.'' *St. Paul Press*, quoted in the *St. Cloud Democrat*, February 6, 1862.

13 ''The Governor's house is a model of home comfort, and small elegancies, showing plain, good sense, and artistic taste in the mistress of the establishment. There is a piano, books, pictures, photographs of distinguished persons &c. — Eureka! Dinner without sauce plates. Oh, dear, but it was a relief to our meat and all the vegetables and sauce to be eaten with it, on a large plate, to be disposed of at leisure and not be required to take charge of half a dozen plates, one of fowl and potatoes, one of oysters, one of cranberry, one of cabbage, one of tomato, &c., &c., and so on according to our St. Cloud company programme.'' Editorial correspondence from St. Paul, in the *St. Cloud Democrat*, February 6, 1862.

she could utilize it; great reputations were as nothing in comparison to her first-hand impressions.

From along in 1863 to the end of the war nursing kept her busy, but when the war was ended something must be found to do. Again Secretary Stanton assisted her by giving her a position as a clerk in his department. What she saw and experienced produced many letters, of which some, particularly those on the question of women in industry, appeared in the *New York Tribune.* Washington, she opined, was the worst place in the country to give this comparative innovation a fair trial; there was no test of fitness before appointment; the male employees were unable to realize that women were trying to earn a living and thought that they must all be treated as "ladies" in a drawing-room. Some women would work and some would not; too many were in the latter category, so that Secretary Harlan solved the problem by turning them all out, neither a just nor a manly way of deciding the issue, according to Mrs. Swisshelm.

The issues raised by reconstruction were naturally a subject of close attention for this woman who had been fighting the southerner and slavery all her days. It was not in her that a prostrate people would find a defender, hence the attempts of President Johnson to put brakes on a radical congress brought down upon his devoted head the invective which she felt was deserved. Since there was no paper ready to be a medium for her own ideas — certainly not for all of them — there was nothing to do but start another, and so the *Reconstructionist* was born. While the utterances of its editor no doubt found a responsive echo in the breast of Thaddeus Stevens, the short-tempered man in the White House was not the sort to brook such emanations from a mere clerk in one of his executive departments, and so he took the emphatic but unfortunate course of dismissing her incontinently, discharging her directly without taking the trouble of having Stanton do it for him. Yet one finds it hard to censure his course after reading the article which provoked it:

When President Lincoln was murdered nearly all loyal people believed that the South had made a serious mistake. A very few thought otherwise. Of these, two said to us: "You are mistaken. They know what they are about. Andy Johnson is their tool."

The thought was too horrible to be entertained. It was too dreadful to believe that the man who had just received such marks of confidence from the loyal millions was simply a skillful actor playing patriot the better to serve the cause of treason. But these shrewd prophets shook their heads and said: "You will see."

One thing was certain. The morning of the inauguration he was drinking freely with blatant Copperheads. . . .

The business was to get the President, and they got him. That it was the South which nominated him through indirect influence — that Mr. Johnson labored cunningly for that nomination by boisterous professions of loyalty, and the thrusting forward of ultra pledges designed to be broken, there is no longer any doubt. That he was prepared beforehand to serve the purposes of treason there can be no doubt; that his administration and its programme were part and parcel of the assassination plot, we have no longer the shadow of a doubt.

This does not make it necessary that he should have known of the intended assassination. We do not think that either Tyler or Fillmore knew that the men who used them intended murdering Harrison and Taylor; but in all these cases the assassins knew their men; and these three Presidents, made Presidents by assassination, are each, with their administrations, as much incidents of the rebellion — emanations from the brain of the arch-fiends and wholesale murderers who plotted that rebellion, as was the starvation of our men at Andersonville, or the poisoning of our armies. Whether known or unknown to Mr. Johnson, his veto message is the further unfolding of the assassination plot.

That assassination was a change of base in the traitor war for the destruction of the Union. The veto is the Sumter guns of this second era of the war, and it will probably be followed by a Bull Run and Ball's Bluff — by disaster and perhaps apparent defeat to the loyal millions whose weapons are once more turned upon them by their trusted agents. Andrew Johnson has his plans matured. He is in full sympathy with the South, and will follow up his present advantage to the bitter end. Let the people nerve themselves to do what they can. They can and will save the government; but there is great danger of a repetition of the mistakes and delays and dreadful disasters of the first stage of this war. There is great danger of a kid-glove campaign under some political McClellan.

Could the people be made to feel that the assassins of President Lincoln are now the honored guests of the White House — that this veto is a part of the murderous programme — Northern Copperheads would not insult a loyal people by their insolent rejoicings, and the traitors of the South would stand aghast before their indignation.[14]

With no clerkship there could be no *Reconstructionist*, and that rocket burned itself out forthwith. Nevertheless, it had scattered its sparks, which flickered out in comments of the editorial variety all over the country.

Worn in body and in mind, Mrs. Swisshelm left Washington for Pittsburgh, where a long lawsuit brought her the old farm at Swissvale and eventually a competence which lasted the rest of her days. St. Cloud, Chicago, and Swissvale, as well as the trains of the Pennsylvania railroad running into Pittsburgh, were favored with her presence during these latter years. While in Chicago, she passed much of her time with the widow of President Lincoln, for the two women seem to have had much in common. These final nineteen years of her life were marked by no extraordinary public activity unless one so reckons an occasional contribution to the *Chicago Tribune*; apparently her life work was done. Her constructive — or was it destructive? — task was completed. Visiting her daughter in Chicago, gossiping with Mrs. Lincoln, or merely sitting quietly at the door of the old house at Swissvale watching the trains go by and gazing at the trees she had planted in earlier years, filled her hours with ample employment, although toward the end of her days she wrote, from memory — for she had destroyed all letters and other documents for fear they would be used for evil purposes — an account of her life down to the closing days of the war. A surcease of labor filled her with a calm content, so that the white-haired woman who made friends with the brakeman of the Pittsburgh local no longer strove to remodel the world. Her day was past. New problems no longer drove her into the noisy conflict of a world trying to forget the war and its causes. The slavery she knew was no more; the south might struggle on, undisturbed by her, toward the dawn of a brighter life.

LESTER BURRELL SHIPPEE

UNIVERSITY OF MINNESOTA
MINNEAPOLIS, MINNESOTA

[14] From the *Reconstructionist*, quoted in the *St. Paul Pioneer*, March 6, 1866.

THE ORIGINAL OF REBECCA
IN IVANHOE

Gratz Van Rensselaer

THE ORIGINAL OF REBECCA IN IVANHOE.

WE believe it is not generally known that the honor of having been the prototype and inspiration of the character of Rebecca the Jewess, in "Ivanhoe," belongs to an American lady, whose beauty and noble qualities were described to Scott by a friend. The friend was Washington Irving, and the lady Rebecca Gratz, of an honorable Jewish family of Philadelphia.

Michael Gratz, the father of Rebecca, was a native of Styria in Austria. Having received his inheritance in money from his father, he emigrated to America in 1750, when a mere youth, and engaged in the business of supplying Indian traders with merchandise. He became wealthy, and in 1769 married Miriam Symons, of Lancaster, Pa. Retiring from mercantile life at the close of the war for Independence, he devoted his time to his extensive landed interests, which in Kentucky included the Mammoth Cave. He warmly espoused the cause of the colonists, and his name appears among the signatures to the Non-Importation Resolutions after the passage of the Stamp Act. The Gratz family mansion in Philadelphia was known far and wide as the home of a refined and elegant hospitality. Gifted and distinguished guests—illustrious statesmen, and eminent persons from abroad whom choice or vicissitude brought to the country—found there an appreciative welcome. About 1811 Rebecca's parents died, leaving a family of eleven children. Many of their descendants filled important public positions, or were prominent as merchant princes of their day. Simon, the eldest son, retired from business in 1825, and purchased a portion of the old Willing estate, in what is now the twenty-ninth ward of the city of Philadelphia, and resided at "Willington" until his death in 1839. He was the founder of the Pennsylvania Academy of Fine

"SUNNYSIDE," IRVING'S HOME ON THE HUDSON.

REBECCA GRATZ. (FROM THE MINIATURE BY MALBONE, IN POSSESSION OF MRS. REBECCA GRATZ NATHAN.)

Arts, and remarkable for vigor of intellect, benevolence of character, and manly beauty. His brother Hyman, a man of elegant presence, was President of the Pennsylvania Insurance Company. Rebecca was born on the 4th of March, 1781, and in her younger days, and even beyond middle life, she possessed singular beauty. Her eyes were of exquisite shape, large, black, and lustrous; her figure was graceful, and her carriage was marked by quiet dignity—attractions which were heightened by elegant and winning manners. Gentle, benevolent, with instinctive refinement and innate purity, she inspired affection among all who met her; and having received the best instruction that the time and country afforded, she was well fitted for practical and social duties. In company with her brother, she was accustomed to spend her summers at Saratoga Springs, where she became the center of a brilliant circle of men and women of position and culture from all parts of the country. Her visits at the home of her brother in Lexington, Kentucky, whither her fame had preceded her, partook of the nature of ovations. On these occasions she received marked attention from Henry Clay, between whom and her brother a warm friendship existed. Several members of her family intermarried with the Clays, the Schuylers and other Gentile families; and the society of few persons was more courted by Christians than was that of Rebecca Gratz.

It is said that, when a young lady, Rebecca won the regard of a gentleman of character, position, and wealth, whose passion was devotedly returned. The difference in their religious faith, however,—the one a conscientious Christian, the other devoted to the ancient creed of Israel,—proved an insuperable barrier to their union. She was never married. Accustomed to the society of Christians, loving them and beloved by them, the attachment to her ancestral faith is rendered more conspicuous, and her firmness in the strife between inclination and duty may be considered an index of the exalted character of the woman. Self-denial and lofty conscientiousness distinguished her life, which was one long chain of golden deeds. There was scarcely a charitable institution of her day in her native city that did not have her name inscribed upon its records as an active officer, or as an adviser and benefactress. As early as 1811 her name appears as an officer of the Female Association. She founded the Orphan Asylum of that city, and was its secretary and warmest friend for more than forty years. She was one of the founders of the Female Benevolent Society, the Foster Home, the Fuel Society, and the Sewing Society. In 1838 she founded a mission Sunday-school for Hebrew children, where prayers of her own composition were in daily use, and for which she procured the writing and compilation of text-books. This is said to be the oldest institution of the kind in America. Gentiles, as well as Hebrews, were made the recipients of her zealous kindness. For a half-century she was thus actively engaged in benevolent enterprises, and for many subsequent years was a valued counselor in charitable work. She died on the 27th day of August, 1869, at the age of eighty-eight.

One of her brother's most intimate friends was Washington Irving, then in the early freshness of his literary fame. When in Philadelphia he was a welcome guest at the mansion, and the "big room" was assigned him to "roost in," as he termed it. The beauty and character of Rebecca, together with the fact that she was a representative of a race whose history is full of romance, deeply impressed him, and the foundation was laid of a cordial friendship and admiration which lasted through life. In the following letter to her, introducing Thomas Sully the artist, Irving expresses his respect and esteem:

"NEW YORK, Nov. 4, 1807.
"I hardly need introduce the bearer, Mr. Sully, to you, as I trust you recollect him perfectly. He purposes passing the winter in your city, and as he will be a mere 'stranger and sojourner in the land,' I would solicit for him your good graces. He is a gentleman for whom I have great regard, not merely on account of his professional abilities, which are highly promising, but for his amiable character and engaging manners. I think I cannot render him a favor for which he ought to be more grateful, than in introducing him to the notice of yourself and your connections. Mr. Hoffman's family are all well, and you are often the subject of their conversation. Remember me affectionately to all the family. Excuse the liberty I have taken, and believe me, with the warmest friendship,

"Ever yours,
"WASHINGTON IRVING."

Miss Gratz passed many of her younger days with the Hoffmans and other old families in New York, with whom she was on intimate terms. Among her friends at this time were the literary wits of Salmagundi. Matilda Hoffman, the object of Irving's first, last, and only love, was her dearest friend. Miss Hoffman, who is described as lovely in person and mind, with engaging manners, delicate sensibilities, and playful humor, faded early and died in April, 1809, at the age of eighteen. Rebecca was her constant companion during her illness, sharing with the family the cares of her sick-bed, and holding her in her arms when she died. Irving was then twenty-six years old, and for the half-century of his later life he cherished faithfully the memory of his early love. He slept with her Bible and Prayer-book under his pillow, and they were ever his inseparable companions. After his death, a package was found containing some private memoranda, a miniature of great

beauty, a braid of fair hair, and a slip of paper containing her name in his own handwriting. In his private note-book he wrote: "She died in the beauty of her youth, and in my memory she will ever be young and beautiful." Portions of his writings convey the impress of the event, as the following passage in "St. Mark's Eve," in "Bracebridge Hall:" "There are departed beings that I have loved as I never shall love again in this world—that have loved me as I never again shall be loved." In "Rural Funerals," in the "Sketch Book," the same tinge of quiet sadness is discernible. The painful experience through which his friend Rebecca had passed, and her grief at Miss Hoffman's death, were well known to Irving, and the delicate sympathy arising from the knowledge each possessed of the other's sorrow was the firmest bond of their friendship.

For many years, during which he studied law and was admitted to the bar, Irving's naturally gay temperament was overshadowed by this grief, and his frequent intervals of depression unfitted him for literary labor. Engaging in business with his brother at Liverpool, he passed much of his time abroad. His mercantile career, however, proved a failure, and he thenceforth devoted himself to literature. It was in the fall of the year 1817 that Scott and Irving met for the first time. With a letter of introduction from the poet Campbell, who was aware of Scott's high estimate of Irving's genius, the latter visited Abbotsford. He was most cordially received and welcomed by Scott himself, who came limping down to the gate, attended by his favorite stag-hound, and grasped his hand in a way that made Irving feel as if they were already old friends. Here Irving passed several of the most delightful days of his life, rambling from morning till night about the hills and streams; listening to old tales told as no one but Scott could tell them; and charmed by the storied and poetical associations of the Tweed. A warm, mutual attachment ensued. Scott was then forty-six, and in the brilliancy of his early fame. Irving was thirty-four, and just rising in literary reputation from the favorable reception of his "Salmagundi," and the "Knickerbocker's History of New York." Scott's opinion of Irving is thus expressed in a letter to John Richardson:

"When you see Tom Campbell, tell him with my love that I have to thank him for making me known to Mr. Washington Irving, who is one of the best and pleasantest acquaintances I have made this many a day."

Irving's opinion of Scott is given in a letter to Paulding:

"I cannot express my delight at his character and manners. He is a sterling, golden-hearted old worthy, full of the joyousness of youth, with a charming simplicity of manner that puts you at ease in a moment."

To this friendship we owe the character of Rebecca in "Ivanhoe." During one of their many conversations, when personal and family affairs were the topics, Irving spoke of his own, and Miss Hoffman's cherished friend, Rebecca Gratz, of Philadelphia, described her wonderful beauty, related the story of her firm adherence to her religious faith under the most trying circumstances, and particularly illustrated her loveliness of character, and zealous philanthropy. Scott was deeply interested and impressed, and conceived the plan of embodying the pure, moral sentiment, that like a thread of silver ran through the story. Although "Rob Roy" was then unfinished, he was already revolving in his mind the plot and characters of "Ivanhoe." He immediately determined to introduce a Jewish female character, and, on the strength of Irving's vivid description, he named his heroine Rebecca.

More than in the Cœur de Lion himself, or in the Knight of Ivanhoe, or in any of the haughty templars and barons so prominent in this romance, its strength and charm lie in the sad, devoted and unrequited tenderness of the Jewish damsel. In almost every one of Scott's works there is a poetical, may we not say impossible, character—some one too good and enchanting to be believed in—yet so identified with our nature as to pass for a reality. Rebecca is the angelic being in "Ivanhoe," and at the last engrosses all the interest. It is by far the finest and the most romantic creation of female character that the author ever conceived, and ranks with any in the annals of poetry or romance. It is, moreover, an exhibition of Scott's wonderful power of will, in view of its composition during moments of intense physical pain. He was obliged to dictate a large portion of the work to his faithful amanuenses, William Laidlaw and John Ballantyne as he lay on a sofa, frequently turning on his pillow with a groan of torment. Yet, when the dialogue became animated, he rose from his couch and walked up and down the room, and vividly personated the different characters. Ballantyne entered with keen zest into the interest of the story as it flowed from the author's lips, and could not repress exclamations of surprise and delight. "Gude keep us a'!" "The like o' that!" "Eh, sirs! eh, sirs!" Laidlaw, too, related the following: "I remember being

so much interested in a part of 'Ivanhoe' relating to Rebecca the Jewess, that I exclaimed, 'That is fine, Mr. Scott! get on—get on!' Mr. Scott, himself highly pleased with the character, laughed and replied, 'Ay, Willie, but recollect I have to make the story—I shall make something of my Rebecca.'"

Scott finished the book in December, 1819, and immediately sent the first copy to Irving. In the letter accompanying it, he asked: "How do you like your Rebecca? Does the Rebecca I have pictured compare well with the pattern given?"

This source of the character was known to Miss Gratz, upon whom Irving had made his first call when he returned to Philadelphia to superintend the publication of his works. Shrinking as she did from any publicity, she would seldom acknowledge the fact, and when pressed upon the subject would deftly evade it by a change of topic. The resemblance is closely marked in many points, which the reader of "Ivanhoe" may be left to find for himself.

In addition to the miniature of Miss Gratz by Malbone, who was famous for the faithfulness and beauty of his art, there is in existence a portrait by Sully, which is said to be one of his most successful works, though he himself was dissatisfied with it.

As an illustration of the regard in which Miss Gratz was held, we may relate the following incident. An aunt of hers was married to Dr. Nicholas Schuyler, of Albany, a surgeon in the Revolutionary war, a friend of Washington, and a near relative of General Schuyler. The Doctor was a Christian, and the differences of religious faith made the marriage very objectionable to the bride's father, who had, however, the highest regard for his son-in-law. A long estrangement ensued, and a reconciliation seemed impossible. During his last illness, the grandfather was attended by Miss Gratz, whose gentleness and skill seem always to have made her in demand in the sick-room. Calling her to him one day, he said: "My dear child, what can I do for you?" Turning upon him her beautiful eyes filled with tears, she replied, in a tone of earnest entreaty: "Grandfather, forgive Aunt Shinah." The old gentleman sought her hand, pressed it, and after a silence said in a broken voice, "Send for her." In due course the lady came, received her father's forgiveness and blessing, and when, a few days later, he breathed his last, the arms of his long-estranged child were about him, while Rebecca Gratz sat silently at his side.

Gratz Van Rensselaer.

"MARIA DEL OCCIDENTE"

Thomas Ollive Mabbott

"Maria del Occidente"

By THOMAS OLLIVE MABBOTT

Robert Southey was very much disturbed. Poet-laureate of England, sometime Radical who became Conservative, historian, biographer, critic, patron of youthful poets, friend of Wordsworth and Coleridge, he found a novel problem confronting him. He had received some letters from an American lady, who told him of how she had been crossed in love, and he believed her a strange person. And now, one day in the year 1831, came a message that she had arrived at Keswick, and was awaiting a call from him. Southey felt that common politeness demanded that he call, but he was determined to stay but fifteen minutes at the most. So minded, he set out—he presented himself, and was so instantly won by the charm of the lady that he remained two hours. And then he and his family entertained the lady for a long visit, and Southey supervised the printing of an epic poem she had written. It was a fine friendship, thus begun between two gifted people—and sometimes I have a notion Southey's gifts were not the greater.

The American lady was Maria Gowen Brooks. She won the respect and admiration of a good many important critics in her own day, and has always found admirers who warmly cherish her work. And I believe my readers will agree her life was a strange one. Probably she told Southey some of the story on her first meeting—certainly she did so ultimately, and he urged her to write it down, so that I may now tell you a tale as romantic as the pen name she signed—"Maria del Occidente."

In 1795 a girl was born in Medford, Massachusetts. She grew up there, and was remembered in after years as a somewhat strange person. Of her parents I know little—but her father died before the daughter was fully mature, and one of his friends married the daughter—to care for her. Mr. Brooks was more than twice Maria's age. He was kindly, he was rich, and, one get an impression he was obtuse. The language of the period is flowery, and it was a time of reticence. Maria Brooks had the literary habit of the time, but she was outspoken with the frankness of an earlier day, and the fearless purity of a noble woman. To her husband she owed what was due also to a parent, she respected him, and never defamed him, but though she bore him two sons she never loved him as a woman loves a man, nor did he realize how sensitive a spirit was wounded by his lack of comprehension. The earnestness of her protest against too early marriage in her notes to Zophiel is witness that she suffered deeply. Yet one should not call her unhappy, for she admitted that at the time she thought of happiness in an active sense as existing only in books.

Mr. Brooks lived in Portland—and there is something pitiful in the picture one sees of a highly intellectual and artistic lady in a provincial part of New England in the days before the War of 1812. The ladies of the neighborhood looked with disfavor upon books and music, as leading to "idleness" and Maria often occupied herself with sewing when it was not needed, from docility of temperament and to escape the censure of these creatures, who managed to mind other people's business without the aid of a Woman's Club. There was an ugly side to the life of the period—and a woman of artistic genius was not expected, or wanted. After all, our an-

cestors were not often troubled by such a problem. But neither are we, and I doubt that Maria would have been much happier at a woman's college to-day. Of course, she might have met one or two men of intellectual power—but she did that in Portland.

But if her marriage was loveless, Maria was soon in love. The experience came in a strange fashion—a violent passion brought her much sorrow —yet at first she was, herself, unaware of its violence, and later when it passed away she could look upon love as the holiest of human experiences. The story, as told in her novel "Idomen," is slightly modified for artistic purposes—particularly is the chronology difficult to follow, because of the author's desire to preserve the classical unities of time and action, which makes her relate a story within a story. But the general outlines are clear enough.

The first meeting between Maria and the one great love of her life took place early in her married life. He was a Canadian by birth, a tall and powerful young man, beautiful in form and feature. In the novel he is called Ethelwald—his real initials were E. W. R. A., but his name I do not know.* He had been an officer in the British

* See Idomen p. 87; Judith, Esther, and other Poems, p. 43.

Army, and returning home by way of Portland, visited the Brooks home in company with a cousin of the hostess. He spent there only a single evening, yet long enough to be much attracted to the lady, who fell instantly and violently in love with him. Of course, however, she gave no sign. But when the guests were leaving Maria kissed her cousin goodnight—and refused to salute his friend in like fashion. Womanlike, she at once regretted her refusal—but composed an ode in his honor, comparing him to Paris, to Phaon, and to the god, Apollo. Although nothing had passed between them, and they saw nothing of each other for several years, Maria knew from that time of her passion. The ungiven kiss was a token more powerful than reality.

But another problem soon troubled Maria, and of a far more dangerous kind. Through her husband she had met, in Portland, a gentleman of literary tasts, who called on her, and brought almost her sole contact with the world of books and music. Welcome as his visits were, she began to feel in his manner too great a warmth. The danger she knew, yet tried to conceal it from herself—to give up all association with him was to cut herself off from her most innocent pleasures. Finally she solved the problem in a romantic way, with a thoroughly characteristic though paradoxical commonsense. To her admirer she addressed a poem with the refrain "Fratello del mio cor" (Little brother of my heart). He took the hint thus gracefully given, ceased the unpleasant part of his attentions, but continued his friendship. He was a rather good sort, I think, as he should have been to be. a friend of Maria Brooks.

Meanwhile Mr. Brooks had suffered financial losses. Like so many New Englanders during the War of 1812, he invested heavily in privateers, and the unfortunate vigilance of the British Navy rendered some of these but a percarious source of income. Mr. Brooks, if not wholly ruined, was in greatly reduced circumstances, and left little or nothing when he died, not many years later. His wife was therefore forced to look to her own relations to support her and her little boys

(for she always treated her stepson as her own). It should be remembered that a woman was rarely able to support herself in those days, and although Mrs. Brooks is said to have contributed poetry to local newspapers, and indeed published a volume of verse in 1820 at Boston, she could not expect to live by her pen. Let us turn aside for a moment and examine her first book. It is a tiny affair, but contains a good many poems in a small type—the principal ones, Biblical narratives, give it the title "Judith, Esther and other poems. By a lover of fine arts." Some of the verses are smooth,

a few may interest the biographer, but I cannot say that they make any deep impression upon me. Maria chose to write in a simple style, which gains great dignity from elevated content, but makes little appeal when the subject is slight. Maturity was to bring the full gift of poetry—the verses of her girlhood are pretty, but little more.

An uncle of Maria lived on a coffee plantation in Cuba, and thither she moved in the early days of her widowhood. But she was not happy there. It was suggested that marriage with a neighboring planter would solve her difficulties. But if the girl had been docile, the woman was firm. One loveless marriage was enough—and a phantom of happiness glowed somewhere in her heart. Shortly she left Cuba, and paid a long visit to a cousin in Canada.

At Quebec she again met the young officer who had attracted her, and very shortly she became engaged to him. Then, for reasons not wholly apparent to the masculine intellect, despite the wealth of detail with which the lady has told of the incident in her novel, Maria broke the engagement. And finally, completely miserable because of the loss of her beloved, she went through a period of mental stress, almost, if not quite, amounting to derangement. She even attempted suicide, though in a very strange fashion. She procured opium and drank it, but prayed that if it were God's will that she live, the poison might be without effect. She was made deathly sick, but recovered. Then she repeated the process with like effect. The kind efforts of a friend were happily successful in recovering the poet to bodily and mental health, and Maria ever after in token of her gratitude wore a small cross which her rescuer had given her.

After this dreadful experience, Maria seems to have become fully reconciled to life, and devoted herself to the education of her children, and to those "literary employments" which she found the greater solace of her life. Her uncle in Cuba died, and she returned to the island, where she was to spend most of the remainder of her life (save for visits to the United States and to Europe) upon a coffee plantation near Matanzas.

Out of her experiences Maria had conceived a poem, and in Cuba, composed the first canto of her epic, which was issued in Boston in 1825. It was a mere first trial, of course, but the title adopted was retained—the name of the fallen archangel who is the protagonist of the tale—a creature gloriously endowed for good and evil, and whose actual existence seems to have been most real to her—Zophiel. I do not know that the volume attracted much attention, but the author contin-

ued her work, and the manuscript of the completed work in six cantos, was finished in January, 1829.

The publication of the full poem did not come for a time, but the nature of the work may well be discussed here. The basic story Mrs. Brooks found in the Apocryphal book of Tobit, where are told the adventures of a Hebrew maiden, whose bridegrooms were successively slain on the wedding night by the evil demon Asmodeus. The imagination of the romantic poets, and I suppose, of their readers, had been fascinated by the idea of the angels who fell in love with mortal women. Byron and Moore had used such themes. And Mrs. Brooks, who had a tase for curious learning, combined other elements in her story, for she adopted the opinion of the early fathers of the church, that the Greek gods (as well as all the gods of the heathen) were fallen angels. She also assumes that absolute damnation was meted out only to the followers of Satan in his revolt against the Most High, and that certain kings of a superior nature were punished by an exile, perhaps temporary, from Heaven. These she supposed to be the beneficent deities of the Ancient World, and indeed it was hard for one familiar with the worship of Apollo—and, let us say, Moloch—to regard both with equal abhorrence, as perhaps strict orthodoxy required.

Taking her story from Tobit, Mrs. Brooks wove into it much from her knowledge of ancient history, and more from her knowledge of human hearts, especially her own. Her heroine, Elga, daughter of exiled Jewish parents during the time of the Captivity, is fated to marry a certain youth, who lives in a far clime—and is also visited by the fallen angel Zophiel, who is identified with the God Apollo. A certain courtier persuades Egla's parents to wed her to him—on the wedding night the bridegroom is slain by Zophiel. Egla is taken before the king, who conceives a passion for her —various followers insist on braving the peril first, and are killed in turn. Meanwhile Zophiel attempts to procure immortality for his beloved—she is imperilled by a jealous sweetheart of the first slain bridegroom, but rescued by her angel lover. Despite celestial warnings, Egla is about to yield to Zophiel, and sings to him the marvellous Twilight Song which has won for its author the reverence of so many great critics—but her destined lover arrives, protected by a good angel, and she weds at last. Zophiel is driven off, but left not without hope of his ultimate pardon and restoration to Heaven.

So brief a synopsis can do no justice to the tale, the adventures of Zameia, Egla's jealous enemy, involve the sacred "Sacrifice of Chastity" connected with the worship of Astarte which one hardly would look for in a poem of the early nineteenth century. Yet the whole thing is told so that a reader hardly realizes the daring element until he tries to tell it in his own words. The author's mind seems to have been perfectly free from all prudishness, and the boldness of her attitude makes what is said inoffensive. Much of the story is an allegory of Maria's own experiences—the loneliness of Egla, the unhappy Zameia wedded to an unloved husband, the dangerous yet fascinating spirit Zophiel—"all of this she knew, and part had been."

The finest thing in the poem is the Song I have mentioned above. Written in Cuba, it seems to hold in it the fire of the blazing stars of that tropic sky—to feel the full effect, one must imagine an evening balmy as a few nights are with us in June. Then, it seems the perfect expression of a lonely heart—unquestioning in its passionate devotion; the words of the singer gradually increasing in vigor from the merely rich description of the first lines, to the utter abandonment at the end, to everything else in a consuming flame of unselfish love.

> Day is melting purple dying
> Blossoms all around me sighing,
> Fragrance from the lilies straying,
> Zephyr with my ringlets playing,
> Ye but waken my distress:
> I am sick of loneliness.
>
> Thou to whom I love to hearken
> Come, ere night around me darken;
> Though thy softness but deceive me,
> Say thou'rt true, and I'll believe thee.
> Veil of ill, thy soul's intent:
> Let me think it innocent!

> Save thy toiling, spare thy treasure:
> All I ask is friendship's pleasure:
> Let the shining ore lie darkling;
> Bring no gem in lustre sparkling;
> Gifts and gold are naught to me:
> I would only look on thee.
>
> Tell to thee the high-wrought feeling,
> Ecstasy but in revealing;
> Paint to thee the deep sensation,
> Rapture in participation,
> Yet but torture, if comprest
> In a lone unfriended breast.
>
> Absent still? Ah, come and bless me!
> Let these eyes again caress thee.
> Once in caution I could fly thee:
> Now I nothing could deny thee.
> In a look if death there be,
> Come, and I will gaze on thee.

These are the lines which Charles Lamb thought "so fine no woman could have written them," the lines that Southey thought worthy of Sappho herself. From the arrangement of the original MS. I believe the song was written earlier than the epic, but inserted in its present place, according to a preconceived plan. Mrs. Brooks hated the mechanical part of writing—she composed her poems "in her head," then transferred them to paper, and, if corrections were needed, made them on the original MS. by cancelling, or pasting strips of paper across rejected portions. But for the Song she left a blank on two pages, and then actually inserted a single leaf, between the blanks.

After the fashion of the day she decorated her poem with learned notes, which give me a high opinion of her scholarship. She had opportunity to use the Dartmouth Library, while one of her sons was a student there, waiting to enter West Point. A fine story is told of how he gained his appointment after several disappointments. About this time Maria made her journey to Europe, on which occurred her visit to Southey. But she went also to France, where she met Washington Irving, and there she was presented to the aged Lafayette, who was charmed, and begged to know if he could be of any service. "Yes," said the lady, "you can get my son into West Point." The general wrote a letter, and to this Horace Brooks owed his appointment, and his country a worthy soldier.

Mrs. Brooks's visit to Keswick was the great event of her life. She had, because of her Welsh ancestry, a romantic admiration for Southey's well nigh forgotten epic "Madoc," and the meeting with her idol was, as I have told, a happy one. He undertook to superintend the publication of "Zophiel," in London, and Mrs. Brooks returned to the United States, whence she occasionally wrote to the laureate, and thus, in a sense, made a claim to be regarded as the one American member of the group of Lake Poets.

Southey kept Maria's letters, and the manuscript of "Zophiel" even after it was printed in 1833, and after various adventures the manuscript and four letters came into the hands of the late Beverly Chew, at whose request Miss Ruth S.Grannis of the Grolier Club, wrote the tiny privately printed brochure "An American Friend of Southey," which contains a great deal of information about Maria. Mr. Chew prized his collection of Brooksiana highly, and at his death I looked to learn if he had willed it to some institution. Mr. Chew did not will the collection. It was sold at his sale, and not bought by any library. Yet I hope he would be pleased to know that a younger collector, who had long admired the poetess, and cherished her writings, ultimately, through the kind offices of a scholarly bookseller who lives at Metuchen, obtained the lot, and has added to it another letter, and photostats of the few MSS. in public collections. And I also hope anyone who has any material about the lady will let me know about it! Some day there should be an edition of her writings—they are "honorable to literature," as Disraeli said of something he wrote!

Mrs. Brook's later life is, of course, easier to chronicle. A letter to Southey from Boston, Feb. 25, 1833, is the earliest I have seen—it tells of her plan to publish her poem in America for the benefit of the Polish exiles, and thanks Southey for his efforts. No copies had yet come to Boston. "Zophile" was printed in 1833 complete in London—it was reissued in America the same year, and then reprinted in 1834. There has also been an edition in 1879, supervised by Mrs. Zadel Barnes Gustfson, herself a poet. Yet the book is rare, and few seem to have read it, even in her own day. But among those who read were critics of discrimination, and they quoted, so that anthologists could glean, the great lines allegorical of marriage, which have so pleased Prof. Saintsbury by their original meter.

The bard has sung, God never formed a soul
Without its own peculiar mate, to meet
Its wandering half, when ripe to crown the
    whole
Bright plan of bliss, most heavenly, most
    complete.

But thousand evil things there are that hate
To look on happiness: these hurt, impede,
And, leagued with time, space, circumstance,
    and fate
Keep kindred heart from heart, to pine and
    pant, and bleed.

And as the dove to far Palmyra flying
From where her native founts of Antioch
    beam
Weary, exhausted, longing, panting, sighing,
Lights sadly at the desert's bitter stream.

So, many a soul o'er life's drear desert far-
    ing,
Love's pure congenial spring unfound, un-
    quaffed,—
Suffers, recoils; then thirsty and despairing
Of what it would, descends, and sips the near-
    est draught.

One can almost hear the rush of wings and the fluttering to earth of the bird in those last lines,—yet if the critics praised the most beautiful lines, they have all, I think, overlooked another very delicate, very ethereal passage—to a tropical flower.

Sweet flower! thou'rt lovelier even than the
    rose
The rose is pleasure,—felt and known as such,
Soon past, but real; tasted while it glows,
But thou, too bright and pure for mortal
    touch,
Art like those brilliant things we never taste
Or see, unless with Fancy's lip and eye,

When, maddened by her mystic spell, we
    waste
Life on a thought, and rob reality.

The critics praised—the public seems to have paid homage, but no more, and the publishers were looking for profits. One firm, to which she proposed some volume, told her frankly "her writings were too elevated to sell"—a reply which she characterized as a libel on her countrymen.

Mrs. Brooks continued to reside partly in Cuba, partly in this country, and occasionally she contributed to the periodicals. Urged by Southey, she had written her own love story into a novel, to which she gave as title the curious name "Idomen," an abbreviation of the heroine's name, Idomenee. This story she published first serially, mainly for the purpose of obtaining a clean copy, in the Boston Saturday Evening Gazette, between February 17 and September 29, 1838.

The story made a considerable sensation, as well it might, since it is one of the most searchingly frank documents ever written, and reveals a woman's heart, and emotional trials as few authors have ever done. The richness of her descriptions of the tropics is unsurpassed—and with less direction, but equal skill, she tells as Conrad has done in "Heart of Darkness," of the rot which comes in those lands of luxuriant growth, where life is so abundant, one comes to regard death without emotion.

Yet Maria herself shared not in this callousness. She had built for herself a little white replica of a Grecian temple, and there clad all in white she sat and composed her poems. In her hair was always a passion flower, about her neck the ribbon with the memorial cross. Her storm of life should have been over—but it was not to be so. During a visit to the United States, two of her sons, one of them, her favorite, Edgar, fell sick. The mother learned of it, and wished to hasten to their side—friends reassured her, she postponed the journey, word of the young man's death came. In the youngest boy's memory she composed a song so simple, so dignified, so touching, that the whole grief seems to become music. The lines have, says

Prof. Saintsbury, a simplicity which does not become silly. To write such a song is the high achievement of a German poet—for an English poet only the peculiar combination of genius, emotion, and complete freedom from self-consciousness made it possible—for the third time Maria del Occidente sang greatly.

My fair-haired boy, long months have fled
Since came the tidings thou wert dead;—
But what are months or years to me?
    Tears flow for thee. Tears flow for thee.

I did not close thine azure eyes
Nor took my lips thy latest sighs
But, in my heart, looks, sighs, will be—
    Tears flow for thee. Tears flow for thee.

Howe'er may change my earthly lot,
My Edgar, I'll forget thee not.
Dear Spirit, thou shalt ever see
    Tears flow for thee. Tears flow for thee.

The lines were published in the Boston Saturday Gazette, September 14, 1839, and a copy sent to Southey, but except in the privately printed book of Miss Grannis have not yet been included in a volume, nor have they been seen by many anthologists. To the memory of her sons Mrs. Brooks wrote also some long Odes to the Departed in a peculiar measure which she herself had invented as early as 1825. The last stanza of one of these odes is perhaps the finest—and aside from its interest metrically, has a fine dignity about it, the mother's love for the favorite child, whose spirit she invokes in Heaven, as among the saints, though perhaps not highest among them.

This song to thee alone! Though he who shares
Thy bed of stone shared well my love with
    thee,
    Yet in his noble heart
    Another bore a part,
Whilst thou hadst never other love than me:
Sprites, brothers, manes, shades, present my
    tears and prayers!

Mrs. Brooks remained in the United States, staying near West Point, and on Governor's Island with her distinguished son, and arranged for the printing of her novel in book form. She made the acquaintance of Fitz-Greene Halleck, who seems to have taken little interest in 'Idoman,' and also of the celebrated critic E. P. Whipple, who was, perhaps, more appreciative—to judge from her letters to the two men, in the Aldis Collection at Yale. Meanwhile she continued her correspondence with Southey—a fifteen-page letter to him dated August 30, 1840, is before me, and has been published by Miss Grannis. But it is doubtful if the laureate, whose mind failed him at the last, could read the message. However, after his death, his executors applied to Maria for copies of his letters to her—she had a set made and sent them. But she refused to make a second set of copies, or to loan the originals to George Ticknor, as her letter to him of May 27, 1843, (now in the Boston Public Library) shows.

Meanwhile, she became acquainted with Rufus Griswold, and in the first edition of "The Poets and Poetry of America" appeared a handsome notice of her work. To quote a few words: "Mrs. Brooks is the only American poet of her sex whose mind is thoroughly educated . . . . Learning, brilliant imagination, and masculine boldness of thought and diction are characteristic of her works. In some of her descriptions she is perhaps too minute; and at times, by her efforts to condense, she becomes obscure." Later Griswold said that, after all he had done for the "Female Poets" he might admit that he felt but one fully deserving of the praise he bestowed— Mrs. Brooks.

She seems not to have met Poe, and late in his life he complained that he had not had an opportunity of thoroughly examining her claims to fame. But his references during 1848 and 1849 make me think he was studying her poetry, and had he lived, might have produced a critique upon it.

"Idomen" after many delays, was printed, and privately circulated, but neither her own nor Griswold's efforts gained her a publisher. One of "Rufe's" ideas was to have her write a review of her own work—the letter in which she discussed the proposition is in my collection, with certain careful erasures by the wily biographer! It was an age of petty trickery in the field of letters—but what modern period is not? I may say that the "self-

review" does not seem to have appeared.

Graham's Magazine published a portrait of Mrs. Brooks in its series of "Our Contributors," and her letter of January 31, 1843 above mentioned, refers partly to the arrangements connected with that. It is a delightful letter—very feminine in its insistence upon the artist's preserving certain details of costume, especially the flower and the cross.

A later letter, preserved at the Boston Public Library and partly published in the "Griswold Correspondence," tells of her approaching return to Cuba. Thence in 1844 she sent a Washington editor one of her long memorial odes, and complained of her want of a competent amanuensis. Alas, that want seems to have prevented her committing to paper an epic on "Beatriz, the Beloved of Columbus" which she had composed, and recited portions of to Griswold. And soon opportunity was gone.

Mrs. Brooks returned to her estate near Matanzas, and the graves of her two sons. Another son (not Horace, the soldier) lived there with her. And suddenly, one of those tropical diseases came upon them, the abundance of death which compensates for the vigor of the life principle. After so

7

Song.

Day, in melting purple dying,
Blossoms, all around me sighing,
Fragrance, from the lilies straying,
Zephyr, with my ringlets playing,
        Ye but waken my distress
        I am sick of loneliness.

Thou, to whom I love to harken,
Come, ere night around me darken;
Tho' thy softness but deceive me,
Say thou'rt true & I'll believe thee;
        Veil, if ill, thy soul's intent,—
        Let me think it innocent!

Save thy toiling; spare thy treasure:
All I ask is friendship's pleasure:
Let the shining ore lie darkling;—
Bring no gem in lustre sparkling;
        Gifts & gold are nought to me:
        I would only look on thee,—

Tell, to thee, the high-wrought feeling,
Ecstasy but in revealing;
Paint, to thee, the deep sensation,
Rapture, in participation,—
        Yet but torture, if comprest
        In a lone unfriended breast.

Absent still—ah! come & bless me!
Let these eyes again caress thee;
Once, in caution, I could fly thee;—
Now, I nothing could deny thee;
        In a look if death there be,
        Come, & I will gaze on thee!

strange, so troubled, so bold, so sad a career, the tired heart ceased to beat —she and her son were laid to rest beside the two young men who had gone before. The spirit was gone to join those it so dearly loved and white marble cross stood as monument for all save one of the family.

A few months back I wrote to Matanzas to ask if that cross still stood—if any now recalled Maria del Occidente. No reply has come. It hardly matters. Her song still is graven deep in some hearts, and such there long must be. The passion flower blooms in purity.

RECKLESS LADY

THE LIFE STORY OF
ADAH ISAACS MENKEN

BY
NAT FLEISCHER
EDITOR, THE RING MAGAZINE

DOLORES

For the tale of our life as it closes
Is darkness, the fruit thereof dust,
No thorns are as sharp as a rose's,
And Love is more cruel than lust;
Time turns the old days to derision,
Our loves into corpses or wives,
And marriage and death and division
Make barren our lives.

ALGERNON CHARLES SWINBURNE

Reckless Lady

The Life Story of
ADAH ISAACS MENKEN

CHAPTER I

IN one of George Bernard Shaw's early novels, "Cashel Byron's Profession," the hero is a heavyweight champion who falls in love with, wins and weds a wealthy young woman, a member of aristocratic British society. In our modern day, Gene Tunney contracted a matrimonial alliance with a rich American socialite.

As a rule, prize ring fiction frequently works out that way, but such marriages are not so common in real life. Several disgruntled critics took Shaw to task for his audacity in conceiving a situation where a heroine of culture and refinement yielded to the glamor of an athletic male personality.

Adverse criticism never troubled George Bernard Shaw, but had he cared to refute the fault-finders, he could have quoted a precedent in the case of John Camel Heenan, bare knuckle heavyweight champion of the Fifties and Sixties, who wed Adah Isaacs Menken, famous American Venus, author, actress, and journalist. No fistic king ever led such a wonder-bride to the altar as "The Menken," celebrated in both the New and Old Worlds for her wit, beauty and intellect.

What sort of a man was this Heenan, who, despite the handicap of belonging to a profession stamped illegal at that time, and represented mostly by ruffians beyond the pale of decent society, still exercised an irresistible fascination over an acknowledged queen of the stage and literati?

Well, the names of John Morrissey, John Camel Heenan, Tom Sayers and John L. Sullivan led the pugilistic field during the last half of the 19th Century. Of this quartet, Heenan and John L., held the most dramatic appeal for the public. And preceding the advent of the mighty Sullivan, the fistic spotlight unquestionably rested upon the Herculean figure of Heenan, the handsome "Benecia Boy," as he was known to the Fancy, or ring patrons. As a gladiator, he had earned a reputation for strength, skill, courage and iron endurance second to none in the arena.

Boxing in the gaslight era of New York flourished in a decidedly malodorous atmosphere of crime and political corruption. Pugilists commonly participated in the gang wars then rampant around Manhattan, wars in which knife, pistol and club worked overtime, and human lives were snuffed out with callous indifference.

Dance halls of shady character ran wide open, pickpockets and strong-arm men plied their trades with impunity, a favorite hunting-ground being around Castle Garden, at the Battery, place of entry for immigrants. Political factions fought viciously to get and retain control of the pugilistic brigade, from whose ranks were recruited bodyguards for the municipal big-shots.

The Native American Party subsidized a formidable army of tried fighting men to protect its interests, headed by Bill Poole, the city's greatest rough-and-tumble slugger. Heavyweight champion Tom Hyer bossed the ring—Poole passed up the formality of ropes, stakes and referee, confining his battling activities strictly to street and bar-room. Later, Bill was to die from a six-shooter bullet that pierced his bold heart during·a saloon row.

Tammany Hall, allied with the Irish-American element against the Native Americans, also maintained a grim band of hard-bitten, tough-as-nails scrappers. Where the Natives gathered only the American-born into their political fold, Tammany's strength lay in the support of immigrants from the Emerald Isle, and others of Celtic descent. John Morrissey was leader of the fighting Irish henchmen. Later Morrissey was to win the heavyweight title, become a member of the New York State Senate, and finally attain the proud prominence of a United States Congressman. He was the first professional boxer to reach the status of legislator, State or National.

Such were the conditions around Gotham when Heenan came from the goldfields of California to issue a challenge for the American heavyweight championship. Heenan, a native of Troy, N. Y., had lived for several years on the Pacific Coast, where he won fame as a two-fisted, slashing fighter, and was first distinguished by the sobriquet of Benecia Boy.

John Morrissey, also born in Troy, knew Heenan from their boyhood days. They were enemies then, because of a sort of family feud dating from a quarrel between their respective fathers, and a nursed hatred for each other increased in strength and reached bitter heights by the time they attained manhood.

During Heenan's residence on the Coast, Tom Hyer had resigned the heavyweight throne, having passed his prime and being a victim to rheumatism. Morrissey was Hyer's natural successor.

and his right to the American championship title was universally recognized, except by Heenan.

The Benecia Boy always believed he could whip John Morrissey, and the Native Americans, opposing Tammany Hall's fistic leader, readily accepted Heenan as their representative. Morrissey was only too willing to settle a long standing grudge with his fists, and a match was speedily arranged.

The men met in the ring at Long Point, Canada, on October 20, 1858. From the start of hostilities, Heenan labored under a handicap of poor physical condition. He had been obliged to break his training owing to an attack of malaria. His friends had begged him to call off the fight, or at least request a postponement. But the Benecia Boy's pride would not permit him

AN EARLY PORTRAIT OF ADAH ISAACS MENKEN

to ask a favor of Morrissey, the man he hated, and he was consequently by no means in real fighting trim for the title-battle.

Realizing that his condition left much to be desired, Heenan fought fast and viciously from the first call of time, knowing that the longer the contest lasted, the greater were the odds against his winning. A quick victory was his only chance. But Fate proved unkind. In the opening round Morrissey ducked a savage right aimed for his jaw. Heenan's driving fist skimmed across the top of his opponent's head and collided with terrific force against one of the ring posts.

They didn't pad the stakes in those hardy days, and that impact with the hard wood smashed Heenan's hand up badly. From then on he could only use his left for offensive purposes, the dangerous right being out of commission so far as punching with it was concerned. Thus crippled, Heenan had absolutely no chance against such a formidable opponent as Morrissey.

Nevertheless he battled on desperately, so long as his fast-ebbing strength held out, but the end came when he fell from sheer exhaustion in the eleventh round, and Morrissey was declared the victor.

This was bad medicine for the Native Americans to swallow and Heenan was greatly depressed. His only consolation was that the defeat reflected no disgrace upon him, as even Morrissey's adherents admited that luck had certainly favored John as much as it had buffeted the Benecia Boy.

Still, the cold fact stood out that Heenan had lost, and there was no way of redeeming himself except by another battle test. But Morrissey, an extremely shrewd personage, had no intention of fighting Heenan again. As a matter of fact, Morrissey's ambitions now headed in a political direction, and the ring no longer appealed to him. It helped him in his political climb to be known as the heavyweight champion, but he could see no reason for risking his laurels in a second meeting with the Benecia Boy, for whose prowess he had intense respect.

So it befell that in response to repeated challenges, the best Heenan could get from Morrissey was a somewhat derisive announcement that the Benecia Boy could have a return match, provided that he first went to England and defeated the British champion, Tom Sayers.

Heenan considered this reply merely a subterfuge to sidetrack him, as it probably was. In bare knuckle days if a champion consistently refused to meet a worthy challenger, it was the ring-custom to declare the challenger "Champion by Default."

This is what happened in Heenan's case. It was universally recognized that Morrissey owed him a return chance at the title. And as both sports and politicans were pretty well aware by this time that Morrissey was no longer interested in pugilism as a profession, the crown passed to Heenan by popular acclaim.

Most pugilists would have been satisfied by public recognition.

But Heenan was not. Physically rugged and as courageous as a pit-terrier, the Benecia Boy had an intensively sensitive side to his nature. He had set his heart on beating his boyhood foe, and brooded over his failure to such an extent that he was seriously contemplating permanent retirement from the ring.

In this disheartened mood Heenan sought the advice of his best friend, Frank Queen. The latter was editor and proprietor of the New York Clipper, cherished bible of the show-folk, and a publication high in favor with the sports fraternity.

None of us know by what seemingly trivial incidents our future is determined. When Heenan walked into the editorial sanctum of the Clipper, Fate had already staged the first scene in the tempestuous life-romance of the fighting Benecia Boy.

Seated by Frank Queen's desk, Heenan's startled gaze rested upon a vision of fairy-like feminine loveliness—the most beautiful woman his eyes had ever beheld. The sound of her voice, a rich, musical contralto, vibrant with the melodious accent of the Deep South, thrilled the stalwart fighter to the innermost core of his being. This dainty, dazzling creature was none other than Adah Isaacs Menken, born Adois Dolores McCord!

When Heenan entered, she was discussing with Queen the probable outcome of the turf events scheduled for that day. Adah Menken was a keen student of equine form. She possessed a positively uncanny intuition in dealing with racing possibilities and the correctness of her forecasts was a constant surprise to Queen, who was arguing with her regarding the favorite's chances in the Goodwood Cup, when his visitor appeared.

The editor greeted him warmly.

"You couldn't have come at a better time," he said. "Mr. Heenan, I take much pleasure in introducing you to Miss Dolores McCord, known to fame as Adah Isaacs Menken reigning queen of the American stage, of whom you, of course, have heard."

The usually cool and self-collected Heenan flushed scarlet, as the actress rose and extended a slender hand, which he took cautiously, as though afraid of injuring it in his grasp.

"Who hasn't heard of her?" he stammered in confused, but very apparent delight, as Adah smiled graciously, sensing the giant's reaction to her beauty.

Heenan was attired as befitted a prosperous sporting man of the period. A tall silk hat, frock coat, striped trousers and high boots completed a costume that set off his splendid, athletic figure to the best advantage.

Frank Queen, viewing the towering form of the young champion beside his charming new acquaintance, inwardly reflected that a handsomer pair could not be found in all America.

The magnetism of her presence, a magnetism that enslaved countless admirers, exercised a magic spell upon Heenan. There was hypnotic power in the shining depths of her eyes, and the Benecia Boy succumbed to its irresistible lure without a struggle.

And even as Adah's glances made him a willing captive, she knew that she herself was on the verge of surrender to an overwhelming personality. It was love at first sight for both!

Few women knew sports as did Adah Menken. She was a gambler of high calibre, her specialty being the bang-tails and bare knuckle fighters. It was therefore natural that, when the conversation turned to ring matters, the actress remarked:

"I am so sorry you were beaten by John Morrissey, Mr. Heenan."

"It was just bad luck," rejoined the pugilist. "Breaking my right hand at the start was too big a handicap to overcome. No one-armed man can whip such a fighter as Morrissey. I would like another trial with him. But Morrissey won't do business, in spite of all my efforts."

"I understand he insists that you must go to England and defeat Tom Sayers, the British champion, before he will consider a return match?" broke in Queen.

"That's what I wanted to talk over with you," responded Heenan. "Of course, John Morrissey has no intention of fighting me again. He's practically through with the ring and interested only in politics now."

"According to 'The Spirit of the Times,'" commented Miss Menken, "Sayers has a previous engagement with Bob Brettle, and won't discuss any other challenge until that fight is over."

"Yes," said Heenan, "but all that makes little difference now. Had I won from Morrissey I would have challenged Sayers for the international championship and belt. But the defeat upset my plans and disgusted me so much with the fighting game that I am just about ready to follow Morrissey's lead and retire."

"Retire!" echoed the actress. Her voice rang out like a silver bell, charged with flaming scorn.

"You would retire—in the prime of your strength and manhood, disappoint the thousands of Americans who see in you the sole hope of wresting the world's championship from an Englishman? Why where is your patriotism, your love of country? Our fighting sailors once taught Britannia that she didn't rule the waves! Are you afraid to do battle for the honor of the Stars and Stripes and show England that neither does she rule the ring? This isn't merely a sporting proposition, Mr. Heenan. It's your duty to whip Tom Sayers!"

Heenan stood abashed, slightly bewildered, his feelings submerged in an emotional chaos. But he was conscious of something within him that responded to Adah's magnificent disdain and compelling entreaty, even as a war-horse responds to the charging trumpet-call. Frank Queen's friendly hand fell on his shoulder.

"She's absolutely right, John," said the editor. "You musn't let one defeat spoil you. If you hoist the white flag, what will folks say? They certainly won't think you fit to be the standard-bearer of the Native Americans."

Heenan looked steadily at Queen. Coming from anyone else he would have resented that "white flag" comment. But Frank Queen was a privileged person. Moreover, the pugilist's pride had reacted to the woman's spirited words. In a flash his resolution was made, as his eyes encountered Adah's rapt, intent gaze.

The champion's clenched fist smote Queen's desk with sledge-hammer force, and the polished surface split across from the heavy impact. His deep voice thundered through the room:

"You win, Miss Menken! I'll fight Sayers and bring the world's championship to America. Frank, old pal, I thank you, too, for helping to make me see what my duty really is. It's up to you now. Turn loose the Clipper's guns on the Englishman and make him come to time!"

Queen's ringing laugh broke the emotional tension, as he slapped Heenan on the back and roared:

"That's the genuine John Heenan talking! If Sayer's jaw isn't a whole lot tougher than my desk, I feel kind of sorry for him. There was gunpowder-shock in that punch, John!"

"I beg pardon, Frank," said Heenan hurriedly. "I'll buy you a new desk. Miss Menken just made me forget everything, including my manners, for the moment."

"Never mind," responded Queen jovially. "I'd give every stick of furniture in the place for the sake of hearing you say what you did, and I'm sure Miss Menken agrees with me."

"I'll show you just what I think about it," said the impulsive young actress.

The next instant her arms were around Heenan's neck, and standing on tiptoe, she drew down the giant's head and pressed her lips upon his.

"Here," said Adah Isaacs Menken, "is a man after my own heart. Frank Queen, we've made history in this room today!"

The challenge to Sayers duly appeared in the columns of the New York Clipper, with Queen named as the American's champion's representative. And thus was born the first International Heavyweight Championship in which two white men participated.

Matched to meet Sayers at Farnborough, England, on April 17, 1860, Heenan became the hero of the hour in his native land. Yet all the fame that accrued to him, all the adulation that was lavished upon him as America's fistic Hope in the coming battle, meant little to Heenan compared with his infatuation for Adah Isaacs Menken.

He had fallen in love with her at first sight, and Adah, always a creature of impulse, responded to a physical attraction for handsome young giant, which speedily assumed the proportions of a flaming love affair.

For several weeks after their initial meeting they were inseparable companions, figuring prominently in the pleasures of
New York's feverish night-life. But Heenan, a willing slave to
Adah's caprices, was not content with the probable transitory delights of a mere love idyl. His heart was set upon making her
his wife.

This was quite in accordance with Adah's wishes. She had
grown really fond of her big athlete, and, having two years previously divorced her first husband, Alexander Isaac Menken,

ADAH ISAACS MENKEN WHEN SHE MARRIED HEENAN

famous Jewish musician, was ready for a second matrimonial
adventure.

So on a fine April evening in 1859, the third day of the month,
the lovers drove up the Boston Post Road to the city's outskirts.
Dawn was breaking as they reached the Rock Cottage Inn, on
the Bloomingdale Road. There they were married, remaining for
a fortnight at the tavern, and were visited by Frank Queen, Edwin
James, the formers' sports critic, as well as members of the stage,

journalistic and fistic fraternities, who came to congratulate and make merry with the newly-wedded pair.

The short honeymoon over, they returned to New York, to live in a boarding house on the Bowery, then much favored by the sports of that era as a residential location. Here the former Dolores, vivacious stage-gypsy of the twinkling eyes and nimble, dancing feet, entered upon a new domestic existence.

For a while she was happy in this environment, having temporarily retired from the stage and apparently content to live upon Heenan's earnings. His boxing exhibitions brought him handsome fees, and no fighter in the past had enjoyed the popularity he attained with the American public.

Always what is known in modern slang as a "good mixer," his dashing young wife won the liking of many friends of her husband who hailed from society's lower strata. In those days it was inevitable that a pugilist should court the favor of the underworld. A majority of the Benecia Boy's tough admirers were members of the Native Americans political faction, but even these gangsters, tamed by Adah's adroit flattery, would have been willing to die in her defense.

This was true also as regarded the nymphs of the city's scarlet trails. A Rudyard Kipling admonition wasn't necessary to make Heenan's clever spouse realize that—"the colonel's lady and Judy O'Grady are sisters under their skins!"

If an adventuress sought her acquaintance, she was blithely welcomed, provided that she was mentally bright and amusing. The question of morals never troubled Adah Isaacs Menken, who looked upon a chaste moron as one of Nature's worst blunders.

She was very fond of Frank Queen and his editor, the noted Ed James, with whom she was even more closely associated after her marriage, and shared their interest in boxing and racing. An expert in many branches of sports, Adah now became familiar with such lusty amusements as cock-fighting, bull-baiting, rat-killing handicaps, billiards and shooting—all pursuits in high favor with the city's bloods. As a matter of fact not even the Wild West ever produced a better feminine shot than Adah Menken, who could hit a target with as precise accuracy as the famous Annie Oakley of later years.

In a word, she was as popular in the sports world as her husband, and this pleased Heenan highly. He was extremely proud of her and his devotion knew no bounds. Yet there were probably times when she must have looked back with a certain nostalgia to the past and yearned for a return to the intellectual plane of her former life.

Heenan and his rude associates could not, after all, completely satisfy the cultured, brilliant mind of the one-time darling of the stage. But meanwhile, she carried on gallantly. If Heenan was living in a fool's paradise, he certainly never suspected it at this period of his life.

As the time for his battle with Sayers drew near, he repeatedly urged her to accompany him to England, but this she steadily refused to do. There is no doubt whatever that she was genuinely anxious for him to win the world's championship, and looked forward eagerly to his triumphal return, after performing an exploit which would enable her to bask in a glow of reflected glory.

Should he fail—well that was a contingency to be considered. Men who failed were objects of scorn, rather than sympathy, from the somewhat merciless viewpoint of Adah Issacs Menken. This seems to have been foreshadowed by a remark she made to the Benecia Boy one day.

Referring lightly to the classic legend of the Spartan mother who told her warrior son on the eve of battle to "return victorious, or on his shield!", thereby indicating a preference for death above defeat, Adah said, with laughing emphasis, that she doubted if her love for him would survive the disgrace of his losing to Sayers.

This was apparently a jest. But Heenan, whose powers of perception were quite acute enough to enable him to read between the lines, knew in his heart that it was a jest which might easily be turned into grim earnest.

There is something extremely pathetic in the dog-like devotion of John Camel Heenan to his brilliant marital partner, whom he was fated never quite to understand because of the intellectual gulf which yawned between them. In the sporting resorts where boisterous admirers paid uproarious tribute to his fighting qualities, he bragged with honest enthusiasm about his clever, beautiful wife, extolling her many accomplishments, her superior education, her wide-spread fame as an actress.

He gave her full credit for his resolve to fight Sayers and uphold America's honor in the ring. In his eyes she was a living idol, a wonder-woman who had no equal on earth. When she praised his prowess and strength, he was humbly grateful and worshipped her for her condescension. In passion affairs of this kind there is generally one who gives in full measure, while the other tolerantly accepts. Heenan was enthralled by his enchantress, body and soul. She, at first influenced by physical transports, was bound to weary of his attentions in the course of time.

Heenan can scarcely be classed as one of Dame Fortune's favorites. Luck was against him in his two most important ring battles. He was beating Morrissey when the accident occurred that put his right hand out of commission, and ended his chances of winning.

Then, in the great international contest with Tom Sayers, the jinx again got in its fine work on the Benecia Boy. Sayers was weakening fast under the terrible punishment administered by the American, when some of Sayer's friends cut the ring-ropes. This was in the thirty-seventh round. Sayers was lying on the ropes, helpless in Heenan's iron grip.

The referee, submerged in the rush of the crowd toward the combatants, quit the ring, and for five rounds the fight went on without that official. From the thirty-seventh to the forty-second round Sayers was so exhausted that he kept on his feet only with the support of his seconds. Heenan, partially blind, and hampered by the leaders of the mob pressing close around the gladiators, was unable to get home a finishing blow.

Finally the mob rushed the ring in such numbers that the contest suddenly ended with the flight of the principals. A few days later the referee officially declared the fight a draw, and so it went down in the records.

The American public knew that Heenan had not been given a square deal, and he was lionized by the sports on his return home. But, in his wife's eyes he had only achieved a half-triumph, and Adah Isaacs Menken was the sort of person whose desires demanded all or nothing. The love-bond was loosening, and little was required to complete its severance.

Once again an evil Fate struck and wounded the Benecia Boy. Adah had been far advanced in pregnancy when her husband left for England. A baby boy was born, a healthy child whose birth seemed to draw the parents closer together.

But one morning as Heenan took the baby out of his crib, the big fellow slipped and fell, with the child underneath him. The weight of the father's body crushed out the hapless infant's life.

No blame attached to Heenan, any more than when Sayer's friends broke the ring and cheated him out of victory; or when a broken hand prevented his winning from Morrissey. Nevertheless, this last tragic stroke of ill-luck was all that was needed to write finis to his romance with Adah Isaacs Menken.

In less than two years from the date of their marriage, they were parted, and finally divorced. Yet to the end of his days Heenan cherished the memory of that stormy passion-interlude. Later he married another famous actress, Sara Stevens, but nothing could ever efface from his heart the haunting loveliness of the erstwhile Dolores McCord.

In a newspaper interview, explaining her reasons for leaving Heenan, Adah coldly and critically summed up the whole affair as follows:

"Every man is more or less a hero in his sweetheart's eyes. Women adore bravery, whether demonstrated on a battlefield, or in the ring. John Heenan has the courageous heart, stately physique and iron sinews of a classical hero. He attracted me physically, in much the same fashion as Marc Anthony's ardent embraces stirred the tiger-blood in Cleopatra's veins. But the finer side of my nature revolted, when glamor died away. This splendid gladiator was, after all, a mere animal, his bravery that of the untamed brute creation. Once I realized that I had sacrificed myself to an entirely false ideal, our separation became inevitable!"

It is worthy of note, however, that, quite apart from her literary and dramatic talents, this charming siren of the Fifties and Sixties was by no means lacking in the practical qualities of a keen business woman.

For example, the apt use she made of her marriage to Heenan as an advertising asset would win the admiration of a modern Broadway publicity agent. She wrote glowing poems and articles about the champion which were published in leading newspapers and magazines, and well paid for.

Even after the divorce, when the Heenan-Sayers battle was still an international topic, she was starred at the National Theatre of New York, not as Adah Isaacs Menken, but as Mrs. John Camel Heenan. She also utilized his name as a box office attraction on the stage in Boston, Philadelphia, Pittsburgh and Chicago.

She was distinctly an opportunist, with the wide world as a stage for the exhibition of charms as irresistible as they were rare. Her magnetic personality may be truthfully said to have fairly hypnotized some of the most distinguished men of letters of her day.

Walt Whitman, Charles Dickens, Charles Reade and Joaquin Miller were numbered among her admirers. In her long list of ardent lovers, the names of Algernon Charles Swinburne and the elder Dumas stand out prominently. A ceaseless craving for adventurous thrills, a temperament electrically charged with the mad joy of fast living, a horror of all that was drab or commonplace combined to thrust her into spectacular roles. According to the whim of the moment, she alternately appeared upon the public horizon as poetess, opera ballet dancer, circus rider, legitimate actress, and created a terrific sensation in this country and abroad as the naked heroine of "Mazeppa," lying bound and helpless on the back of a galloping wild horse.

CHAPTER II

THIS daring heart-breaker, who so boldly scorned all conventional rules, was born in Milnesburg, a New Orleans suburb, on June 15, 1835. Baptized Adois Dolores McCord, she had a sister, Josephine and a brother James, the latter dying in infancy.

Despite general belief to that effect, she was not a Jewess by birth. Her father was a Scot, James McCord, who emigrated to America and opened a general merchandise store. He was born of Scottish parents in Holborn, England. He married a French girl in the Crescent City, who later became the mother of his three children.

James McCord died when Adois Dolores was seven. Her mother wed Dr. Josiah Campbell, chief surgeon of the U. S. Army at Baton Rouge. Campbell, impressed by the grace of his step children, visualized a possible career for them as operatic ballet dancers. At his suggestion, they studied dancing and became remarkably proficient in that art.

When Adois was thirteen, her literary talents were already developing, a local paper having published several of her poems. These verses were signed, "Dolores," as she disliked the sound of "Adois," which she finally dropped altogether.

At this juncture, Dr. Campbell died, leaving his family in very poor circumstances. Not long afterwards, through the influence of a suitor, one Senor Zalva, Mrs. Campbell obtained stage engagements for both girls at the French Opera House.

The debutantes were an immense success, but with Dolores winning premier honors. At fourteen she gave full promise of her mature beauty attained in future years. After the first night's performance, she became one of the most sensational attractions in New Orleans. Throngs flocked to see her, and at her farewell appearance, she was the recipient of presents valued at $3000.

When the French Opera House season was over, Mrs. Campbell embarked for Havana with her Cuban lover and the two girls, where the sisters were billed at the Tacun Theatre. They were again a tremendous success, but, as before, Dolores scored the greater triumph, becoming the city's stage darling and winning the sobriquet of "Queen of the Plaza."

Unfortunately, Josephine was her mother's favorite, and Mrs. Campbell resented angrily the preference for Dolores shown by audiences.

This jealousy was exhibited in another way, for Mrs. Campbell, still a beautiful woman, was intensely distrustful of the attentions bestowed upon Dolores by her mother's lover, Zalva.

Although the girl did not encourage him, Zalva lost no chance of making love to her. Returning from the theatre one day, Dolores found herself alone with Zalva and at his mercy. In an instant she was clutched in his arms, and despite her desperate struggles and cries for help, he criminally assaulted her.

Her screams brought Mrs. Campbell on the scene, and then, strange to say, this unnatural mother exhibited more indignation over the Cuban's infidelity than the outrage committed upon her daughter.

The outcome was the breaking of all relations between the girl and her maternal parent. Dolores was then fifteen, and even at that early age, was not lacking in the quality of determination for which she was noted all through her stormy career. She left the stage and obtained a position as a teacher of the French, Spanish and English languages at a young ladies' seminary.

While there, she made the acquaintance of Jacques de Vaillet, a New Orleans ballet dancer, then engaged in Victor Franconi's Hippodrome. She won the liking of Jacques' little two-year old son, Henri, and in this way, without arousing any suspicions on the part of Jacques' wife, the pair became lovers.

At de Vaillet's suggestion, Dolores forsook school-teaching and joined his show, traveling through Texas and to Mexico under the stage nom-de-plume of Adah Bertha Theodore. She was a success wherever she appeared. Besides being a skilled horsewoman, she danced beautifully and was an imitable male impersonator. As a matter of fact, she could do everything required of a veteran trouper.

It was while touring Texas that she experienced what she afterwards described as—"the most romantic episode of my life, my kidnapping by a band of Indians who held me prisoner for three weeks, and made me a member of the tribe."

This incident occurred while she was on a hunting trip, shooting buffalo, with several friends. Some of the party got away, but the redskins captured her and Frederick Varney. Taken to the Indian camp, Dolores bided her time, watching for an opportunity to escape. With the magic which never failed her when it came to the problem of winning the good graces of male acquaintances, she managed to make herself so agreeable to the red men, that, as before stated, they adopted her into the tribe.

When a chance of getting away did present itself, Varney, who appears to have been a very poor specimen of manhood, notified the chief that his pretty prisoner was about to make a dash for freedom, with the result that the girl was so closely guarded that she was obliged to relinquish the idea.

Finally a band of Texas Rangers struck the trail of the Indians, and made a successful night attack on the braves, capturing the chief and killing several bucks. Released, Dolores said nothing regarding Varney's dastardly action, not caring to see him shot or hanged from a convenient tree by the indignant Rangers.

But it was characteristic of her that she did not allow him to go without punishment. Later on, she lured him to an assignation at a lonely spot, and, keeping her victim under the muzzle of a six shooter, horsewhipped him mercilessly.

When the rescued captive met General Harney, chief of the

Rangers, the veteran soldier was completely fascinated by her, offered to adopt her, placed her with his family, and employed a young tutor to perfect her studies in painting and sculpture.

But the fine arts expert also yielded to the seductive powers of this amorous pupil's glances, the teacher became merged in the role of lover, and another tender romance developed. Somebody—report had it that the vengeful, soundly thrashed Varney was the source of secret information—told Harney what was going on. The General, consumed with jealousy, lost no time in ordering her to leave his home.

Dolores complied willingly enough. She was tired of Harney, tired of her latest love-conquest, and impatient to play a part in the big amusement world again. There was no trouble about getting booking, and at the age of seventeen, in the Spring of 1852, she joined a traveling hippodrome managed by the noted Victory Franconi, with which she continued until May 7 of the following year.

Then she returned to New Orleans, her escort being none other than her old flame, the ballet master, Henri de Vaillet. In his memoirs, subsequently published in this country, de Vaillet frankly states that no other woman ever exercised such a compelling influence over him, and had not his wife refused to grant him a divorce, he would certainly have married her—provided that he could have obtained her consent.

However, the past can not have held any very serious regrets for Dolores, so far as Vaillet was concerned, for she did not linger long in his company, but flitted gaily to Memphis, Galveston, and finally to Cincinnati, Ohio.

It was in the last-named city that she met Alexander Isaac Menken, a musician of high reputation, but whose name was to win far greater and wider-spread fame through the agency of the remarkable woman who now entered his life.

Again Dolores assumed her favorite artistic role for conquest purposes, for she became a pupil under Menken, and while he labored to improve her musical talent, she, with probably less exertion, but equal, if not superior facility, gave him lessons in the art of loving. On April 3, 1856 they were married.

Expounding her love philosophy, Dolores once explained to Charles Reade, the British author, that marriage was to her merely a "means to an end." Divorce was a simple process of separating two people, one of whom, at least, badly needed release from a situation which had grown intolerable. She could imagine nothing more horrible than being compelled to live with a man for whom the fires of passion no longer flamed. In this respect she was thoroughly pagan in her views.

That there was something more than infatuation behind her interest in Menken seems probable, or it does not appear likely that she would have adopted the Jewish faith just for his sake. Moreover, all through her short, tumultuous life, she held loyally

to the Hebrew religion, and clung to the name of Adah Isaacs
Menken, excepting for the interval when, purely for advertising
purposes, she allowed herself to be billed as Mrs. John Camel
Heenan.

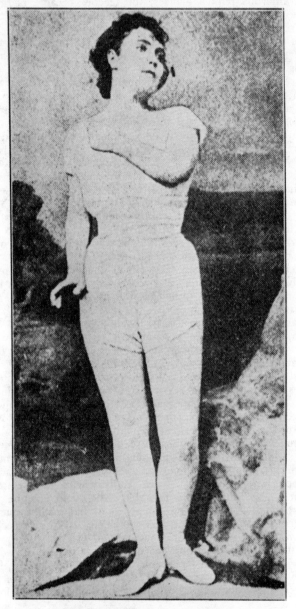

ADAH MENKEN AS MAZEPPA

Yet Menken in vain tried to cage this wild bird and induce her to rest permanently in the domestic nest. Nor would she yield to his repeated requests that she should abandon the stage. For a few months she did remain away from the footlights, but the roving spirit moved too strongly in her to keep her forever in a quiet home atmosphere.

Also, there were other distractions. During this period of inactivity, de Vaillet maintained their old friendship and called frequently at the Menken residence. One afternoon he informed her that he was about to leave on a tour, and as he rose to go, he embraced her, and she kissed him fervently.

As she did so, the parlor door opened and Menken walked in, just in time to witness the affectionate parting scene. Husbands have seldom behaved calmly under such circumstances, and Menken was no exception to a well-proved rule.

The indignant musician raged furiously and ordered the disturber of domestic peace out of the house. He went, and Adah endeavored to pass the incident over lightly, on the grounds of de Vaillet being such an old acquaintance, for whom she naturally entertained warm feelings of friendship, born of their stage associations.

Menken would not be pacified and continued to storm. Suddenly there came a great calm, as the husband ceased talking in response to his wife's imperious gesture of protest.

"That will do, Alexander," she said coldly. "I am not your slave, nor am I accustomed to submit to verbal abuse. You will have no further cause for complaint. I am leaving this house, never to return!"

Menken was fully aware that when the lady who bore his name resolved on a certain course of action, she could not be turned aside. Panic-stricken over the notion of losing her, he apologized abjectly and begged her to forget the incident and remain.

But the die was cast, and as she had ever done, the reckless female gambler with Fate would abide by the throw of the dice. Within the hour, Adah Isaacs Menken had rejoined de Vaillet. She was back again in the environment she loved—that of the stage. In the Spring of 1857 she was starred in the drama "Fazio," at the Varieties Theatre, New Orleans, playing to crowded houses.

"Fazio" had a long and lucrative run, and from the date of this engagement, which brought thousands of new admirers to the ranks of her supporters, the South began to pay homage to this versatile beauty as one of the brightest stars on the dramatic horizon. She was fast becoming a national character, men referred to her as "The Menken," as one might say—"The Queen!" Even in the critical East, there was gossip concerning the theatrical prodigy over whom the South was raving.

Like Napoleon, she believed in her star, and being a fatalist, neither success nor disaster could surprise her to any great extent. Had a fortune teller then predicted that in the not-so-distant

future Adah Isaacs Menken would be the most talked-about
woman in the world, the idol of Paris and toast of the London
literati, she would not have deemed it an idle prophecy. According to the conquering Menken code, there were many probabili-
ties, and few impossibilities to be encountered on the royal road
to triumph.

Women envied, men worshipped her, were willing to kill for
her sake. In the time-yellowed, crackling sheets of The Mascot, a
weekly New Orleans paper, published while "Fazio" was de-
lighting huge audiences at the Theatre Varieties, a short, but significant paragraph states that—"Shots were exchanged early yes-
terday morning between Monsieur Duprey, and Mr. Harold
Sheenan. A bullet in the hip of Monsieur Duprey ended hostilities. His antagonist was not hit. The affair is said to have proceeded from an argument over the beautiful Miss M—the actress
whose piquant charms are a constant source of rivalry among
the gilded youth of New Orleans!"

Duelling was a common practice in pre-Civil War days, especially in the Deep South, where no gentleman of recognized social
standing dare refuse an invitation to "the turf before breakfast,"
with the cheerful stage properties of "Pistols for two and coffee
for one!" It is said that more than one duel took place, with
The Menken as the lovely cause, a not unlikely statement regarding a time when lethal weapons were openly carried by fiery
youths who asked for nothing better than to fight to the death
for the possession of a prospective mistress.

When the run of "Fazio" ended, its leading lady went North
to Memphis, and later to Louisville. In both cities she filled successful stage engagements, but her versatility shone forth in other
lines of endeavor for the edification of the good folks of the Kentucky burg.

In her early teens it had been her custom to contribute verse
to the New Orleans papers, and at intervals during succeeding
years she was the author of poems favorably received by the
public. But Louisville was to become acquainted with her, not
only in the aesthetic role of verse-maker, but that of sporting
authority.

It has already been stated that Adah Isaacs Menken was a daring rider, and skilled circus performer. But her knowledge of
horses went much further than the mere ability to tame and handle
them. For she was a keen turf student, and could furnish the
history of every prominent horse in the racing calendar without
consulting a stud book. In a conversation with the sports editor
of a local paper, the scribe was so impressed by Adah's clear-cut
dissertation upon the racing situation that he invited her to contribute to his columns.

This she did promptly, quoting odds on an important race. Her
selections finished first and third, and overnight she won the
reputation of a sensationally successful handicapper. Thenceforth

her newspaper articles were eagerly looked forward to by the turf-followers.

The region of the Blue Grass has ever been celebrated for the breeding of the best in equine aristocracy, and it was but natural that the Kentuckians should have become enthusiastic about a young women who combined in her extraordinarily fascinating person, dramatic talent, poetical genius and "horse sense" that endowed her with mass popularity as a sports-writer.

Even Horace Greeley, least likely of all elderly journalists to be carried away by the lure of feminine accomplishments, was evidently impressed by public opinion of Adah Isaacs Menken. Wrote the New York Tribune sage editorially:

"If all that has been said and printed regarding this woman is true, and there appears to be no reason for believing otherwise, she is entitled to rank as a female Admirable Crichton!

High praise that, even if given with a certain shade of grudging admiration, by the gruff, plain-spoken Greeley! Yet it was not undeserved, for no one could anticipate what new light might at any time be thrown upon the diverse, colorful character of this brilliant adventuress.

While appearing as leading lady of Crisp's Dramatic Company at Dayton, announcement was made that Adah Isaacs Menken had been appointed Captain in the Light Guard, a military organization. In our time, one hears of similar honors bestowed upon screen stars, but there is no record of any actress taking an active part in professional exercises of the Sons Of Mars.

But it was no empty honor in Adah's case. During her connection with the Texas Rangers, General Harney had given her a Captain's commission in that band of rugged fighters. At once she plunged into a study of military tactics, and mastered the intricate details of drill in a marvelously short time.

Therefore, as a company officer of the Light Guard, she was perfectly familiar with military duties. Appearing in full uniform during a review, trig, agile and quite at home in her surroundings, she thrilled all beholders and astonished His Excellency, the Governor of Ohio, by the ease and correctness with which she drilled her men.

After her Dayton engagement, she came to New York, where her romance with John Camel Heenan, already referred to, began and ended. When hostilities broke out between North and South she obtained an assignment as war correspondent for a Gotham paper, but her activities in this direction were short-lived.

Because of her birth and long residence in the South, her sympathies were naturally with the Confederate cause. Resuming her stage career, she was starred at a Pittsburgh theatre in July, 1861. With her usual recklessness, she had not been backward in either private or public life in expressing her hopes for a Southern victory.

One night, when on the stage, Adah's observant eyes noted

three gentlemen seated in the front orchestra row, whose talk and general demeanor indicated that they were Southerners. Adah began a flirtation, and when the act was over, sent them a note, inviting them to meet her in the wings, and they complied.

"Are you gentlemen Southerners," queried the actress.

"Yes, Madame, but we now reside here," responded one of the trio.

"Where are you from?"

"Down Memphis way," rejoined the spokesman.

Adah smiled significantly.

"I trust you are doing well for the cause," she said, and handed a bottle of wine to each of her visitors.

Concealed in the wrapping of one bottle was a note which read: "To the health of Jeff Davis!"

The men thus honored were members of the U. S. Secret Service, assigned to watch Adah because of her pro-Confederate attitude.

JOHN C. HEENAN, THE BENECIA BOY

As she was leaving after the performance, she was placed under arrest. Given a court hearing, she protested that she was innocent of any intent to do wrong.

"Your Honor," she pleaded, "I have not broken the law in any way. I was born in the South and my people still live there, but I have done nothing which should offend the Federal authorities."

Said the Judge sternly:

"You have been a constant trouble-maker. Government reports show that your seditious speeches have been responsible for several outbreaks in theatres where you attempted to arouse sympathy for the South. Yet, you are earning your living among the people you try to betray. You were married to a great Northern sportsman, although you have separated from him.

"The note placed by you in that parcel was a plain act of treason against the United States Government. We are in the midst of all the agony and travail of a bloody war, and there is no reason for clemency toward an enemy of our country. Your guilt is unmistakable. I sentence you to thirty days imprisonment!"

Adah turned pale, but left the dock with her head erect and smiled slightly as she glanced around the court-room. Yet the prison sentence was a decided shock, for she had counted upon escaping with the payment of a fine, and the care-free demeanor she assumed was sheer bravado.

Taking everything into consideration, however, she got off very lightly. Justice meted out to offenders in wartime is usually of extremely merciless type, and Adah's indiscretions had been of such a glaring nature that it was in the judge's power to have treated her far more severely.

The popularity she enjoyed was widely manifested by the interest of the public in her case, and the attempts made to aid her. Influential friends rallied to her side, some of the greatest literary men of the age brought pressure to bear in her behalf. But the Government remained adamant in its determination not to parole her.

She served full time, and upon her release was inundated with offers from Northern papers to write her experiences. Again she accepted a post as war correspondent, but, as might have been expected, Government officials interfered. They didn't want a self-confessed Southern sympathizer fooling around the Union Army lines. She was refused permission to enter war areas which were open to other correspondents, and resigned from the coveted post.

Among her many staunch supporters was Robert Newell, known to the literary world as "Orpheus Kerr," editor of "The Mercury," and a writer of juvenile stories. Newell accepted and published a number of her articles and poems, and in the course of time their acquaintance ripened into love.

Although her divorce from Heenan was not yet declared, a little technicality didn't worry Adah Isaacs Menken, and at Newell's earnest solicitation, she went through a wedding ceremony with him. Included in their matrimonial agreement was the stipulation that she must quit the stage, but though the bride blithely promised, she probably had not the faintest intention of so doing. Menken had extorted a similar promise, but when the spirit moved Adah to hit the sock and buskin trail, the marriage bonds snapped with surprising suddenness. Newell had a whole lot to learn about his unconventional spouse.

The marriage took place in New York and the honeymoon was spent in Washington, D. C. Much to the amazement of Washington society, Adah and her husband were invited to have luncheon with President Lincoln. It was a great triumph for the Southern belle, all the more so because of her recent imprisonment on what was practically a treason charge, and provoked plenty of adverse comment.

But in some matters, setting aside infringements on the moral code, Old Abe could spurn conventions as haughtily as Adah Isaacs Menken. He was not concerned with her private life record or political beliefs, it was her dramatic ability that made her a welcome guest.

For Lincoln always had a warm spot in his heart for the player folk. He loved the theatre—it was in a theatre that an assassin's bullet struck him down—and as he once remarked, "Stage people were pleasant men and women whose company was soothing in times of trouble." The great Joe Jefferson, James K. Hackett, Lester Wallack, Edgar Loomis Davenport, Edwin Forrest, John McCullough were numbered among the stars whom the martyred President delighted in playing host to.

Lincoln was an ardent admirer of Shakespeare, and as Adah had frequently performed in "Macbeth," one of the President's favorite plays, the nation's chief executive and the actress met upon common ground, with the Bard as a topic of conversation.

The day after her White House visit the Washington papers listed her as one of the President's callers. Wilke's "Spirit of the Times" reported as follows:

"Among the President's callers at the White House was Adah Isaacs Menken, her husband, and her booking agent, Ed James, Dramatic Critic of the New York Clipper. Miss Menken and party had luncheon with the Nation's Chief Executive, after which the President and his fair guest entered upon a long discussion of stage topics. According to Miss Menken the President was particularly interested in 'Macbeth,' and players who had taken part in that play. Miss Menken, it will be recalled, began her profesional acting career as a member of a 'Macbeth' cast, in Memphis, Tennessee." She played the sleep-walking scene for Lincoln.

In a letter to Frank Queen, proprietor of the New York Clipper, dated October 17, 1862, Adah wrote:

"Think of me, a Confederate at heart, sitting at the same table and conversing with the President of the United States. Did I feel happy? Yes, I was overjoyed. At first I felt slightly embarrassed, because of my recent troubles with the Government, and even somewhat ashamed. But in a few moments all was changed. He made me feel right at home. His quiet smile, his soft-spoken words, his cordial manner, his intimate knowledge of the profession dearest to my heart—made me forget everything except that I was being treated as a friend by Abraham Lincoln.

"He is a marvelous man. Perhaps I was wrong in my stand against what he represents. I now see things differently. Looking at his wise, kind face, with a nation's worries imprinted on it, listening to him, has made me decide definitely to abandon all thoughts of a journalistic career, I shall return to where I really belong—on the stage. Henceforth let the wrongs and rights of North and South be settled by those best qualified to handle them. I am preparing to go to California."

It was even so! Domesticity shared with the fastidious, literary Robert Newell had already begun to pall upon Adah, and the bridal vow to desert forever the garish atmosphere of the stage, belonged in the limbo of lost things. Mr. Newell didn't like the new setup. The thought of a Western tour annoyed him.

ALGERNON CHARLES SWINBURNE AND ADAH MENKEN

CHAPTER III

SO it was Westward Ho for Adah and her hubby, and off they went, stopping temporarily at Chicago, and then entraining for the Pacific slope. Ahead of them was Edwin James, whilom dramatic critic of the Clipper, and now The Menken's advance agent. She was wont to refer to James as her best friend, and this was probably true. James was a prince of good fellows, a smart writer on both sporting and theatrical events, who was always loyal to Adah, gave her excellent advice, and saved her more than once from the consequences of her wilful indiscretions.

It was at James's suggestion that booking had been made for California, the then Gold Coast of America, where money was plentiful. "Beautiful Adah" was likely to prove a sensation on this virgin territory.

She made her debut at Tom Maguire's Opera House in San Francisco on April 24, 1863, opening with "Mazeppa". There had been considerable competition for her services among the Coast showmen, but Maguire had corresponded with James prior to the latter's arrival, and secured the star's services, much to the disgust of his rivals. It was "standing room only" from the start.

People went wild over her performances, and when she went to Sacramento, it was the same story over again, crowds fighting to get in and police called out to hold back the frenzied throngs. Then back to San Francisco, and fresh sensational triumphs!

Without any effort on the part of press agent James, the newspapers "ballyhooed" the show tremendously by publishing thrill-tales of Adah's meteoric career, her many love affairs, etc. And ignoring her previously expressed intention of forsaking journalistic work for good, the volatile star of "Mazeppa" and "The French Spy," took to her pen again, and wrote a hectic description of her impressions of California, which was published and played up under shock-headlines, and made a great hit with the Native Sons.

The disconsolate Robert Newell lurked in the background of this continuous triumph-fate, a morose and sombre figure. So far, this Western trip had brought him nothing but regret. He loathed San Francisco and cordially detested Sacramento, and longed pensively for the more aesthetic atmosphere of his beloved East. His wife's announcement that Columbia was the next stopping place aroused no enthusiasm in Newell's melancholy heart. He feared that there would be no balm there for his bruised spirit, and guessed correctly.

Columbia was then one of California's boom mining towns, known, because of its seemingly exhaustless supply of rich gold ore as—"The Gem of the Southern Mines!" In time its mines petered out, its inhabitants faded away, its day was gone. But while the boom times flourished, with thousands of seekers after wealth carousing, making and losing fortunes, gambling, living furiously and dying violently by stab of knife or flash of gun, Columbia prospered feverishly.

It was a motley crowd that greeted Adah Isaacs Menken. Representatives of every civilized nation on the face of the earth were there—yellow men, black men, red men, white men—a regular crazy quilt pattern of mixed humanity. All had money to burn, and spent it recklessly. There were gambling houses galore to cater to the demands of this lusty, uproarious mob for games of chance, three theatres were in operation, one of which had only Chinese and Mexicans for patrons, and ricketty dance halls, of the rough-and-ready type peculiar to Western mining camps, with their varied assortment of female habitues, were plentiful.

This exotic, exciting atmosphere was just to Adah's liking, and equally distasteful to her husband. She visited a circus that had just arrived, mingled with its performers, and gossiped with them about the days when she too was on the road, with the "Big Top." They entertained her royally and she had a gala time, while Newell, alone in the hotel, sulked like Achilles in his tent, and to as little purpose.

"Mazeppa," billed for three days, opened to an overflowing house. Never had its leading lady received such a tumultously enthusiastic reception. Columbia's city officials led the cheers of its robust, leather-lunged miners for this dazzling siren, whose daring feats and flaming beauty had made her famous across the length and breadth of the North American Continent.

Among those present on the opening night was William Thompson, better known as "Handsome Billy," who had struck it rich and was reputed to be worth millions. His features were fine and regular, a silk black moustache decorated his upper lip, he was broad-shouldered, over six feet tall, supple and muscular—in every way worthy of the sobriquet the dance hall dames had bestowed upon him. A "ladies' man" of course, and a marked success in that role.

When Adah's lithe, almost nude figure sprang lightly from her horse after the mad, galloping dash up and down the incline, in "Mazeppa," she was greeted by "Handsome Billy," who leaped from his box-seat to the stage, and as the actress took her curtain bows, threw a gold nugget worth five thousand dollars at her feet. Robert Newell was in the wings and an agitated witness of this formation of a new friendship, which he dolefully reflected, boded no good to his already demoralized domestic bliss.

He made the mistake of remonstrating, a mistake other men had made before him, for interference never served any purpose with Adah, except to spur her forward at a faster pace toward her chosen goal. When he learned that Thompson had arranged a party in her honor for that night, he lost his temper completely, and told her that she must not go. The heroine of "Mazeppa" only smiled disdainfully.

"My good Robert," she said mockingly, "do I understand that you are actually trying to dictate to me—to Adah Isaacs Menken? You must have lost your senses, my poor boy. Calm yourself and let us have no more of this infantile nonsense!"

So that was that! Obviously, Newell felt that he was wasting breath. As well attempt to check the progress of a hurricane as try to halt The Menken in her stride. He said no. more, and accompanied her to the big combination saloon, dance hall and gambling den where the partakers of Thompson's hospitality were already gathered.

It was a wild night, with liquor and wine flowing like water, and "Handsome Billy" paying unremitting attentions to Adah, acknowledged queen of the festivities. Newell, sullen, but helpless, watched the proceedings moodily. It irked him sorely when Adah brought down the house in thunders of applause by performing several specialty dances with fiery verve and abandon. Worse yet was the mutual infatuation drama staged by her with Thompson. "Handsome Billy" never left her side all night, they played the roulette wheel together till dawn, his every gesture was pregnant with possessive meaning, and Adah's melting glances spelled sweet surrender. Newell returned to the hotel alone.

Adah had won a new cavalier and plenty of cash. On the other hand, she had lost a husband, for Newell shook the dust of Columbia from off his neatly-shod feet and returned to the safe haven of New York. It was his intention to seek a divorce, a fact which exactly suited Adah's plans, for the author-husband had long since become excess baggage, so far as she was concerned.

Advance agent James, with a true showman's intuition, knew that the time was ripe for an invasion by his star of the European theatrical world. Much had been written about her in the London journals and French papers, James had seen to it that press material for that purpose had not been lacking, and aroused public curiosity promised capacity houses.

On April 22, 1864 they sailed for England by way of Cape Horn, then a sufficiently exciting and stormy voyage which it took the fast clipper ships four months to make.

Wherever Adah Isaacs Menken went the figure of Romance was sure to be flitting around the neighborhood, and the glamor spells were a'weaving as soon as the good ship left the harbor. For aboard was a man of wealth and substance whose eyes had already drunk their fill of Adah's beauty on the stage. He had booked passage solely for the purpose of making contact with her in that intimate atmosphere peculiar to long sea voyages.

His name was James Barkley, a gambler of national reputation, owner of a mansion at Seventh Avenue and Tenth Street, New York City. He had been making a brief stay on the Gold Coast when he first saw Adah, and resolved to win her at all costs.

Barkley's plan succeeded to a certain extent. Adah accepted his addresses graciously. They were constantly together through-

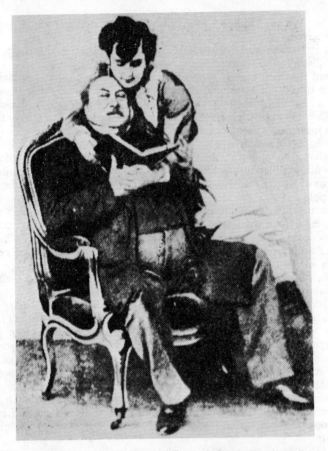

ALEXANDER DUMAS AND ADAH MENKEN

out the voyage, with only Ed James as chaperon, and James was wise enough to do his chaperoning at a distance.

But she would not be rushed into marriage. In the first place, Newell hadn't got his divorce yet, and anyhow, she preferred the state of single blessedness for the time being. But Barkley had the consolation of knowing that later he would be added to the list of Menken husbands. Adah's reception by the British public exceeded even the golden hopes entertained by James. She took the house by storm in Astley's as the voluptuous heroine of "Mazeppa." The staid Londoners lost their heads over her as completely as did the rude mining population of Columbia, California. When she toured the provinces, her success was as marked as it had been in the metropolis.

Undeniably, Adah Isaacs Menken had become the reigning fad in Great Britain. In London, her rooms at the Westminster Hotel were frequented by such men as Charles Dickens, Charles

Reade, Watts Phillips, John Oxenford and Algernon Charles Swinburne.

In Paris, she was the intimate friend of Alexander Dumas, pere, and Theophile Gautier.

Had she been merely a beautiful doll of limited mental capacity, Adah would not have won the admiration and unswerving friendship of so many men of genius. It was her intellect. and really brilliant talents which elevated her above the level of a Circe, this born adventuress and passionate pagan.

Robert Newell had obtained his divorce and when Adah returned to New York, there was no longer any obstacle to the fulfillment of her promise to wed Barkley. That amorous gambler remained as true to his declared love as the magnetic needle to the pole.

Arrangements for the marriage were rapidly concluded and the wedding was duly staged on a scale of magnificence that made New York society gasp in envious astonishment. For a wedding gift, Barkley presented his bride with a gorgeously furnished residence on Seventh Avenue and Thirty-Seventh Street.

To this mansion she gave the name of "Bleak House," after her favorite novel by her friend, Charles Dickens.

Of all Adah's marriages, that which made her the legal partner of Barkley had the shortest span and ended most tragically. They were wedded on August 21, 1866. Just two months after the honeymoon, the luckless bridegroom passed into the Great Beyond.

Some said his death was a suicide, others, including the authorities, set it down as an accident. However that may have been, the facts were that the pair separated a fortnight after the wedding. Barkley appears to have brooded over the separation to such an extent as to bring on nights of insomnia. To relieve this condition, he took to opiates, and succumbed to an overdose of sleeping tablets.

Adah accepted the situation philosophically. Her grief for the untimely deceased gambler never seemed to attain very acute proportions. Whatever sorrow she may have felt was doubtless assuaged by the fact that he left her mistress of a comfortably large fortune.

Had she so desired, she could have lived a life of luxurious ease on the dead man's money, but her restless disposition impelled her in the direction of fresh stage triumphs. She reappeared at the Bowery Theatre in "Mazeppa" for a week, and played to record-breaking houses. Her popularity was greater than ever, and offers of engagements came in a flood from Philadelphia, Boston, Chicago, and other metropolitan centers. But the lure of foreign travel still held her. She signed for a short tour of the Eastern circuit, and then sailed for England again.

As before, she was a terrific sensation. All London thronged to see the sylph-like form and beautiful limbs of the young American actress, and for four months she appeared in "Mazeppa" with unvarying success.

According to the British papers of that date she was being paid the highest figures of her entire career. Her contract called for a weekly salary of 250 pounds, amounting to $1,250 in United States currency. This was in addition to a bonus for each extra performance, of which she sometimes gave eight in seven days.

Such earnings were unprecedented in the theatrical world of that time, and established a high-water financial mark not to be equalled or surpassed until the advent of moving pictures in the next century boosted players' salaries to new heights of affluence.

Then came her romance with England's great poet, acknowledged master of passionate lyrics and melodious verse, the Titian-haired Algernon Charles Swinburne. They were kindred souls, for from childhood, Adah's devotion had been one of her marked characteristics, and her published tributes to the Muse won unlimited praise from the world's most celebrated literary critics.

This was a genuine love affair on both sides and aroused a lively scandal, as neither made any attempt to conceal the connection, but rather gloried in its attendant publicity. On one occasion she was photographed sitting on Swinburne's knee.

As before stated, Adah was always a good business woman, so far as permitting what we would call "ballyhoo" today was concerned. So she did not object when her press agent, scenting a fine chance for free advertising, sent out copies of these pictures to papers all over the world. This incident raised a storm of protest from some of Swinburne's friends, who even exerted their influence to obtain a Government order for Adah's expulsion from the British Isles, on the plea that she was a menace to public morals.

This attack by members of the "unco guid" clan, as Bobby Burns puts it, came to nothing. The lovers continued to meet and develop their idyl. It was not until the fierce flames of passion had begun to flicker, and finally died away into cold ashes that they severed relations.

As an aftermath of this affair, Swinburne wrote his famous poem entitled "Dolores," the heroine of which, an enchanting symbol of carnal joys, was undoubtedly none other than the erstwhile Dolores McCord, whose exhibition of her charms in "Mazeppa" ensnared the impressionable author. One stanza illustrates vividly the reaction of Swinburne to the seductive beauty of Adah Isaacs Menken:

> Thou art fair in the fearless old fashion
>   And thy limbs are as melodies yet,
> And move to the music of passion
>   With lithe and lascivious regret;
> What ailed us, of gods, to desert you
>   For creeds that refuse and restrain?
> Come down and redeem us from virtue
>   Our Lady of Pain!

Not to be outdone in the poetical expression of dead longings,

Adah, cleverly adapting the meter of "Dolores," dedicated the following swan-song of a vanished idyl to her former lover:

To A. C. S.

We drank the red wine of desire,
    My heart at a conqueror's feet,
And there flamed into celestial fire
    A love that was bitter as sweet;
Now the idol I worshipped lies broken,
    Its shrine is deserted and lone,
And over the desolate token
    Time's black weeds have grown!

It was during this period, that of her greatest stage triumph, that she published her fugitive poems in a volume entitled "Infelicia." The lines addressed to Swinburne, following the publication of "Dolores, were not included in the edition of her collected poems, perhaps because of the antagonism displayed by Swinburne's friends to his entanglement with her. The verse to A. C. S., quoted above, was discovered among her papers after her death, and was printed for the first time in an article on Adah Isaacs Menken by her most trusted ally, Edwin James.

When she informed Charles Dickens that she had dedicated "Infelicia" to him, the great novelist, accepting the dedication, wrote to her as follows:

Gad's Hill Place, Higham-by-Rochester, Kent.
          Monday, the First of October, 1867.

Dear Miss Menken:
I shall have great pleasure in accepting your dedication, and I thank you for your portrait, a highly remarkable specimen of photography.

I also thank you for the verses enclosed in your note. Many such enclosures come to me, but few so pathetically written and fewer still to modes of sent. (sentiment—Ed.)

Adah's last poem, written at a later and more somber stage of her eventful career, entitled "Infelix," reflects the mood of depression caused by the desertion of many of her so-called friends when misfortune descended upon her:

Where is the promise of my years
    Once written on my brow?
Ere errors, agonies and fears
    Brought with them all that speaks in tears,
Ere I had sunk beneath my peers;
    Where sleeps that promise now?

Naught lingers to redeem those hours,
    Still still to memory sweet!
The flowers that bloomed in sunny bowers
    Are withered all; and Evil towers
Supreme above her sister powers
    Of sorrow and deceit.

I look along the columned years
  And see Life's riven fame,
Just where it fell, amid the jeers
  Of scornful lips, whose mocking sneers,
Forever hiss within mine ears
  To break the sleep of pain.

I can but own my life is vain
  A desert void of peace;
I missed the goal I sought to gain,
  I missed the measure of the strain
That lulls Fame's fever in the brain,
  And bids Earth's tumult cease.

Myself! alas for theme so poor,
  A theme but rich in Fear;
I stand a wreck on Error's shore,
  A spectre not within the door,
A houseless shadow ever more.
  An exile lingering here.

During her last English appearance she also played the role of
William in "Black Eyed Susan." This was a famous old British
marine melodrama in which Adah looked sweetly wistful and
bewitching in her sailor-laddie uniform. Later, she appeared at
Sadler Wells Theatre as Leon, in Brougham's "Child of the Sun."
She scored distinct hits in both instances, although nothing in her
repertoire ever equalled the furore created by "Mazeppa."

Touring Britain's principal cities, she never failed to draw large
audiences everywhere. At Birmingham her performances broke
all records for the Prince of Wales Theatre. It was there she
quarreled with the manager, who objected to her smoking a cigarette behind the scenes.

It was not until many years later that cigarette smoking became
a fixed habit with the fair sex, and the manager was shocked at
this breach of conventionality.

With austere dignity, he informed her that only wayward
women would be guilty of such an action in public, and insisted
that he would not tolerate such an iniquity in his theatre.

A hot argument ensued. Adah terminated it in a fashion
worthy of the former wife of a heavyweight champion. She suddenly cuffed the upholder of propriety on the jaw, sending him
sprawling into the wings. The stricken one arose and staggered
away. The situation was too much for him to cope with. Thereafter, the spunky leading lady smoked as she pleased without
molestation during the run of the play.

Following her provincial tours she went to Paris. During her
closing performance there of "Pirates de la Savane," at the Theatre
de las Gaite, Napoleon III and his son occupied the Royal box,
in company with the King of Greece and the Duke of Edinburgh.

All applauded her enthusiastically. Later, Prince Jerome visited her dressing-room and presented her with a diamond ring, with the greetings of the Emperor.

While in France, the goddess of romance beckoned once more. This time it was none other than France's noted novelist, Alexander Dumas, pere, who won her heart. At the time, Dumas, ever improvident and heavily in debt, was being hounded by his numerous creditors. He lived, as a means of entrenchment, in small, humble quarters, and was often visited by Adah, who, in her usual generous way, aided him financially.

A national scandal, similar to that which developed as a result of the Swinburne affair, developed out of Dumas' infatuation for his enchantress. They went to a picnic, and in the course of an afternoon of festivity, she posed with him for photographs in various enticing attitudes.

The unscrupulous cameraman retained prints of the pair kissing each other, of Dumas lying with his head on Adah's bosom, and the actress sitting on his knee. He made many copies of these pictures, which were sold freely all over Paris.

Whereupon the younger Dumas hastened to reclaim his father from the siren's toils, and made what was generally considered a rather unnecessary fuss over a rather amusing incident. Adah saved the situation by advancing her elderly admirer sufficient funds to take him to Italy.

It was characteristic of Adah Isaacs Menken that when she rescued Dumas from his predicament at her own expense, she was on the verge of financial disaster. Always she spent money recklessly, giving her bounty unsparingly, wherever distress called. She had also been very unlucky in the making of certain investments which turned out badly. Of all the great sums of money she had possessed, including the fortune left her by James Barker, but little remained.

In addition to her financial troubles, her health was failing rapidly.

That gala night at the Theatre Gaite, when Royalty smiled graciously upon her, was the last time Adah Isaacs Menken's radiant beauty graced the stage. The glory of the sun had departed, and the shades of night were enveloping her.

For some time she had been aware that the dread disease of cancer had her in its inexorable grip. But, like the gallant trouper she was, she carried out the old stage tradition of—"the show must go on." So long as her fast-ebbing strength held out she continued to act, and only her most intimate acquaintances knew that a secret malady was devouring her vitals.

While rehearsing in "Pirates de la Savane," which was scheduled for a return engagement in Paris, in July, 1868, she collapsed, and was unable to continue.

An illness of several weeks followed, during which she steadily grew weaker. When she knew that the end was near, she gave instructions that she should be buried according to the Hebrew ritual, thus holding loyalty to the last to her profession of the Jewish faith.

She passed away on August 10, 1868, aged thirty-three years. In accordance with her wish, a plain tombstone, bearing the cryptic words—"Thou Knowest," marks her grave in the cemetery of Pere la Chaise.

That the tender memory of her early marriage to Alexander Isaac Menken clung to her throughout all her years of roving is obvious. No matter what other ties she contacted, she always retained his name, only adding a final "s" to Isaac. There must have been a glamor about that particular matrimonial adventure of singular endurance, for it seems never to have been dissipated, despite her other numerous love affairs.

Of the many laudatory tributes paid to the deceased actress by the press on both sides of the Atlantic, that of the Boston Courier, in its issue of August 18, 1868, is especially worth quoting:

"Adah Isaacs Menken's stormy life is over; her passionate heart is at rest; the queenly body of this brilliant and beautiful woman who, during her short span of life captivated two continents, will soon be dust. One of the most peerless beauties that ever dazzled human eyes, she had fascinated all who knew her. Now that strange and gifted girl is gone—gone forever. The restless spirit that could not find peace in life, has found peace in death!"

Adah Isaacs Menken's faults all lay on the surface. With all her shortcomings, she was a noble creature and had many virtues. Her generosity was unparalleled. A request from a friend, or even an ordinary acquaintance, brought quick, responsive relief.

Even strangers were the subjects of her pity. Frequently, on her way home from a performance, she would thrust handfuls of coins or bills on human derelicts of the streets who attracted her ready sympathy. No one cared less for money than she did. Which accounts for the fact that she let several fortunes slip through her slender hands, and died practically penniless.

In that narrow space of thirty-three years she acquired a reputation for physical loveliness and intellectual brilliancy unequalled by any female contemporary. There was only one Adah Isaacs Menken!

Appendix

HEENAN'S TRIBUTE

WHEN the news of the death of Adah Issacs Menken had reached John C. Heenan, the American heavyweight champion said, when interviewed:

"I loved her. She was my inspiration when I fought Tom Sayers. She instilled me with new life after I had lost my battle with John Morrissey. She awakened a new spirit in me, something I can't explain.

"Many stories have been printed about our separation and divorce, but not one is true. I have refrained from telling the world the reason for our break. Two things caused it—the death of our child through a mishap and my failure to bring back the championship belt.

"Her heart was set on me winning the international heavyweight title. She adored by strength. She worshipped my fighting qualities and she admonished me not to come back to her without that belt. Had I defeated Sayers in the eyes of the British as I did in the eyes of the Americans who were present, including my dear friend and hers—Ed James, I would have won the belt and she would have been the happiest woman on earth. She then would have remained with me. I know it, I'm confident of it. That's why I was so eager to take back to America the belt that was at stake for our fight at Farnborough.

"She loved hero worship and she was keenly disappointed in my failure. Despite her waywardness, she held powers of fascination over me."

AS EDWIN JAMES SAW HER

THERE were three influences in the early life of Adah Isaacs Menken that moulded her character and career:

First, the literary and art education she received from her stepfather, Dr. Josiah Campbell.

Secondly, the necessity, through Campbell's premature death, of earning her living at an early age.

Thirdly, her experiences while teaching English and French at a young ladies' seminary, followed by her engagement as a circus rider.

She liked to look like a boy. Her short black hair, boyishly bobbed, coming down close on the forehead, her dark eyes and eyebrows, the firm, straight lines of her mouth and imperious carriage of her head radiated a distinctly masculine suggestion. Her favorite stage roles were male impersonations. Daring, determined, her bright, fearless spirit significantly prominent in a conventionally hide-bound age, heralded the future emancipation of womanhood.

Because she specialized in the wearing of breeches-pants on the stage, she shocked many members of her own sex, but made a hit with the men.

The Wild Horse of Tartary in "Mazeppa," carried her from Broadway to the gold fields of California, and thence across the ocean to Europe.

Critics gave her full credit for her wealth of poetical imagery as expressed in her writings, listing her in this respect as a feminine prodigy, as well as for her inimitable work on the stage. They also deplored the fact that so many prudish folks could only see Adah's faults, without acknowledging the immense amount of good she did for those of her profession. A more generous creature never lived. She delighted in making the outside world believe that she was as bad morally as she was lovely. But with her close friends she dropped this pose entirely, and they found her just one of themselves, companionable and laughter-loving.

She could not endure a drab atmosphere, always she wanted the sparkle of life, color, and fast action. There can be no question as to her status as a genuine intellectual. Few women of her time were her equal in artistic ability and versatility.

When she was playing "Mazeppa" in California, she appeared on the streets clad in a single garment of yellow silk that attracted considerable attention. The costume was as daring as it was simple, setting off her exquisite figure to great advantage, yet probably no other woman could have worn it without looking ludicrous.

Her London life, was brief, brilliant and at times bitter. She was fearfully extravagant, but it must be said that she never refused to help a friend in need. She counted among her acquaintances and admirers some of the greatest men and women in England, who thronged the salon where she reigned as a veritable Queen and patron of the arts.

When illness and financial misfortune prostrated her, she commented philosophically on the rapidity with which so many fair-weather friends deserted her. A true citizen of the world, she had experienced the ups-and-downs of fortune from childhood, and had no illusions regarding human nature.

When she left London, her days were numbered, although she was to score a final triumph on the Paris stage, winning Royal approbation from Emperor Napoleon III and Prince Jerome. But the curtain was soon to go down forever on her life drama. With shattered health, her wealth squandered, her great lover of former years, Alexander Dumas, fleeing to Italy to avoid scandal, she was alone and neglected in her hour of bitter need. Her lingering illness ended in death on August 10, 1868.

I imagine that had John Camel Heenan won his international battle with the British champion, Tom Sayers, Adah Isaacs Menken would have remained his wife, and her subsequent romantic career might never have expanded as it did.

HER LAST DAYS

As Described in London Press of May 11, 1878
By Dr. Martin, of Guy's Hospital

I N one of our picture galleries is the picture of a beautiful actress, Adah Isaacs Menken, who died some ten years ago. Looking at it the other day, I recalled an incident in her life that has never been made public.

When she first came to England thousands flocked to see her perform nightly at Astley's, in "Mazeppa." As a doctor at Guy's Hospital, I often watched her drive along the Mall behind a gorgeous team of horses. Later I was, in a sense, to become accidentally a part of her later existence.

With another doctor, my immediate superior, we went to see "Mazeppa" one night. The big thrill came when the wild steed galloped into view, through scenery representing the mountains of Tartary, appearing and disappearing in the distance, until through clever staging, the horse and the living form bound on his back appeared small in perspective.

Suddenly the house re-echoed to a woman's scream. The curtain was rung down. The manager came forward. He stated that Miss Menken has sustained a slight injury, and requested that, if there was a doctor in the audience, he would go back stage to her.

We were in the front row, and immediately responded to the call. Miss Menken was lying in the Green Room. "I'm not much hurt," she said, smiling. "When turning a corner the horse went too close to one of the flats. My leg was grazed and the flesh torn."

The wound was not serious, though painful. We dressed it. She was advised to go to the Continent for a rest. So she went to Paris.

Four months later she sent me a message pleading that I should visit her before she died. I answered by letter, gently upbraiding her for lack of faith, and telling her she would soon be well. In reply came a telegram:

"Come and see me, please hasten, before I die!"

I went at once to Paris, but got there several hours too late. The newspapers gave the cause of death as consumption, but that was not the case. She died from a complication of diseases, brought on in the first place by the shock sustained in the accident at Astley's. A cancer growth formed. Her case was incurable.

Well, she knew what doctors feared to tell her, the truth about her illness. Though she had many love affairs, the person who was uppermost in her mind at the last, was the man whose name she bore to her grave—Alexander Isaac Menken. Often when I sat and chatted with her by her bedside, she recalled her early life with him, the man she loved and respected most, although she divorced him.

AMELIA BLOOMER AND BLOOMERISM

Paul Fatout

THE BLOOMER POLKA

COMPOSED & INSCRIBED TO

M^{RS} COLONEL BLOOMER

BY

J . J . BLOCKLEY .

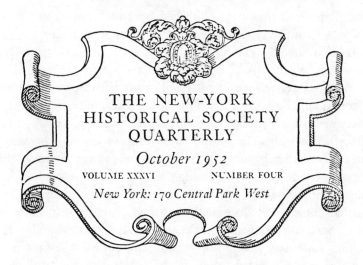

THE NEW-YORK HISTORICAL SOCIETY QUARTERLY

October 1952

VOLUME XXXVI NUMBER FOUR

New York: 170 Central Park West

AMELIA BLOOMER AND BLOOMERISM

by PAUL FATOUT

Department of English, Purdue University

AT THIRTY, Amelia Jenks Bloomer was an auburn-haired, petite and comely creature whose dainty fragility belied the resolution of an independent spirit. In July 1848 she attended the first public meeting on woman's rights in Seneca Falls, New York. She was deputy postmaster of that town, and a contributor of articles, signed "Gloriana" and "Eugene," on morality, temperance, social questions, and politics to the *Temperance Star, Water Bucket, Free Soil Union,* and *Seneca County Courier.*

In the fall of 1848 she audaciously proposed that the local ladies' temperance society sponsor a journal for women. The ladies endorsed the proposal, but before the project materialized they succumbed to timidity or masculine ridicule, and washed their hands of the unprecedented enterprise. Nevertheless, stubborn Amelia, against the advice of her Quaker husband, Dexter C. Bloomer, and with the dubious assistance of Anna C. Mattison as co-editor, launched in Seneca Falls on January 1, 1849, the

first American magazine published by and for women: "*The
Lily. A Monthly Journal Devoted to Temperance and Litera-
ture. Published by a Committee of Ladies.*"[1] The title, said Mrs.
Bloomer, "I never liked...but the society thought it pretty...."[2]

After the second number Mrs. Mattison withdrew, and thereafter Amelia Bloomer carried on alone, determined that no top-
lofty male should sneer that a woman was a quitter. Although she
described herself as "a simple young thing with no experience,
no education for business, in no way fitted for such work,"[3] she
set up shop in a room adjoining the postoffice, wrote industri-
ously, contracted for printing, read proof, edited, wrapped and
mailed copies, and drummed up subscriptions at fifty cents a
year. Scraping along with little money, she performed all publishing functions except typesetting and presswork. Her per-
sistence was a superbly courageous rebuttal of the prevailing
opinion that, outside the domestic sphere, women should be seen
and not heard. Amelia Bloomer was a daring pioneer.

"It is Woman that speaks through the Lily," said the first
editorial:

...upon an important subject.... Intemperance is the ... foe to her ...
happiness.... Surely she has a right to wield the pen for its suppression
... without throwing aside the modest retirement which ... becomes her
sex....

...we shall not be unmindful of ... a healthy and moral Literature....
the Lily will ... strive to please all who delight in productions of the ...
fancy—striving to have them ... tempered with a chaste ... sentiment,
that shall not offend even the most fastidious....

...we shall strive to make the Lily the emblem of "sweetness and
purity"....[4]

Sermons on the evils of the wine-cup and the rum-seller,
together with genteel literature, continued to be standard fare,

[1] Vol. I, No. 1 (January 1, 1849), 1. The "Committee of Ladies" was a fiction.
From the start, the publisher was Amelia Bloomer. For the publication history of *The
Lily* and the location of extant volumes or partial volumes, see Dr. Vail's account immediately following this article.
[2] D. C. Bloomer, *Life and Writings of Amelia Bloomer* (Boston: Arena Publishing
Company, 1895), 49.
[3] Unpublished letter from Amelia Bloomer to Lillian G. Browne, March 21, 1893,
New York State Library, Albany, N. Y.
[4] *The Lily*, Vol. I, No. 1 (January 1, 1849), 4.

but Mrs. Bloomer soon revised her slogan to the more inclusive "Devoted to the Interests of Woman." "Sweetness and purity" apparently offering little scope, *The Lily* in its second year plunged boldly into the turbulent arena of woman's rights, winning the acclaim and contributions of such combative champions as Lucy Stone, Susan B. Anthony, Frances D. Gage, and Elizabeth Cady Stanton. More virile than its bloodless title, the magazine argued its side of the woman question with lively pungence. By 1853 subscriptions had zoomed to four thousand.

The twentieth century, however, remembers Amelia Bloomer less as a laborer for suffrage than as an earnest advocate of dress reform, which was a spectacular offshoot of the struggle for emancipation. Her name, attached by common consent to the combination of short skirt and loose trousers, sometimes called pettiloons, draping hitherto hidden female legs in the eighteen fifties, is immortalized as a common noun. Hers was a spirited effort to free women from their voluminous and constricting haberdashery: heavy skirts raking the muck of streets, multiple petticoats, bustles, miscellaneous padding, and lung-crushing whalebone—all told, some fifteen pounds.

In late 1849, when Fanny Kemble and other ladies of Lennox, Massachusetts, startled the town by allegedly promenading "equipped in coats, vests, and pantaloons," Mrs. Bloomer cast a favorable eye upon the unconventional costume, saying:

...the... "man's clothes" which Mrs. Kemble has been guilty of putting on, is ... a loose ... dress falling a little below the knees, and loose panteletts ... confined to the ancle [*sic*] by a band.... Every change in a lady's dress ... must be ... criticised by ... gentlemen of the press as though it were a subject of serious consideration for such superior beings ... to take action upon .... we maintain that we have the right to control our ... wardrobe....[5]

Amelia Bloomer did not at the moment follow the Kemble example, but she was converted by Elizabeth Smith Miller, daughter of the ardent abolitionist, Gerrit Smith. Visiting Seneca Falls in the winter of 1850–51, this lady, no mean reformer

[5] "Mrs. Kemble and her New Costume," *The Lily*, Vol I, No. 12 (December 1, 1849), 94.

herself, shocked some and pleased others by wearing "a loose costume with long, full Turkish trousers of black broadcloath, a short skirt and Spanish cloak of the same material, dark furs, and a beaver hat trimmed with feathers."[6]

By February 1851, Amelia Bloomer was enthusiastically praising the new costume, and taking further pot-shots at "our self-constituted lords and guardians":

... now that our cautious editor of the *Courier* recommends it, we suppose there will be little harm in our doing so . . . . ladies, will it not be nice? . . . no . . . dresses drabbled in the mud . . . . In getting . . . out of carriages . . . no fear of the wheels . . . . we can even sit down in a puddle of tobacco-juice without endangering our Sunday suit . . . . we shall be allowed breathing room; and our forms will be what nature made them.[7]

Within another month, feeling "the necessity of putting . . . principles into practice," she had herself donned the so-called Turkish dress, described for correspondents as:

... skirts robbed of about a foot of their former length . . . loose trowsers . . . to the ankle . . . gathered . . . and buttoned . . . or . . . plaited up . . . and left sufficiently wide . . . to . . . allow of their falling over the top of the gaiter . . . . the dress with a sack front . . . tight back . . . skirt gathered in . . . mantilla . . . nice fitting boot or gaiter, and a round hat[8]

"We do not say," she remarked, "we shall wear this dress and no other, but we *shall* wear it for a common dress; and we hope it may become so fashionable that we may wear it at all times . . . without being thought singular."[9] She had immediate support from the more aggressive of the woman's-rights contingent—Lucy Stone, Susan Anthony, Elizabeth Stanton, Sarah Grimke, and Lydia Hasbrouck—who also adopted the new style.

The Boston *Journal* proposed that the outfit be called "The Camilla Costume," after Camilla, the Volscian maiden dedicated to Diana, and as a fleet-footed follower of the chase not im-

[6] Alma Lutz, *Created Equal: a Biography of Elizabeth Cady Stanton* (New York: The John Day Company, 1940), 63; see also Alice Stone Blackwell, *Lucy Stone* (Boston: Little, Brown, and Company, 1930), 103.

[7] "Female Attire," *The Lily*, Vol. III, No. 2 (February 1851), 13.

[8] "The New Costume," *The Lily*, Vol. III, No. 5 (May 1851), 38.

[9] "Our Dress," *ibid.*, Vol. III, No. 4 (April 1851), 30.

mobilized in a chrysalis of corset and petticoats. This name did not find favor. "... rather far-fetching a name to go to Greece for it," observed the Boston *Carpet-Bag*, "and the name of 'Bloomer' is equally musical: Mrs. Bloomer, if not its inventor, has done more than any other to secure its adoption, and we give our voice for the dress retaining the name it first received, by almost universal sanction, the 'Bloomer Costume.'"[10] By late spring the name had been so thoroughly bandied about that it was well fixed in the public mind.

The revolutionary change, sensible if not glamorous, furiously agitated a hidebound society schooled in the sentimentality of woman's unobtrusive rôle as the laced and swaddled adornment of decorous seclusion. Around Amelia Bloomer and her proselytes swirled a tremendous hubbub. Ladies from Maine to California deluged her with hundreds of inquiring letters, and *The Lily* went out to them in far-off places. For months newspapers talked about Bloomerism. Approving, condemning, laughing, raging, sputtering, they worried the subject as feverishly as they discussed abolition, the Fugitive Slave Law, Louis Kossuth, and Jenny Lind. The petticoat suddenly became as momentous as the eternal verities, and its summary shucking was like flouting immutable law. Shortening the skirt by a foot was roughly equivalent to a major earthquake.

Ladies appearing in public in the new costume, even in so presumably sophisticated a city as New York, precipitated flurries of excitement, minor stampedes of boys and young men, rude jeers, nose-thumbing, and occasionally literal mud-slinging. The press throughout the nation reported these cataclysms as statistically as a financial page on the stock market: "It is ... reported that one of our most beautiful belles, a leader of *ton* ... will shortly make her appearance on the public *pave* in an elegant Turkish short dress, and breeches"; "... butterflies of fashion parading Baltimore streets in short skirts and full satin pants ... with embroidered bands"; "So anxious were citizens of George-

[10] *The Carpet-Bag*, Vol. I, No. 12 (June 21, 1851), 1.

town . . . to see the . . . display at the Capitol . . . of the Turkish female dress, that the Union Line brought seventeen omnibus loads of ladies and gentlemen . . ."; "Forty ladies made their appearance in the Bloomer costume, at Battle Creek, Mich. . . ."

Elaborate variants of Amelia Bloomer's sober workaday version fascinated reporters, whose dithyrambs rivalled a fashion editor's. In Washington a dazzling young lady perambulated in what was described as:

trowsers . . . of deep pink satin, covered with white figured lace. . . . frills of white lace fell on white kid boots. . . . tunic . . . to the knees . . . of materials similar to the . . . trowsers. Around the hem . . . a quilling of pink riband. . . . sleeves full and tight at the wrists. Frills partially covered . . . white kidded hands, in the right of which was a . . . beautiful fan. . . . front hair . . . braided and turned back . . . turban of pink silk and white lace. A brilliant ornament . . . clasped . . . two white feathers, tipped with red, which gracefully waved as she walked . . . with a male companion, supposed to be her father.[11]

At a Boston wedding the bride was attired "in the poetry and bloom of a Bloomer costume . . . of elegant white satin . . . fitted like love among the roses, reaching around the waist and close up in the neck, the spencer opening in front like a naval officer's vest, and interlaced *a la* Swiss mountaineer . . . white satin slippers, hair . . . plain with . . . orange blossoms over the brow. . . ."[12] The Brooklyn *Eagle* gurgled over "a young lady, apparently in the bloom of her teens, and beautiful as a bouquet of roses . . . her limbs . . . symmetrical as the chiselled pedestals of Venus, encased in . . . yellow pantaloons, which displayed . . . an ankle on which the closest scrutiny could discover no defect. . . ."[13] Perhaps no other vagary of feminine dress has ever so stimulated the avid attention of journalists, from editor to legman, as the Bloomer.

The noisy chorus of comment rose in a confused medley of cheers and anguished howls. "Every day," moaned the Boston *Post*, "we hear that the 'unutterables,' the very 'unwriteables,'

[11] Washington, D.C., *Republic*, n.d., quoted by Lockport, New York, *Daily Courier*, July 15, 1851.
[12] Lafayette, Indiana, *Daily Courier*, July 17, 1851.
[13] Brooklyn, New York, *Eagle*, June 7, 1851.

and 'unprintables' are fast getting into favor with the women, to the entire abandonment of petticoats!"[14] Gordon Bennett's New York *Herald* huffed and fumed:

. . . the attempt to introduce pantaloons . . . will not succeed. Those who have tried it, will very likely soon end their career in the lunatic asylum, or, perchance, in the State prison.[15]

We . . . presume that women who . . . throw off the delicacy of their sex . . . are of no . . . reputable stamp. This dress has been . . . for . . . twenty years . . . worn in disreputable houses as a lure to the imagination. . . .[16]

Horace Greeley's New York *Tribune*, conceding the desirability of a short skirt, turned thumbs down on the pettiloons: "Diminish the skirt . . . and you reduce the fair revolutionist to silence.—No? she . . . claims . . . that the figure . . . in that case will look 'dumpy?' But is . . . any . . . effect half so dumpy as that produced by a pair of Turkish pantaloons? We have never seen a female thus attired without an emotion of aversion."[17] And the New York *Courier and Enquirer* unctuously opined:

Nothing could sooner break down our respect for woman . . . than the . . . wanton examination of that which . . . regards her personal sanctity. . . . lead her . . . into the broad glare of . . . publicity . . . and the gentle . . . spell she now weaves is broken forever. The sun belongs to man, the shade is woman's. Notoriety is the foul fiend at whose feet she falls and perishes. . . .

Such suffocating complacence, epidemic in mid-century, made thoughtful women resent dogmatic masculine ordination, and the hardy ones delighted to affront convention. Still, the sisterhood, vexed with subservience to fashion and mores, did not rally around with unanimous Bloomer support. Mrs. C. H. Nichols, editor of the Windham *Democrat*, expressed a characteristic blend of secret approval and outward caution when, hoping that ladies would foster "every improvement promising

[14] Boston *Post*, n.d., quoted by Albany, New York, *Argus*, May 20, 1851.
[15] New York *Herald*, May 21, 1851.
[16] *Ibid.*, June 11, 1851.
[17] New York *Tribune*, June 12, 1851.
[18] New York *Courier and Enquirer*, n.d., quoted by *The Lily*, Vol. III, No. 9 (September 1851), 66.

comfort and health," she nevertheless confessed that ". . . we would not cut a single inch from our skirts simply for convenience' sake, while there is the least danger that . . . we might cut away an iota of the influence . . . we have or may win, to carry forward reforms vital to health and . . . morality."[19] Charlotte Cushman, the popular actress, hailed as a Bloomer adherent, issued a disclaimer indignantly asserting that the story grew out of her wearing an india rubber suit in a rainstorm. Mrs. Jane Swisshelm, a strong-minded member of the woman's-rights brigade, was yet squeamish enough to reject the dress as immodest: "We should not subject ourself to the rude gaze of a man on the street, or the insolence of ruffians and boys, for anything less than the salvation of the soul."[20]

Godey's Lady's Book, barometer of the mass female mind, handed down an adverse judgment muffled in mystical words about "differences . . . in the peculiar points, and in the shape and structure of the human form": ". . . prevailing . . . fashions," it said, "are . . . most appropriate for the . . . diversity . . . in . . . female form and stature. . . . they must . . . prevail so long as . . . diversities are thereby equalized, or rendered . . . uniform, to the exclusion of the most formidable innovation that ingenuity . . . may attempt to introduce."[21] Even so staid a journal as *Blackwood's* solemnly spoke its piece, which could not resist a discreet snicker: ". . . the dress . . . is not unbecoming. . . . But it is indecent . . . Because . . . it removes the separation wall . . . between the sexes. Men may break it down, and rudely, but no woman should . . . 'stand in the breech.'"[22]

Among the ribald, criticism degenerated into hilarity, and the puns (—"Let a husband take his Bride full Blooming"; ". . . the

[19] Windham, Connecticut, *Democrat*, n.d., quoted by *The Liberator*, July 11, 1851.

[20] Pittsburg *Saturday Visiter* [sic], n.d., quoted by Albany, New York, *Evening Atlas*, May 31, 1851.

[21] "The New, or Proposed New Costume," *Godey's Lady's Book*, Vol. XLIII, No. 3 (September 1851), 189.

[22] "Husbands, Wives, Fathers, Mothers," *Blackwood's Edinburgh Magazine* Vol. LXXI (January 1852), 82.

design proposed by such as would *dare all things*, and boldly rush
into the *breech*-es") richocheted interminably. The Boston
Transcript, reporting an entire Bloomerized family—Mr. and
Mrs. Bloomer, Miss Bloomer, and the little Bloomers—humor-
ously varied the usual story by describing Mr. Bloomer:

> ... black hat, worn jauntily on the left of the perpendicular, light ...
> cravat, standing dickey ... checkered Marseilles vest, frock coatee, skirt
> very short, Turkish pants, large legs and gathered ... to a close fit, black
> gaiter boots, small walking stick, with the top in his mouth. It was
> acknowledged by all that he was the man, and he was congratulated
> accordingly.[23]

Punch cartoonists, joyfully deriding outlandish Americans,
exaggerated the absurdities of Bloomerism. *Punch* writers invented Bloomer conventions, the Ex-Unprotected Female, and
"Theodosia Eudoxia Bang, of Boston, U.S., Principal of the
Homeopathic and Collegiate Thompsonian Institute for developing the female mind." One "Thomas Snarlyle" cried:

> A mad world this ... since ... rampant ... Bloomerism ... came
> over.... Bloomerist ... affectations ... I take to be ... dumb ... clamor-
> ings for the Rights of Women ... and mutinous female radicalisms grown
> termagant.... But here are we ... amid ... hallooings ... bawlings
> ... guffaws ... imbecile simperings and titterings, blinded by ... No-
> vember smokefog of coxcombries and vanities, stunned by hallelujahs of
> flunkies, beset by ... simpletons in ... great lunes and ... petty lunes;
> here ... we, with Bloomerism ... bubbling uppermost, stand, hopelessly
> upturning our eyes for the daylight of heaven, upon the brink of a vexed
> ... gulf of apehood and asshood simmering forever.[24]

Notwithstanding much merriment and harsh criticism on both
sides of the Atlantic, Amelia Bloomer had gallant defenders. Of
the "fashionable female costume," the Springfield *Republican*
heatedly observed:

> ... if ... a man ... can look upon ... this leg-tangling, back-heating, hip-
> depressing, chest-compressing, arm-imprisoning, breath-stopping, dis-
> ease-inducing apparatus [*sic*] known by the name of a woman's dress, and

[23] Boston *Transcript*, June 13, 1851.
[24] "A Latter-Day Fragment. By Thomas Snarlyle," *Punch*, Vol. 21 (November 15, 1851), 217.

not cry "down with the miserable humbug," he is a very small pattern of a man.[25]

The New Haven *Palladium* hoped that the new style would "lengthen the lives of the fairer sex, by dispensing with . . . wet skirts around delicate feet, and increase the happiness of young bachelors, by affording an occasional glimpse of a pretty ankle [*sic*] or handsomely arched instep."[26] The Auburn *Advertiser*, admiring a Bloomer girl, remarked that she appeared "more like a celestial being than one confined to earth. The lady seemed ready for any emergency . . . ."[27] The Boston *Carpet-Bag*, one of Mrs. Bloomer's most loyal supporters, and the first to print pictures of the new costume, reproved fellow journalists for their levity:

> We are sorry to perceive a disposition . . . to ridicule the change. . . . A reform . . . is much needed, and we do not perceive anything in the . . . change to excite the risibles of our amiable contemporaries. They must covet petticoat government . . . who wish that ancient authority to maintain its supremacy. . . . We commend the ladies who have become pioneers in the movement, and wish them success in what they have so courageously undertaken.[28]

So the battle raged during the summer and fall of 1851, enlivened by subsidiary fights. A Reverend Mr. Stone of East-hampton, Massachusetts, acquired a brief notoriety by forbidding two Bloomer girls to enter his church, and threatening them with excommunication. Whereupon gentlemen of the press momentarily ceased feuding with each other and with Mrs. Bloomer, the while they unanimously denounced Mr. Stone for his unwarranted assumption of tyrannical authority, Gordon Bennett's *Herald* assailing him as roughly as it had condemned Bloomerism.

Amelia Bloomer, taken aback by the onset of an unexpected

[25] Springfield, Massachusetts, *Republican*, n.d., quoted by Lockport, New York, *Daily Courier*, June 13, 1851.
[26] New Haven, Connecticut, *Palladium*, n.d., quoted by Albany, New York, *Evening Atlas*, May 28, 1851.
[27] Auburn, New York, *Advertiser*, n.d., quoted by Plattsburgh, New York, *Republican*, May 17, 1851.
[28] "For the Amusement of the Reader," *The Carpet-Bag*, Vol. I, No. 8 (May 24 1851), 1.

furore, quickly recovered her poise and rode out the storm with magnificent aplomb. She stuck to her principles and to her Bloomer dress, printed in *The Lily* a box score of opinion pro and anti, ranging from metropolitan dailies' to the *Water Cure Journal's,* and retorted with sense and vigor. "We have at present," said she after over a year of bouquets and buffets, "no idea of giving up the short dress—fashion or no fashion."[29] When a famous divine, Dr. DeWitt Talmage, invoked the authority of Moses against Bloomerism, she polished him off by citing the more ancient authority of Genesis, which specified no difference between the fig-leaves of Adam and Eve. Besides, if Moses were accepted as law-giver to the nineteenth century, then a hundred other customs and ordinances were being violated by men, including the eminent Dr. Talmage. No sensible woman, she concluded, should "sit under" such absurd preaching.

Annoyed by the nice-nellyism of her own sex, she observed with forthright modernity: "There is a mock modesty among women which we cannot sympathize with or tolerate."[30] The cantankerous Swisshelm, characterized by Amelia as "a very queer woman . . . forever saying something we wish unsaid," rated her reproof in a similar vein: "Women of intellect should . . . raise woman to . . . the dignity of self reliance and a noble independence, and not encourage her weaknesses by talking to her about her 'delicacy,' 'helplessness,' and 'physical disabilities.'"[31]

A valiant fighter was Amelia Bloomer, feminine as a figurine, yet never asking quarter because of delicacy, helplessness, or physical disability. "We know . . . ," she said, " that many frown upon us for daring to be different from the mass; but having experienced the blessings of freedom, we cannot rivet the chains upon ourself again, even to gain the good will, or to avoid the frowns of slavish conservatives."[32]

Despite her efforts, however, the Bloomer never became

[29] *The Lily*, Vol. IV, No. 6 (June 1852), 54.
[30] "Our Dress," *ibid.,* Vol. III, No. 5 (May 1851), 38.
[31] *Ibid,* Vol. III, No. 7 (July 1851), 51.
[32] "Our Fashion Plate," *ibid,* Vol. IV, No. 1 (January 1852), 1.

popular, perhaps because, as editors shrewdly surmised, the design did not originate in Paris, and was not taken up by leaders of fashion in New York and Boston. As one paper remarked: "The sex have treated the subject as they do their shopping,—ransacked it,—turned it over,—talked of it,—dwelt upon its beauties, and—left it."[33] Converts were so sporadic that no concerted movement toward the new style animated women, who by and large clung to their street-sweeping skirts, petticoats, and formidable stays. By midwinter of 1852 the excitement had subsided, and interest in the subject had, like the weather, cooled off.

Yet the experiment, not entirely a failure, did result in at least one permanently Bloomerized woman, Lydia Sayer Hasbrouck. Among the first to wear the costume, she later edited the *Sybil*, "A Review of the Tastes, Errors, and Fashions of Society," agitated for dress reform, and wore the Bloomer until her death in 1910. The commotion in 1851 also left an aftermath of memories. Fifteen years later, the New York *Times*, reporting an equal-rights convention, recalled Bloomerism: ". . . no woman was in attendance wearing the bloomer or 'short' dress. . . . Mrs. Stanton has abandoned it, and Mrs. Bloomer has adopted the garments of Paris and London."[34]

Amelia, who wore the short skirt and trousers for about eight years, retreated gracefully. Mistakenly assuming that good sense is more potent than senseless custom, and meeting the defeat often suffered by those who step out too far ahead of the crowd, she was not embittered as she carried on the battle for temperance and suffrage. Modern women, more free than she ever dreamed of being—and all others who believe in Emersonian non-conformity—owe her a debt of gratitude for assaulting the rock-bound front of sentimentality and tradition. Of her adventures with *The Lily* and with Bloomerism, she said: "I had a great struggle, but did the best I could."[35] She did, indeed, and her best merits tribute.

[33] Albany, New York, *Evening Atlas*, June 21, 1851.
[34] New York *Times*, November 22, 1866.
[35] Unpublished letter from Amelia Bloomer to Lillian G. Browne, March 21, 1893. New York State Library, Albany, N. Y.

Seneca Falls N.Y.
Nov. 26. /53

Dear Mrs Janney

Please tell me the
day of holding the Annual
Meeting of your State Temperance Society = I shall
probably ... attend I
would like also to give notice
of the time and place in
The Lily for Dec 1st .... My
paper circulates largely in
Ohio, and should contain
notice of such meeting = ...

Write immediately
Yours Truly
Amelia Bloomer

AMELIA BLOOMER TO MRS. R.A.S. JANNEY, OHIO WOMEN'S RIGHTS LEADER
(The dots indicate original passages deleted in the reproduction)
ALS at The New-York Historical Society

WOODCUT PORTRAIT OF AMELIA BLOOMER FROM "THE LILY" SEPT. 9, 1851

The Bella C. Landauer Collection, NYHS

FOUR SISTERS

DAUGHTERS OF JOSEPH LA FLESCHE

Norma Kidd Green

FOUR SISTERS: DAUGHTERS
OF JOSEPH LA FLESCHE

BY NORMA KIDD GREEN

THERE were four of them; four sisters[2] born into a cul-
tural atmosphere which was rapidly changing. In.fact
to a trained, intelligent observer it was rapidly vanishing.
But there were no trained observers looking on and thinking about this over-whelming change, unless the girls'
father might be considered one.

He was not trained, as a later period would use the
term, but he was experienced and extremely wise. Moreover, he was a member of the group and could not completely stand aside and be detached in his observation.

---

[1] Joseph La Flesche (Iron Eye) was the last recognized
chief of the Omaha tribe and appears in many histories of the
Indians and of the West. Unless otherwise stated the sources
for this article are the *La Flesche Family Papers* in the Nebraska
State Historical Society and personal interviews made by the
author.
    [2] The author is well aware that Joseph had a fifth daughter
— Lucy. But Lucy was a half-sister of the "four," spent most of
her life on the Reservation and continued more in the Indian
manner of living.
    J. Sterling Morton, *History of Nebraska* (1907), II, p. 222.

*Norma Kidd Green, wife of Dean Emeritus Roy M. Green
of the University of Nebraska College of Engineering, will
be remembered for her article, "Ghost Counties in Nebraska," in a recent issue of NEBRASKA HISTORY.*

Nevertheless, his wider experience led him to see the possible destiny of these people with whom he had cast his own fate. He was outside of them and yet one of them, recognized as their leader. He believed the old order would vanish, whether or no, and that it was important for the Omaha Indians to follow the path of the white men.[3]

He had, therefore, with others signed the treaty of 1854 by which the Omaha tribe relinquished all rights to their hunting grounds west of the Missouri and accepted in its place a Reservation, bordering on the Missouri and farther north than their former home near the mouth of the Platte.

The steady trickle of white settlers increased after 1854, then slowed down a little during the Civil War; it seemed there might be time for the Omaha to establish new habits and sluff off old customs, if only the white men would remember their promises and continue to treat them as individuals and as adults, instead of as savage beasts or stupid children.

The Omaha chief, Iron Eye—Joseph La Flesche—had worked at Peter Sarpy's trading post and, with a partner had operated a ferry across the Elkhorn during 1846-47 when the Mormons were moving west from Winter Quarters. He had seen the energy, and the irresistible drive of white men when they had a visionary or an actual goal in sight. He had traveled with his French father and seen other tribes and the cities of white men. But even these glimpses of the force which would change the old tribal ways could not have prepared him for the advance of the railroads, for the white man's inexhaustible desire for land or for the increasing and devastating slaughter of the buffalo, which had meant food, clothing, and shelter to the Indians.

His daughters, Susette, Rosalie, Marguerite and Susan were born between the year of the treaty, 1854, and the

---

[3] Fannie Reed Giffen, *Oo-Mah-Ha-Ta-Wa-Tha* (1898), pp. 33-4.

closing year of the war, 1865. Their childhood, young womanhood and years of increasing responsibility were in the crucial time when one old custom after another was dropped, smothered by the onward rush of the white men or forbidden by a power which was indistinct and little known when Susette hung in her cradle board in her father's earth lodge. They all four, however, grew to spend a great part of their lives, begging, cajolling, working with, petitioning, adjusting to and, at times, defying and openly fighting that power—the United States government.

Joseph believed the Indians must learn to live as the white men did, to use their tools, their skills and their learning; to speak, dress, act and think as the white men did. Susette, Rosalie, Marguerite and Susan La Flesche surmounted many difficulties and reached this goal. They did all these things in a manner that was acceptable, in many ways, professional by twentieth century standards. They accomplished it, moreover, before they were fifty years old.

Susette excelled in three lines. She became a lecturer, a painter and a writer. Above all she was the spokesman of her people, not for the Omaha alone but for all the Indians. She was first of her tribe to go to an Eastern school; then, after distressing months at home, she began to teach on the Reservation.[4] The Indian Bureau had said Indians would be given preference for agency positions, but Susette was not readily welcomed and the whole situation was difficult.

When the Ponca tribe was removed to Indian territory, she accompanied her father on a visit of inquiry to them. When white men brought the case of Standing Bear to the courts and Judge Dundy handed down his famous decision "that an Indian is a person"[5] in the eyes of the law, they saw the American people must be better informed on the Indian problem.

---

[4] J. Sterling Morton, *History of Nebraska* (1907), II. p. 157.
[5] *Ibid.*, II, p. 226.

With Chief Standing Bear, her younger brother, Francis, and her future husband, the newspaperman T.H. Tibbles, Susette traveled widely throughout the eastern part of the country. She spoke boldly of the injustice to the Indians and their consequent suffering. With Thomas Tibbles she appeared before committees for three sessions of Congress.

Extremely pretty, possessed of a modest dignity and speaking beautiful English,[6] she stirred the consciences and opened the purse strings of her audiences. Many large and small projects for the Indians were organized by a wide variety of philanthropically inclined persons, including both aggressive "near-professional" reformers and the quieter Society of Friends. Organizations active today had their beginning in the altruistic emotions aroused by Susette. Many individuals continued a patient, practical helpfulness and became beloved friends of all four of the sisters.

Since her Indian name, Inshata Theumba, proved difficult for English-speaking tongues, its translation "Bright Eyes" was widely used. It suited her exactly and was poetic and beautiful. Probably very few realized it had been given her in contrast to her father's name of Iron Eye.

As Bright Eyes she became the Symbol of the Indian Maiden to a romantic sentimental public that had been nourished on Longfellow's *Hiawatha*. The poet, himself, added the final touch, when on welcoming her to his Cambridge home said, "This could be Minnehaha!"

Susette and Tibbles were married in 1882 and carried the message of the Indians to England and Scotland. For the next twenty years Susette lived more in the white man's world than in that of the Indians', yet she was always, emotionally, carrying their problems with her.

She also followed the frequently changing career of her journalist-politician husband. Probably much that she

---

[6] *The Woman's Journal* quoting from The Worcester Spy (Mass.), November 29, 1879.

wrote is lost in the unsigned pages of newspapers, but
several magazine articles and parts of two books can be
identified. She joined with Fannie Reed Giffin in writing
the now rare book, *Oo-mah-ha Ta-wa-tha* (Omaha City),
published at the time of the Trans-Mississippi Exposition
in Omaha,—1898. She illustrated this book with small
sketches and colorful paintings; the first time, it is said,
any book was illustrated by an American Indian.

Until shortly before her death she was working with
Tibbles editing *The Independent* in Lincoln. She was increasingly ill, however, and they retired to Susette's allotment on the Omaha Reserve and more and more of the
editing and writing was done by mail and by short trips to
Lincoln. She died at the age of forty-nine, and is remembered as the first woman to speak for the Indian cause.

Rosalie is almost unknown to history but she carried
one of the more difficult roles in the changing drama.
She remained close to the old and yet she took on the new.
She was the center of the family; the one who stayed near
home and yet could understand the experiences of those
who traveled. She represented the stability of home, yet
a home in which the outside world was welcomed.

She was an efficient business woman, the "business
head" of her Irish husband's stock feeding business. When,
in the 1890's the "Farley pasture" and the Farley leases of
Indian Allotments were questioned by white men who
coveted the land, she made use of the white man's own
institution—the courts. When her persecuters went further and tried to cover their duplicity by appeals to race
hatred and more law suits, she clearly analyzed the issues
involved and waited for her vindication with patience and
dignity.

Not only did she keep the books of the business but
the accounts of many small funds inspired by Susette's appeals in the East. Several different "Indian Associations"
and many private individuals sent money to assist the
Omaha Indians. These were often "named funds," intended
for specific purposes. The donors soon recognized Rosalie

and Ed Farley as reliable agents and administrators of their gifts and Rosalie as an accurate bookkeeper.

She stood between two worlds; befriending the older Omaha men who had been of her father's young men's party in the '60's; after his death in 1888 they turned to Rosalie for sympathy and understanding. Yet she looked forward to the world in which her children would live. Realizing that many of the tribal habits would still remain when they were grown, she sent the two older boys to the Reservation to learn Omaha, but to the public schools to learn English.

She had ten children, eight of whom survived her. All the details of business and Indian affairs which she executed with precision and understanding were carried along with the endless washing, cleaning, baking, sewing, nursing sick children and taking part in the work of a lodge and of the church.

As far as can be learned she had no formal schooling beyond that offered on the Reservation through the Presbyterian Mission and the Government schools. But she kept steadily reading and inspired her children to do so; established the accepted fact that higher education was to be expected. All but one of them went to college, several graduated with fine records. Many of her grandchildren have continued into graduate work and occupy positions of influence in education, in business, in public service and in professional life.

She died three months after she had turned thirty-nine. The stone at her grave carries the fitting epitaph "The nobility and strength of two races were blended in her life of Christian love and duty."

Marguerite has been described as "delicate," both by her family and by white friends. She was frequently ill and her school days were constantly interrupted. She and the younger sister Susan went to the Elizabeth Institute for Young Ladies at Elizabeth, New Jersey. There, beside the "common branches," they studied philosophy, physiology and literature.

Back in Nebraska Marguerite applied for a position as teacher in the Mission and Agency Schools, giving as her qualifications the superior training she had received at Elizabeth, the fact that she spoke fluent Omaha and felt she could manage the children, "although strangers may not think so."[7] She was employed and the teachers began to depend on her as an interpreter in both the literal language sense and in the extended meaning of the word. From this time on, Marguerite never completely ceased being a teacher and an interpreter. She did, however, become a student again at the Hampton Normal and Agricultural Institute, where she graduated in 1887.

Hampton also brought her a romance, for she came to care for a fellow student, Charles Felix Picotte, half-French and half-Sioux from the Yankton Agency. His father, also Charles F., had been official government interpreter at Yankton. Charley wanted to be a lawyer, but the years of study looked overwhelming and teachers advised against it. At the same time Marguerite was urged to forget any idea of marriage and devote a single life to teaching or to missionary work. It must have all looked difficult and separation impossible, for they were married in 1888. Charley, himself, was far from well, but he assumed certain family burdens coming after Joseph's death and, for a time, traveled with Susette and Tibbles among the Sioux. But he became more and more ill and died in 1892.

After Hampton, and during her brief marriage, Marguerite was either matron or teacher at the Agency School. After Charley's death she continued as a teacher until, in 1895, she was married a second time—to the Agency's farmer and industrial teacher, Walter Diddock.

They were busy at the Agency for a number of years and then lived briefly in Pender and in Bancroft. Five children were born to them; a baby boy died at fifteen

---

7 Letter, Marguerite La Flesche to Commissioner of Indian Affairs, August 30, 1882; Records of Indian Bureau, item 16156; National Archives.

months, but two sons and two daughters survived both parents and are busy, able and useful citizens today. Walter Diddock bought lots on the second public sale when Walthill came into being. He built a comfortable house and moved his family there in the spring of 1907. The Diddock's became outstanding leaders in a new and growing community.

Marguerite continued informally as a teacher, for she was repeatedly sought as an interpreter for congressional committees, at court sessions, at funerals and at tribal meetings. Beyond this she met the constant stream of requests for advice, for letter-writing and for general assistance from her Omaha neighbors, both on and off the Reservation. Often she served as an interpreter of the Omaha way of living and thinking as she spoke to small informal groups and large public meetings.

This drew her into a second phase of her life and a farther step along the path of the white man. With a pleasant, adequate home, a knowledge of the old ways but with skills in the new, the habit of steady reading and with many friends engaged in educational activities, Marguerite became known as a hostess.

Many groups of the town and the church met in her home; former teachers, leaders and students of Indian affairs, artists, musicians, writers, clergymen and anthropologists were house guests overnight or for many weeks. The smiling little Indian girl shown in a picture taken in Elizabeth had become the dignified, dark-eyed club woman, reserved and retiring but constantly contributing to the community. Ironically, the "delicate" sister survived all the others, for she alone, passed her "four score and ten."

Susan the youngest, was born in 1865, years after the family was settled in the "make-believe white man's village,"[8] so ridiculed by the conservative Indians. After the tribe had become settled on the Reservation, the young

---

[8] Alice C. Fletcher, *Historical Sketch of the Omaha Tribe of Indians in Nebraska,* (Washington, D. C., 1885), pp. 6-7.

men's party, led by Joseph La Flesche, had built houses of log and frame. The two-story house in this village was the home of the La Flesche family for many years after the fall of 1857.[9] It may be that only Susette was born in an earth lodge, certainly the younger sisters,—even Rosalie, had no visual memory of a lodge. In 1898 their mother had drawn a circle on the earth behind her own newer frame house, had put sticks into the ground to mark the position of the upright supports and explained the plan, the process of building and the arrangement of a lodge to Rosalie and Susan.[10]

The frame house was a big move toward the white man's world. Then before Susan was eight or nine, Susette had returned from school, the three older sisters were speaking English, encouraged by their father. The fourth sister started out in the new society from a different background than had the first. Susan, also, had a large share of the firmness and the intensity which characterized their parents. It is not entirely surprising that she went farther and faster than the others.

Besides two and one-half years at the Elizabeth Institute she had two years at Hampton Normal and Agricultural Institute where she graduated in 1886 with special honors.[11] That fall she entered the Women's Medical College of Pennsylvania. The next three years in Philadelphia opened to her the world of western art and music, made her at ease in beautiful homes and brought her many lifelong friends. In this way she approached Susette's experiences among white people of wealth and education. She finished in 1889 at the head of a class of thirty-six earnest and dedicated young women, many of whom had had preparatory work at outstanding universities.[12] She

---

[9] Letter, Dr. Charles Sturgis to Dr. Walter Lowrie, *Presbyterian Missionary letters*, No. 57, Presbyterian Historical Society, Philadelphia, Pennsylvania.
[10] Letter, Rosalie Farley to Alice C. Fletcher (October), 1898; Bureau of American Ethnology, Smithsonian Institution, No. 4558.
[11] *The Woman's Journal* (Boston), May 27, 1886.
[12] Women's Medical College of Pennsylvania, *Fortieth Annual Announcement*, May, 1889.

was appointed as one of the six internes for the Women's Hospital.[13]

Then, as the first Indian woman physician, she returned to her people to serve as doctor at the agency school and later to the whole tribe. This was heavy work, for the Indians were widely scattered, and most of the time she traveled on horseback, day or night, in all kinds of weather. Four years later she resigned and (to everyone's surprise) married Henry Picotte, a brother of Marguerite's Charley.

They lived on Susan's allotment near her father and not far from her "sister-mother," Rosalie. Two sons were born to them and for a time they lived in Bancroft; but wherever she was, Susan continued to care for the sick of both races. Seldom did her own affairs detain her and when she was at home, each night she placed a lighted lamp by the window where the light would shine on the doorstep. Many white people as well as Indians found their way in the dark to ask for help.

Henry died in 1905 and when the new town of Walthill was founded (1906) Susan joined Marguerite and Walter Diddock in this new community. Their comfortable, modern homes were just across the street from each other and Marguerite and Susan often worked together in interpreting and in meeting the constant requests of the Indians.

Susan became an outstanding leader and citizen. She was one of the organizers of the County Medical Society, health officer for the town and a member of the State Medical Society. She was on the Board of the State Federation of Women's Clubs and lobbied at the legislature for better laws on public health. She established the hospital in Walthill, which was named for her after her death. It was said that in twenty-five years she had treated every member of the Omaha tribe and saved the lives of many.

---

[13] Letter, Susan La Flesche to the Commissioner of Indian Affairs, June 13, 1889, Records of Indian Bureau, item 15736, National Archives.

She led a delegation to Washington and obtained the stipulation that every deed for property in Walthill (or in any community established within the Reservation) should forever prohibit the sale of liquor. She became an eloquent temperance speaker carrying on her father Joseph's long battle against whiskey.

She was the only Indian ever appointed medical missionary by the Presbyterian Board of Home Missions.[14] But her missionary efforts extended beyond physical care and she labored earnestly in ever possible way for the economic, social and spiritual advancement of her people. In Bancroft and in Walthill she led the young people's groups and firmly supported the church.

Like Marguerite she became known as a hostess; musicals, family parties, legislative committee meetings, parties for close friends or distinguished guests were held in her living room with its great mantelpiece carrying the words, "East, West; Hame's Best." At last this room was the scene of her funeral conducted by two Presbyterian clergymen and closed by a prayer in the Omaha language.

Susette, accompanied by her husband, had been the first of the four sisters to present the Indians' problems to Congress. She was followed later by Rosalie and Susan. Marguerite, with many actual years under government appointment, met the impact of its power and its red tape in her day-by-day work. Susan was drawn into the most open battles against governmental bureaucracy.

Less than thirty years after Susette faced her first audiences Susan was moved to a passionate outburst. When it was suggested that the trust period for Omaha lands be extended ten years, the Omaha tribe was restive, resentful and definitely rebellious in mood. Susan was their most articulate voice. Speaking before the Secretary of the Interior and others she said:

> We have suffered enough from your experiments— we have been practically robbed of our rights by the gov-

[14] Rev. Julius F. Schwartz, D. D., *History of the Presbyterian Church in Nebraska*, Golden Anniversary Edition, (1924), p. 35.

ernment—In the name of justice and humanity—we ask
for a more liberal interpretation of the law.[15]

In an open letter to the newspapers, she said:

> As for myself, I shall willingly and gladly co-operate
> with the Indian Department in anything that is for the
> good of the tribe, but I shall fight good and hard against
> anything that is to the tribe's detriment, even if I have
> to fight alone.[16]

The sisters had made their place in the new culture,
had become competent and accepted citizens in the white
man's society. Now it seemed another task remained—to
make both groups, both the white world and the Indians
understand what they had accomplished and what their
people could become.

---

[15] *Walthill Times*, March 4, 1910.
[16] *Walthill Times*, December 31, 1909, reprint of Dr. Picotte's
letter to the *Omaha Bee*.

Susette LaFlesche Tibbles, 1854-1903

Rosalie LaFlesche Farley, 1861-1900

Marguerite LaFlesche Diddock, 1862-1945

Susan LaFlesche Picotte, 1865-1915

PAMELIA MANN

TEXAS FRONTIERSWOMAN

William Ransom Hogan

Pamelia Mann: Texas Frontierswoman

By WILLIAM RANSOM HOGAN

THE most isolated settler in the Republic of Texas knew of Mrs. Mann. Whatever she did was news: and not without reason, for she had an astounding variety of attainments, the mere enumeration of which suggests many-sidedness, and most of which indicate a life of notoriety and adventure. Alertness in thinking and versatility in profanity combined with proficiency in the use of firearms and the bowie knife and in horseback riding to enable her to hold her own successfully in pursuits commonly considered masculine. Yet on occasion she could become a leader in society, and according to the enemies of Sam Houston achieved a close friendship with the General and President. Withal she was the central figure in more than one rousing incident, the details of which were recounted with gusto in tavern and cabin and found their way into reminiscences and contemporary records. Though these records are unfortunately too cursory to afford more than glimpses of a few dramatic scenes in her life, they are sufficiently full to show that the early Texans had a healthy respect for this woman who blazed her own very characteristic trail on the frontier.

Her most famous adventure was in connection with the oxen which she furnished to the Texan army in the spring of 1836. In spite of the tissue of legend which the passage of time has spread over the events of the Texas Revolution, this story appears to have had a solid basis in fact; certainly it created an enduring impression. Veterans of the Texan army, relating the story of the San Jacinto campaign after the lapse of a quarter of a century, still remembered Mrs. Mann and her oxen.

All Anglo-Saxon Texas—the army as well as civilians and their families—was in full retreat before the advancing Mexican force

under Santa Anna. The dirt of the trails which passed for roads
had been turned into slushy mire by a lengthy season of rain, and
the sore need of the military for means of transportation had been
further aggravated by the non-combatants' use of the available
horses and oxen. When the army reached Groce's plantation, it
found Mrs. Mann provided with a wagon and teams. General
Houston obtained a yoke of oxen from her, with the express understanding that they should be used only so long as the army
continued its march toward Nacogdoches. But after following this
road for a few miles, the Texan army left the Nacogdoches route
and turned toward Harrisburg. About ten or twelve miles farther
on, Mrs. Mann, with a pair of pistols and a long knife on her
saddle, overtook the army on a "bit of prairie hog wallow & full
of water, & a very hot day."

The woman defied the whole army. She rode up to the General
and addressed him: " 'General, you told me a·d-m lie, you said
that you was going on the Nacogdoches road. Sir, I want my
oxen'." Houston replied that the cannon could not be moved without them. Her rejoinder came ripping back: " 'I don't care a d-m
for your cannon, I want my oxen'."

> She turned a round to oxen [wrote R. H. Hunter in his diary] & jumpt
> down with knife & cut the raw hide tug that the chane was tied with, the
> log chane was broke & it tide with raw hide, no body said a word, she
> jumpt on her horse with whip in hand, & way she went in a lope with
> her oxen.

As she rode off, Wagon Master Roher, who saw the difficulties of
his job being thus multiplied by the loss of animal power, volunteered to overtake Mrs. Mann and bring back the oxen. Houston
thought that the army would have to proceed without them, but
when Captain Roher insisted, he allowed the Wagon Master and
another soldier to follow her. The General did not allow his sub-
ordinate to leave without a parting verbal shot, for when Roher
had ridden about a hundred yards, Houston rose in his saddle and
shouted: "Captain . . . that woman will bite." The Captain
yelled back, "D-m her biting." Houston dismounted into mud
that came very near to his boot tops and put his shoulder to the

wheel of the cannon: "8 or 10 men more lade holt, out she come, & on we went."

The sequel is equally interesting:

> We got down about 6 miles & campt. . . . a bout 9 or 10 oclock Capt Rober [Roher] came in to camp, he did not bring the oxen, the Boys hollowed out, hai Capt where is your oxen, she would not let me have them, how come your shirt tore so, & some of the Boys would say Mrs. Mann tore it of him what was that for, she wanted them for baby rags.

Other accounts of 'Houston's Defeat' agree in substance if not in detail. S. F. Sparks, an eye-witness, left this version:

> We had a yoke of Oxen pressed that belonged to a Mrs. Mann. She was said to be a notorious woman, and just as we had got through with one of the cannon, her oxen were working in that wagon, this woman rode up to General Houston and said: "General, I have come for my oxen and am going to have them." Houston said: 'Madam don't irritate me.' She said 'Irritate the Devil. I am going to have my oxen.' and drew a pistol and rode up by the side of the team and said, 'Wo!' The team stopped. Houston ordered the driver to drive on. The driver fell in the water and said, 'Oh, Lord, I'm shot.' The woman unhitched the oxen and drove them off. We called this Houston's defeat.

Mrs. Mann's very introduction to Texas had been in the face of danger. In 1834 she had been a passenger on a schooner from New Orleans which ran the Mexican blockade at Galveston Island and landed at Harrisburg.

The passenger list also included her husband, Marshall Mann. Despite the paucity of material concerning him, it is only reasonable to give him credit for considerable hardihood, for in the process of acquiring his redoubtable helpmeet he also took into the family two stepsons, Flournoy Hunt and Sam Allen, both of whom accompanied Mrs. Mann to Texas. Marshall Mann died before the end of 1838, but not before he had bequeathed to two other stepsons in the United States—William H. C. Bartlett and S. Bartlett—one-fourth league of land. In his will he appointed "my loving wife, Pamelia Mann" as administrator.

Conflict seems to have been her fate. Our first glimpse of Mrs. Mann after her arrival in Texas finds her in a belligerent mood. The Reverend O. M. Addison records in his unpublished reminiscences that in 1835 his father removed to Robertson's Colony with two large ox-drawn wagons. In the course of the journey one teamster tore down a fence obstructing the trail and drove

through an enclosure surrounding a house, instead of properly driving a short distance around. The premises belonged to Mrs. Mann, who though a woman, had the reputation of being able to take care of herself, and ready, on short notice to redress her grievances. Her absence from home at the time of the outrage alone saved the teamsters from summary vengeance. We had not been informed of this circumstance, and all unknown to us the teamster proposed to repeat the act of throwing down the fence. On reaching the place we were surprised to find a young man confronting us with gun in hand who ordered the teamster in advance to turn his course & not approach the fence. The only reply to this challenge was a rush to the wagon for a gun, with which the teamster advanced toward the young man.

At this juncture, Mrs. Mann, standing in the door-way of the house near by, cried out to the young man in strong, angry tones: 'Shoot him down, Nimrod! Shoot him down! Blow his brains out!' ["Nimrod" was Flournoy Hunt, her son.]

Horrified at such language, and from a woman, too, and fearing a murder would actually take place, I momentarily expected to see the teamster fall. But for some cause Nimrod wavered. He had taken his gun to use it—In a moment of great excitement his mother had commanded him to kill the teamster, and every thing conspired to justify the belief that her orders would be promptly obeyed. Irresolute, intimidated, or unwilling to im . . . e [immerse?] his hand in human blood, the young man still hesitated, when my father taken advantage of the pause, interposed, and the matter was pacified by the wagons going around.

After the battle of San Jacinto, Mrs. Mann moved to the vicinity of Harrisburg, and when the near-by city of Houston was laid out for a new capital, she was among the first inhabitants.

She earned a livelihood by operating a hotel, an occupation which had become important because of the rigors of the struggle for existence on the frontier. The border territory was, according to one immigrant, a "free fighting, stock raising, money hunting country," and naturally attracted more men than women as permanent settlers. Many of these men came on trips of investigation before bringing out their families or friends. Furthermore, the period of the Republic was an era of speculation, and Americans of means frequently came out from the States seeking speedy augmentation of their capital. Although a large number were wary to the point of departing without investing their money, they had to be accommodated with sleeping quarters and food and drink. The Mansion House was no shrine of gourmets, but sensitive palates were rare in that day of five- to fifteen-minute meals. When it was desired, feminine companionship of a robust and none too virtuous nature must be provided. Boarding houses, often dignified with the name of hotels, were set up to care for this portion of the male population which had to exist without benefit of wifely solicitude. In this last respect, Mrs. Mann and her 'girls' achieved a satisfying success.

The problems of hotel-keeping in Houston were many and formidable; often a number of men were forced to share the same room. Sometimes the roommates were congenial, sometimes not. In 1837 the famous Laurens-Goodrich duel resulted from one of the less fortunate pairings in Mrs. Mann's hotel. Dr. Benjamin Goodrich, swashbuckling Mississippian, killed his innocent opponent, whom he accused of stealing a thousand-dollar bill from him during the night. The innocence of the slaughtered Laurens became even more completely apparent when his one-time bedfellow, Marcus Cicero Stanley, 'absquatulated' with the bill (in the phraseology of the 'thirties) and was caught redhanded trying to cash it in New Orleans.

Indeed, the question of how to deal with intractable guests furnished one of the major worries of the boarding-house keepers. Mr. Baldwin of the Houston House once approached a guest who was several weeks overdue in payment of his account. Upon his making a civil request for settlement, the delinquent one replied, "If you come to insult me again, sir, By————I'll shoot you, sir."

Nevertheless several women found this occupation a means of earning a living. Mrs. Jane Long, wife of the filibuster, General James Long, and Mrs. Angelina Eberly, heroine of the Archives War, were boarding-house proprietors. But none gained a wider reputation than Mrs. Pamelia Mann, who was in charge of the Mansion House in Houston when that city was the capital and was filled with a miscellaneous population scaling downward to include the scum of humanity that invariably accumulated in the boom towns of the West.

The available information concerning her career as a hotel-keeper is biased; but despite the necessity of taking it with reservations, it has a foundation in truth. One of Houston's enemies, who wrote anonymously under the pseudonym 'Milam,' says that Houston introduced the Reverend Timothy Tarbuck, who arrived from Tennessee, to "Mrs. Mann and Mrs. Raimon, ladies of some notoriety about the city of Houston." And Edward Stiff, in his *Texian Emigrant* (1840), refers to Mrs. Mann as "a most notorious character."

The early court records of Harrisburg (now Harris) County, on file in Houston, show that from 1836 to 1840 she was involved in more litigation and was prosecuted for more different crimes than any man of her time. At various times she was indicted for counterfeiting, forgery, fornication, larceny, and assault with intent to kill.

Punishments meted out by the courts were swift and stringent. The sixth and seventh pages of the first volume of the court records show that one James Adams was ordered to "restore to Laurence Ramsey Two Hundred and ninety-five dollars as well as the papers and notes specified in the indictment. It is further ordered and adjudged by the court that he receive thirty-nine lashes on his bare back, and he branded in the right hand with the letter T" in some public place in Houston. Nor was the court lenient in dealing with women. Mrs. Mann was condemned to death for forgery, and was saved only through executive clemency granted by President Mirabeau Buonaparte Lamar.

She ran afoul of the law in this case in 1839. On May 22 a jury found her guilty of forging a four-hundred-dollar check, an offense punishable by death under the laws of the Republic. When the prisoner was brought before the bar, she refused to speak. Then the Honorable B. C. Franklin, District Judge, solemnly intoned the sentence: "That the said Pamelia Mann be taken to the jail of Harrisburg County from whence she came—and there re-

main in close confinement until the twenty-seventh day of June
Eighteen Hundred and Thirty-Nine, and from there to the place
of execution to be erected for said purpose—and then and there
between the hours of twelve and two o'clock of said day she be
hanged by the neck till she is *dead*, and may the *Lord* have mercy
on her Soul."

This Houston jail must have turned the prisoner into a raging
virago. The local grand jury with Ashbel Smith as foreman once
made the following report on its condition: "The building is small
and badly contrived; the cells are only two in number, of narrow
dimensions and very imperfectly ventilated. Into each are frequently crowded half a dozen human beings—sometimes more."
In this "reproduction of the black assizes of England" sanitation
and privacy were non-existent. A continuous foul stench rose to
high heaven as a reminder of the vindicatory justice of early Harrisburg County and as evidence of the difficult jail-housing problem of a newly settled town on the frontier.

After Mrs. Mann had been confined nearly twenty-four hours
following the pronouncement of the sentence, the twelve jurors
recomended to the President that she be treated with leniency.
Their petition stated that their verdict had been reached

> with the understanding that the accused should be recommended to the
> mercy of the Court and Your Excellency.
> That considering the peculiar situation of the accused, being a female,
> a mother, and a widow, and an old settler of the country; and more
> especially seeing that the punishment of Forgery is Capital, and there-
> fore in the estimation of the Jury, severe and bordering on vindictive
> justice.

The Houston *Morning Star* in its editorial column also thought
that the death penalty for such an offense was too severe and im-
plied that a lighter sentence might well be given the prisoner.
President Lamar went even further, and despite the fact that he
had not always been on the best of terms with Mrs. Mann, granted
her a full pardon. The case was followed with interest throughout the Republic and reports of the verdict and her release appeared in several newspapers.

During her career as hotel-keeper, Mrs. Mann put the Houston

police force to rout on two different occasions, both of which had a
tinge of opéra bouffe. A local doctor complained to the civil authorities that she had stolen his trunk, and a warrant was accordingly issued and placed in the hands of the city constable. On his
first attempt this limb of the law was not only decisively out-
tongued but was speedily ejected from Mrs. Mann's quarters. The
officer then obtained the aid of other members of the force and
tried again. But

> The Madam [says Edward Stiff] seems to have committed to memory the
> whole vocabulary of Billingsgate, which she in no measured terms dealt
> out; called to aid a band of renegades which she retains in her service,
> and emphatically declared that her house shall inherit the fame of Goliad
> if the invading army did not immediately beat a retreat. The official band
> of heroes soon took the hint, and it was amusing to see some half dozen
> lusty constables with the rear brought up by Doct. B——, scampering
> across the common.

After this fiasco a group of men decided "to test the moral hon-
esty" of the city authorities. They allowed Mrs. Mann to understand that another trunk contained articles of considerable value
and then gave "this female freebooter an opportunity of gratifying her natural propensity." She stole the trunk and took it to her
office. The Sheriff arrested her but arranged for the investigation
to be carried on at her hotel, "she being rich and there not being
more than forty women among some thousands of men composing
the population of Houston." The officers of the law thus managed
to combine business with pleasure. "The spectators were numerous
and were occasionally regaled with delicious refreshments." The
robbery was proved, and during a brief recess the prosecutor left
the house. On his return he found that the doors of the hotel were
barred, the whole party held within, and the house "defended by
no small garrison." "A siege under such circumstances was useless,
and the officers and spectators were finally liberated on the condition of immediate departure and a nolli prosiqui!!" Thus wrote
Edward Stiff, who was undoubtedly prejudiced against the Houston police force as well as against the defendant, but was entitled

to speak with some.authority since he had once been constable himself.

Mrs. Mann had to deal with many persons of shadowy reputation and callous character. None was more notorious than Dr. Benjamin Goodrich, yet even Goodrich had a neat respect for his landlady. After his killing of young Laurens, public agitation compelled him to leave town. He wrote back to Dr. Ashbel Smith, requesting him to take charge of his Negroes and incidentally paying the tribute of one hardened individualist to another:

> Sam, (my negro body servant) is also under your charge. he says he will pay to you Seven Dollars Pr. Week. and the money must be paid without fail, if he does fail to do so, hire him to the most Sever. Master (say Mrs. Man.) *She will train him.*

Yet there is evidence sufficient to show that this Texas Calamity Jane had social standing in the community. Early in 1838 her two sons attended Mr. Hambleton's school in Houston. And on June 15 of the same year one of these sons, Flournoy Hunt, married Miss Mary Henry. One of the attendants wrote that it was a "grand affair," in which President Houston served as best man, and Dr. Ashbel Smith and Dr. Alexander Ewing, both gentlemen of high repute, acted as second and third groomsmen. Despite the fact that the youthful Dilue Rose was edged out of her rightful place of acting as maid of honor by a designing widow who wished to accompany Houston, Miss Rose, in later life, remembered that "everything passed off very pleasantly."

Death came at last to this feminine swaggerer along the paths of crime. The probate records of Harrisburg County show that on the fourth of November, 1840, Pamelia (Mann) Brown died intestate, leaving Flournoy Hunt and Samuel Allen, aged fourteen, as her only children and heirs. Hunt was appointed administrator under bond of seventy thousand dollars. The court allowed the administrator to sell the household furniture, cattle, and hogs to pay Mrs. Mann's funeral expenses.

This sale brought out a list of her belongings which furnishes an interesting insight into the household effects of a boarding-house proprietor and also into the depreciated value of Texas money. Beds, coffee mills, tumblers, and silverware were sold. One "8 day clock" went for "$8.50 or $51 Texas currency." Rugs and candlesticks came under the auctioneer's hammer, and a "musquito" bar went for "$0.31 par or $1.86 Texas." The total as rendered by auctioneers Wm. White & Co. amounted to $2,652.24, of which the customary ten-per-cent commission went to the company in charge of the sale.

The settlement of the remainder of the estate dragged on for several years. The administrator, Flournoy Hunt, died, leaving a "widow of about fourteen years," but no children. An appraisal in 1842 showed still remaining in the estate of Pamelia, "relict of Tandy K. Brown," seven slaves, a claim to a quarter of land, and the Mansion House Hotel and surrounding lots in Houston. The assets thus listed on June 1, 1842, exceeded five thousand dollars in value, though the estate was by no means free from claims.

Mrs. Mann does not deserve to be placed among those Damaged Souls of history whom ill-founded judgments have left with besmirched characters defenseless before the bar of so-called scientific research. The judicious and sympathetic conclusion of one of her contemporaries (a Methodist minister) might well serve as a model for many of the scandal-hunting writers of the New Biography as well as for his brethren of the cloth:

> I introduce Mrs. Mann not as a typical Texas women of half a century ago [wrote the Reverend O. M. Addison in his "Reminiscences"], but simply as a specimen of on[e] abnormal class, rarely met with, the product of life in a new country, with rude surroundings, in the absence of law and order and the restraints of refined society—A woman, who, perhaps, under happier environments, might have proven an honor to her sex, and left her impress for good upon the sphere in which she moved.—A widow and forced, perhaps from the injustice of others to step forward in her own defense, and meet lawless men on their own grounds; it was but natural that she should have developed the rude and free-spoken temper of the times and people among whom she lived.

Mrs. Mann was of a type common to boom towns in all parts of the West. Her character was essentially the result of her environment; such hardihood could never have been developed within the tradition-bound borders of the eastern seaboard states.

It is true, of course, that many women who migrated westward retained all that excessive modesty of action and bearing which the 'thirties and 'forties professed to admire. But whether Mrs. Mann deliberately elected her free way of life or was forced to it by necessity, one must, in all conscience, remain thankful that the stuffy tediousness of the over-pious was relieved by her vagaries. In an age in which self-effacement behind a family front was held to be a high female virtue, the self-reliance of her kind adds bold and welcome strokes to a cross-section picture of the womanhood of her time.

WOMEN AS LAND-OWNERS
IN THE WEST

Emma Haddock

WOMEN AS LAND-OWNERS IN THE WEST.

BY MRS. EMMA HADDOCK.

New England farms had grown old : two centuries of seed-time and harvest for them had passed before the land of which I speak had bared the bosom to the opening furrow. The East had become rich and populous, had made itself a place in the history of nations, and yet the great Father of waters—nature's dividing line between East and West—for at least one half of its course, was known only to Indian fable, or in the wild tales of the adventurous trappers. The riches lying hidden away in the mountains of the far west was yet nature's secret, known only to him who placed them there. The vast praries bordering this magnificent river, grand in their very vastness, were the home only of the "Noble Savage": there he painted his face, decked his person with the skins of wild beasts, danced his war dance and wooed his dark maiden without intrusion, except it were by Spanish or French Monk or Priest, who, from devotion to his religion was risking life for the spread of his faith.

Scarce half a century has witnessed the peopling of this great west. Its development in all the industries, in internal improvements, in its rapidity has outdistanced history itself. Its progress in the arts, and sciences, in education, in general intelligence rivals the oldest states. In 1833, not more than a score of white families were making their homes in Iowa. In 1850, six years before the iron horse had crossed the Mississippi, there were nearly 15,000 farms in cultivation on Iowa soil.

To what may we look for the causes of this rapid growth? Though largely inherent in the country itself, though later, largely due to that great modern civilizer, railroads, yet, in those early days, occasioned or effected by the courage, energy and strength of the hardy men and women who went before to prepare the way for those who should come after. And, that our "lines might fall in pleasant places" our mothers did their full share of pioneer work. The courage, the energy, that built up this great west belonged equally to the emigrant's wife. Amid a solitude more dreadful than hermit ever knew, she strengthened her husband's hands by her own strong courage. A noble example of this true wifely devotion is given by Mrs. Hemans in the "Death of the Emigrant's Child". The mother sits in the door of their tent in desolation and agony, holding her dead boy to her breast. The strange, wild country, the gloomy woods, the broad, lonely river. even the red sunrise, frighten her; and homesickness tears at her heart. And, as she mourns her baby dead, she half wishes that they all lay under English sod, with primroses blooming above them. Her husband chides her; tells her his spirit sinks if she regrets. This rouses her strong woman's nature, and she exclaims—

> "My Edward, pardon me.................
> ....Thou art my home
> ....where e'er
> Thy warm heart beats in its true nobleness,
> There is my country............

We need not, however, look to poetry for examples. Real life was full of sacrifice, of suffering, and ofttimes of sorrow. But the wives who came to this great west, who crossed the "lonely" river, came not to hang their harps on the willows and weep, but to labor hard and long that the land that was their husbands' might make a home for them and for their children. Each was content if merely a living came to her, and if the husband died. was content with the life interest the law allowed her in the one third of her husband's land. For, as you know, these early settlers brought with them the principles of common law ; and common law took special pains to make it clear that if a woman had the advantage of a husband. she should, at the same time. have no legal advantage ; that two such good things were entirely too good to be possessed at one and the same time. Born and reared under the workings of this ancient law, wives accepted it as they accepted their religion—with veneration, as something sacred, because of the many generations of wives it had protected ! But, as our lives are all more or less shaped by our environment, so, too, the ideas of those early pioneers received the impress of their surroundings. The new earth responded to the ploughman with a generous abundance ; and the nobility and the honor that were supposed to belong only to those of high birth found their place in the breast of the common farmer. The new air whispered to him of a freedom as broad and wide as heaven itself. The reverence for old ideas and old customs melted in the clear sunshine of this new world ; and he saw that there were *new* things better than the old.

Another factor which is not to be overlooked, that assisted in broadening public opinion as to the married woman's true legal status, was the influence of the civil code of Louisiana after its purchase by the States, and the Mexican law after the annexation of Texas. These laws recognized the legal existence of married women ; and all property owned before the marriage, by either husband or wife, was the separate property of each ; and as to the property acquired during the marriage, the law established a partnership between husband and wife, making the wife an equal partner with her husband, and giving her a substantial one-half interest, so that, at the husband's death, one half of such gains vested absolutely in the wife. The husband had the control and dispostion of the common property, with the restriction that he could do nothing in fraud of the rights of the wife.

These laws, which were very much in advance of common law ideas, are the foundation of the laws regulating the property rights of husband and wife in California, Nevada, Washington, Idaho and Arizona, though modified somewhat by common law. In all of the other western states and territories, where common law principles prevailed, laws were early passed changing the status of married women, giving to them a legal life, with rights to own and control property.

I am, however, to treat this subject from a practical, not a legal standpoint ; so let this suffice.—The law never placed any restriction on the property rights of unmarried women : the legal disabilities of married women are largely removed by statute. It now remains to consider,—Do women avail themselves of their right to own and cultivate lands? And what are the results of women's experiments as landholders?

As to anything like reliable statistical information on the subject, I am entirely at sea. True, the United States Census of 1880 gives the number of women who are farmers or planters, throughout the whole states (56,809), but from that no conclusion could be drawn as to the proportion we of the west might claim. The Census further gives the number of women who are engaged as agricultural laborers, set out by states and territories. By this I find that, taking the Mississippi as the boundary line, the number of women engaged in agriculture in all the states and territories lying to the west, and not including any of the former slave states, is, in the aggregate only 4841 (of these, nearly one fourth are located in Iowa.) The number of women in these states and territories who are reported as engaged in gainful occupations is 144,526, making the proportion of those engaged in agriculture, as compared with those making some other work furnish them a livelihood, about one to thirty. While the number of men engaged in agriculture equals the combined mumber of men engaged in *all other occupations.*

The question now arises, what proportion of those reported as agricultural laborers own or have an interest in the soil? Here, statistics are as silent as the tomb. Census reports are full of surprising information on all questions relating to agriculture, mechanics and manufactures ; the population is given with sex distinctions ; the working people are given with sex distinctions; the number of farms and the number of dwelling houses are given; but care is taken not to disclose ownership by sex distinction. The exact taxable property of a state may be learned from statistics; but care is taken not to disclose how much of such taxable property is owned by women. There is, perhaps, method in the madness of those who direct the reporting of these statistics; for, if these things were known, the old colonial cry might be raised, and a war for an independent government of women be the result. However that may be, the exact number of acres planted with sorghum in Iowa is of more consequence than the number of women who own and cultivate farms: and this, too, in a state where one woman out of every eighteen is engaged in some gainful occupation, outside of the usual home duties.

However, by a play upon figures, we are enabled to come to some idea of the extent to which women owned and cultivated farms, at least in the older states of the west, in 1880. In states that may be termed rich, and where such wealth is quite evenly distributed, where there are no Goulds nor Vanderbilts centering immense capital and thus creating a necessity for a large population of the intensely poor, it may be safe to say that no women are employed to do farm labor who have no interest or ownership in the land. True, there are some colonies, largely foreign, whose women do farm work—such for instance, as the Polish women in one locality of Minnesota, who are sought for and employed on farms because they do more and better work than men. But such exceptions as this will not balance the number of men reported as agricultural laborers who do not own the land. Taking it therefore, for granted that agricultural laborers in the west, as a rule, have an interest or ownership in the land, then, having given the total number, of those engaged in agriculture within a state, we may determine by division the number of working persons on a farm. Then, having given the number of women engaged in agriculture, we again, by simple division, find the number of farms owned and cultivated by women.

Applying this rule, we find that in 1880, the date of the last United States Census, there were in Iowa 815 farms owned and cultivated by women; in Kansas, 605; in Minnesota, 512; in Nebraska, 447; in California, 277. These figures can give, however, only an approximate idea of the present condition of things: for it is only in the last few years that women in the West have, to any considerable extent, turned their attention to land as something out of which to realize a profit.

As an example of the rapid increase in this regard, take Iowa, which is one of the oldest of these states, and in which the increase has, perhaps, not been so great as in other states and territories. The census of 1870 gives only 356 women engaged in agriculture in Iowa, as against 1386 in 1880. Applying the rule as above, the number of women who owned and cultivated farms in 1870 was only 197, as against 815 at the close of the decade. At the same rate of increase, there are in Iowa to-day more than 1,000 farms owned and cultivated by women out of the nearly 200,000 farms within the state.

These figures do not include any of those women, who at that time, owned wild land as an investment. Then, too, scarcely any advantage was taken of the U. S. homestead, tree claim, pre-emption or desert land acts until within the last few years. Pre-emption provisions were made as early as 1841 ; but my earliest remembrance of women taking advantage of their rights under the law occurred about fifteen years ago, among the school-teachers in northwestern Iowa, a few of whom pre-empted within the state, went to the expense of locating and building little houses, only with the result of losing all by the acts of gallant monied knights !

The homestead act, passed in 1862, was munificent in its provisions, but excluded married women, and widows did not, for many years, take any advantage from the law. Indeed, the earliest case of which I could learn was in 1879. The timber culture act, passed in 1873 and 1878, limited its privileges to heads of families, widows, or unmarried persons over the age of twenty-one. The desert land act, while open to all alike without restriction as to married women, was not passed until 1887. It will be seen, therefore, that none of the now numerous cases in which women have availed themselves of this right to own government lands is reported in any census or collection of statistics.

Because of these facts, and because of the further fact that it is only within the last six or eight years that there has been an awakening of women to a knowledge of their rights to own and control land, with any appreciable results from that knowledge, I deemed it unwise to conclude this paper with merely what information could be gotten from the books. And the information needed could only be obtained by begging it from individuals in different sections of this great West. This I found involved an amount of letter-writing which neither time nor patience warranted. I therefore prepared a list of questions which it then seemed to me would cover the topic, together with a circular letter giving my reasons for asking the favor. These I had printed, and, with enclosed stamps, distributed throughout all the states and territories of the West.

Lawyers, land agents, bankers, and business men generally responded promptly and kindly. I regret to say I was not so successful in obtaining replies from women, though the few who interested themselves in this subject gave me much valuable information.

As a result of this investigation, I learn that in the Western states, according to the best judgment of business men, the amount of land actually owned by women is about five per cent. This estimate does not include real estate owned in cities and towns. In the older and more thickly settled states, as in Iowa, Minnesota, Eastern Kansas and Nebraska, where real estate transfers are not so rapid as in the territories, where land booms have subsided, and where customs are quite fully established, women do not, to any very considerable extent, avail themselves of their right to buy, hold or sell land as a mere matter of business or gain, though many instances have been given me from all of the above mentioned states, of women who have realized profit out of the ownership of wild or uncultivated lands. And in nearly all of the towns and cities of the West, intelligent American women of means buy property—town lots and the like—as do men—as a business investment. And the verdict of business men generally all over the states is that where women have turned their attention to the purchase and sale of real estate, they have proved successful speculators. They are careful and close in their dealings and good money makers; and one of my informants assured me, their intuitions were quite equal to men's judgment! It is sometimes refreshing to learn that, although women do not possess the reasoning faculties, they have, at least, some property of mind that serves the same purpose.

A sad example of the use of such *intuitions,*—three sisters in Kansas bought 480 acres of railroad land at the rate of $5.00 per acre. They held the land and farmed it quite successsfully for five years, when they sold at sixteen and two third dollars per acre, thus realizing a profit out of their intuition venture of $5600.00.

Granted—that such examples are the exception, not the rule ; that few women make a dollar for which they do not do so many hours of hard work;—granted—that in these older new states few women become rich by dealing in land;   yet such examples go to show what women have done, and if their repetition will but incite or encourage some other women to do likewise, it is so much gained towards the business education of women in general—and another convert is made to the old advisory maxim to "let the head save the hands."

In California, I learn that women invest quite largely in real estate. The climate attracts many women from the East, and nearly all invest their surplus money in lands. Many women are managers of small nurseries, flower gardens or fruit farms. The culture and raising of fruit, as a business, received an impetus by the abundant success of Miss Austin, now Mrs. Blachley, who was the leading spirit in a company formed some ten years ago for the purpose of fruit growing and raisin making. The company consisted of four school teachers, who put their small earnings together, and bought a hundred acres of uncultivated land near Fresno village. Two of the girls continued teaching, and the other two, Miss Austin and Miss Hatch, went energetically to work on the land so purchased. They employed help for the harder work, but a great deal of the lighter work was done by their own hands. They *learned* their business as they worked, and spared no pains to master all the details from the planting of the vine, all through the cultivation, the picking of the fruit, the evaporating, the packing and boxing and shipping, etc. The company is known as the Hedgerow Vineyard Company, and their raisins are labelled the Austin brand. They now have a large business, shipping many tons of the very best raisins yearly. Thus an encouraging example has been set before California Women, and now many are doing well for themselves and their families by this kind of work, and many more are just making the venture. And I am assured that if industry, energy and economy will succeed, *they* will; for, as a rule, they are the embodiment of all these virtues.

Last Summer there was formed in California "The Pacific Coast Association of Collegiate Alumnæ." This association has undertaken the investigation of the subject of agriculture as an occupation for women. The committee which has the subject in charge have circulated questions to which they have asked the out door working women to respond. Upon the information thus gained, they expect to formulate a reliable report. The chairman of the committee writes, "Answers come in slowly, and I fear the report cannot be completed in time to be of service to you." It is, however, of service to us to know that such work is being done. It shows the trend of women's thoughts and acts—out of the gas-light into God's sunlight—out of the school room, the art room, the music room, the offices and counting rooms, and in fact, all kinds and condition of rooms, into the vivifying air of heaven, which women have, for so many generations, been afraid to breathe. But the agricultural work of women in California is not confined to fruit growing. Hundreds of cases are reported, from every state and territory in the far west, of woman who own and manage, or superintend the management of large farms, with great success—of women who have achieved creditable results in large ranches, in stock raising and dairy farming. And even in a state so well settled as California, there are cases reported that bear upon the heroic.

Near Santa Ana, a woman owns a cattle ranch. She hired a man to cut a piece of alfalfa, on land given her by her father-in-law. The said father-in-law forbade the cutting and emphasized his order with a revolver. The hired man retired in good order—whereupon, the woman took her seat upon the mower, flanked by a shot-gun, and cut the alfalfa, the aforesaid father-in-law retiring also in good order. This is a case of commendable pluck, but, I am happy to say, is not often necessary to the ownership of land.

Miss Carson, the Sheep Queen of Montana, has erected for herself a most enduring monument among the mountains and valleys of her chosen home. The memory of Miss Mc Arthur, of whose sad death we learned last August, will long be enshrined in the hearts of women—not alone because of her heroic venture to save the lives of a drowning family, but because of her daring and prosperous business venture of conducting a cattle ranch amid the wilds of the Upper Sun River in Montana.

In Oregon, women are land owners to such an extent that it has almost ceased to be a matter of comment. And women land holders are rapidly increasing in numbers—indeed, it is fast becoming the fashion there for women to own their homes, many husbands voluntarily conveying the home to the wife, thus, in a measure, making her independent of her husband's speculations. Mrs. Abby Duniway says there are scores of wondrous feats of manual farm labor and care of cattle and sheep that have been accomplished alone by women's hands—that women work harder than men on farms, and are, consequently, more successful, on an average. However, farm work is, after all, no greater hardship–if there is cash to back it–when we consider the perfection and ease with which machinery does its work. The riding of plow and planter and cultivator the broad cast sower, the mower and horse rake—which last has driven Maud Muller out of the meadow into poetry. The Maud of to-day wears a sun-hat of the latest fashion, which is not torn, and not only are her feet clothed but her hands too are protected with the chamois skin glove, and she rides like a queen, the meadows o'er—if, indeed, she is allowed to do such easy work at all. Then, there is that little, compact machine called the binder that does the work of cutting, raking and binding all at one and the same time, throwing the golden sheaves aside, at regular intervals, with a triumphant air, as if to say, See how I save my master. And the farmer who understands his machine and manages his horses is doing a far lighter work than the chosen work of thousands of women.

Another class of land owners in the West are the German women who invest in small lots near cities, and cultivate their land for market garden purposes; and, the first growth of the spring that does not taste of the hothouse is the result of their labor.

However, that which is of most interest to me in this subject is the fact, that, to a very much greater extent than formerly, widows who take farm lands as a part of their husband's estate remain thereon and manage or superintend the farm work. And women farmers are really no longer a curiosity. I think I am safe in saying that, in Iowa, there are from ten to twenty in every county, and, from what I am able to gather, I think the same is true of Minnesota. And in almost every letter I have received, the success of the woman farmer is attested. In many cases she is left with her house filled with little children, and her land burdened with debt; yet, by frugality, industry and careful management, she has cleared her home of its mortgage and raised her family to be aids and helps in the world, rather than weights upon it. To such women, all honor is due, and their sons instead of merely rising up "to call them blessed," will do more—they will go out into the world and vote the suffrage ticket—for such a mother in the eyes of her boy, is good enough and wise enough to be the president of the states. But, I hear you ask, do not widows in the West marry? Oh yes! but it is fast becoming the fashion for farmer's widows to marry their farms—and in such an alliance, as a rule, a comfortable support is insured.

To my inquiry "When widows take farm lands as a part of their husbands' estate, do they continue to cultivate, or do they dispose of the land?", one answer came "Usually marry if the lands are valuable, then sell or mortgage the land for the benefit of the second husband." This was an exceptional answer and I am ashamed to say, came from one locality in my own state. One of the objects of this paper is to arouse women to the fact that when they own property, it is but wise and just and proper that they should continue to own it, even though they should take to themselves husbands. And the widows with children who marries again, and who thinks she is doing a gentle, and womanly, and wifely, and altogether lovely thing when she passes her property into her husband's hands, is so much mistaken that no good can be imputed to or grow out of the action. The act is unjust to herself, to the memory of her dead husband, and to the manhood of her living one, and unkind and cruel to her children.

In conclusion, with reference to this branch of our subject. Though there are many successful real estate speculators, though there are actual women farmers who have been fortunate and prosperous, yet, in the opinion of many Western men, the most successful women land holders have been their wives who have held thousands of acres safe from the claims of creditors. For, no sooner did the law endow the wife with rights to own and control property, with full power to make good and valid contracts with her husband equally as with a stranger, than advantage was taken of the law by the husband, who really wished to avoid his debt—and his wife was found to be a useful instrument in effecting his dishonest purposes. So the cases are numerous where men have failed in business, paid only a few cents on the dollar of a large indebtedness, and, by the perversion of this most just law, been enabled to save to themselves fortunes. Voluntary conveyances in good faith, or gifts from husband to wife, as they are usually termed, should be encouraged even though improperly named. For the wife who cares for her children and her home does a work that is equal to, if not greater than his; and such so-called gifts as come from him to her are merely her just dues. The law that made contracts between husband and wife valid, certainly had for its object the setting right of all property questions between the parties themselves. And she who complains that the law is unjust because it does not absolutely give her a share in the property acquired by their joint efforts before his death, is in the wrong. The fault is not in the law, but in the business relations between husband and wife.

We come, now to that division of our subject which relates to women as holders of government lands. It is wonderful—the rapidity with which claims have been located, provisions of the law complied with, payments made and titles secured during the past five or six years. Some idea of the results of this land mania can be obtained by comparing the government receipts from public lands. Take, for instance, the time between 1875 and 1885. During the first five years of this period, the government receipts from such lands were only $7,000,000.00, while the receipts from the same source during the last five years—that is, from 1880 to and including 1885 —were over $25,000,000.00. Take another example in figures. There were, in 1875,, nearly three million acres of land taken under the homestead and tree claim acts, while in 1885 there were nearly twelve million of acres taken under the same acts.

These figures will give a faint conception, at least, of the land fever that has been and still is raging in the country. And the excitement has not been confined to rich or poor, to class or sex. Land companies with capi-

tal, by fraudulent means, have realized immense gains. As an example—
a land company in California hired six hundred American citizens to make
entry of 160 acres of land each, then to transfer their patents to a member
of the company for a trifling sum. The company thus came into possession
of 96,000 acres of the best red wood timber land in California, at a cost of
about $2.50 per acre. This land was afterwards sold at $20.00 per acre.
The case is now being investigated. Business men with means have made
investments on smaller scales. For instance, four working girls each over
the age of twenty-one years, were induced, for a compensation, to spend
six months on the prairies of Dakota, holding pre-emption claims in their
own names, for the benefit of their employer, and thus realizing to one man
640 acres: not an acre of which he was actually entitled to under the law.
And in very many cases, women take claims for the benefit of male relatives who have already been benefited to the extent of the law.

These laws, passed especially for the advantage of the poor, that they
might secure homes at reasonable rates, have thus often been taken advantage of by the rich. But when we consider the great good that has grown
out of them, the numerous homes and healthy competence that has come to
many a laboring man and woman through the government's munificence,
we cannot but see that in the end, the good far outweighs the evil. The
poor have flocked to these open lands. Old men have suddenly torn themselves and their families away from all the connections of a lifetime to die
on the prairies of their new homes, but to leave an inheritance for their
children. Middle aged men, blessed with numerous of the Roman matron's
jewels, but to whom gold is a quantity unknown, are seeking it in government lands. Young men, whose fortunes are yet in the future, have
risked their hard earned dollars in a like venture.

And this fever has not thus raged without touching the working women.
The opening up of the country by railroads made it possible for women to
respond to the general cry "land ahead." The dry bones of the worn out
school-teacher have been shaken, and she has been induced to look beyond
the four walls of her school room into the great world outside, and learn by
actual measurement the exact size of a 160 acre lot. The excitement has
extended to women in all avocations—those in professional life, teachers,
clerks, copyists, dressmakers, seamstresses, even kitchen girls have added
their mite to the general treasury, and made their choice out of Uncle
Sams broad domains. Indeed, the earnings of working women all over
the West have made a large factor in the government receipts from public lands during the past few years; for women very much oftener pre-

empt land—that is, live upon it for six months, then pay the government price of $1.25 per acre than they take either homesteads or tree claims. Of course, I cannot give figures as to the exact number of women who have taken government lands. It would be the work of years to study the land office records to that effect. But, from every state and territory in the West where government lands are located, except the territories given over almost wholly to mining interests, comes the general statement—many women avail themselves of their right to take government lands, and many claims are taken under all of the several land acts. To women who have money, there is no great hardship in complying with the requirements of the law. It is only a very prolonged, quiet picnic, with not the very best picnic provisions. From one locality in eastern Kansas, there went out eight young girls into the western part of their own state, took adjoining claims and built their little houses, or shacks as they are termed, so that two of the company could live together. Thus each little home was at least two miles from its nearest neighbor. They were twenty miles from any railroad station, and their picnic fare was bacon with pancakes made without eggs or milk. And yet they returned to their homes looking so well and strong and brown that their friends could not be induced to sympathize with them, or conceive that they had endured great hardships. As a mere matter of recreation, it was *gold* to them, even though they never realized profit out of their land. I give this as only one, and perhaps as bright and cheery an instance as any of the thousands upon thousands of women throughout the West who have taken government lands.

In Colorada, although farming is a difficult business on account of the necessity of irrigation, yet many hundreds of women have taken claims there, and quite a large per cent have remained upon their land and identified themselves with the growing country. And report states that this is much oftener the case with unmarried women who take government lands than with unmarried men; though there are cases where unmarried men have had attractions that kept them there. For instance, sometimes betrothed couples from the East go West, each takes a pre-emption claim, and after six months, prove up, and each get certificate of title; then shortly after, they together get a marriage certificate and the young husband takes a homestead, and the pair settles down to grow up with the country on a farm of 480 acres.

In all these open public lands, there is perhaps none that has filled up so rapidly as Dakota. And Dakota certainly takes the palm for women landowners. The reason for this is perhaps its position with reference to so many populous states, and the enterprise of railroad companies in so rapidly pushing their lines to the west and north. Yet many women have taken claims twenty, even thirty, miles away from the railroad terminus, hoping soon to have their lands rise in value by the completion of a projected road ; and all over the thinly settled portions of Dakota, hundreds of women live alone under their own shack and garden patch, and none "dare molest or make them afraid". Ineeed, the woman who has the fortitude voluntarily to accept such a life would not brook intrusion ; and, as to fear, she has certainly conquered that feminine weakness, if, indeed, she had ever possessed it. Widows with families generally take homesteads, and, of course, live upon them, and after a time, gather many comforts about them. Unmarried women who take pre-emption claims, after proving up, live in the cities or towns, doing some kind of work until they are able to sell so as to realize something out of their claims, then often invest in town or city property. (Indeed, pre-empted land, as a rule, changes hands once or twice before it reaches the *bona fide* farmer.) Women who take tree claims do a great deal of the work of seeding and transplanting small trees with their own hands. But women in Dakota do not more often than in the states, buy land for farming purposes, and voluntarily assume such work. When they do it, it is largely a matter of necessity. Yet many thousands of women in southern and middle Dakota own government lands. In fact, the woman who has not some kind of a claim proved up is either a new comer or a curiosity. The grown-up daughters in the very best and wealthiest families take claims, as do also their serving girls. Even Dakota wives often become land owners through the munificence of their husbands, who wish to be poor, that they may honestly claim government land. But by far the greater number of women land owners in Dakota went there from the contiguous states for the express purpose of taking land,—many seeking health and gain, many seeking gain alone, and finding both : and often a husband in the bargain. They have very generally made their homes there ; and this ownership of land has been of great benefit to the women of Dakota. There are fewer dependent women there in proportion to the population than in any country in the world. This, the boast of Dakota, arises from the fact that so many energetic, self-reliant working women, who were unable to make more than a bare living in the states, have taken their energy and courage and spirit there, and by their business ability secured to themselves an income beyond the mere drudgery of their daily labor. To my inquiry "what class of women are land holders" the answer universally came—"here there are no classes. The woman who can support herself by any honest work is as good as another ; and those who take land are generally intelligent, educated, and refined." This condition of things must make its impress on the coming generations of women.

I would not, however, leave the impression that this going West and taking land is always a grand holiday. Those who go are usually poor—have merely the bare necessities: then if reverses come, want and suffering must follow. Raging fires and violent storms sweep over that new country, leaving distruction in their wake. Last summer two young girls left Iowa to seek their fortunes in Dakota. Their claims were located, their shacks built, and a few weeks of the brightest days they had ever known had passed, when there came a night, as Burns says,

> "A child might understand
> The De'il had business on his hands."

One of those sudden, driving wind and rain storms so common to large prairies, struck their frail shelter and battered it in pieces. The rain came down in torrents: and, with no covering but their night garments, they took hands to prevent losing each other in the darkness.

> "And such a night they tak' the road in
> As ne'er poor sinner was abroad in."

Thus, in the pelting rain and driving wind, they sought shelter at their nearest neighbor's more than a mile away. This is one of the variations of claim life. It breaks up the monotony—and lessens the time for meditation.

To conclude—there are true tales of the work of energetic, heroic women in the far west, before which the heroism of the soldier pales; and which should stand out as monuments in the history of woman's determined efforts at self support and self reliance. From Washington Territory came numerous accounts of women who shrank not from the most difficult labor under the most trying circumstances. Intelligent, educated women who had known ease, gave the history of their pioneer work, with no grain of regret or shadow of complaining. One, alone, without child or mother or sister, is living on a heavily timbered homestead. She says she has done all the work of grubbing and clearing her land, plowed it with a mattock and cultivated and harvested her crop of potatoes, ruta bagas and beets for feed for her cattle, mowed grass with a scythe and carried it from the swamp to her house load by load in a blanket:takes care of and does the dairy work from five cows, hunts them in the deep forest, with no trail to mark their course or her own; chops her firewood from the growing forest —trees a foot or more in diameter—and saws and splits it for use. Yet, when she commenced this work three years ago she was not strong. But strength came with exercise, and she expects, after a while, when the dairy advantages of her land are improved, to live more easily. She has planted and in bearing on her place, all kinds of small fruits, so that she even now has some of the luxuries.

Another example. Three years ago, a woman left a worthless and cruel husband who could not support her, and a wash tub which had been her only support for many years, and with her mother and four children, started in pursuit of a home. The only encouragement she received was the assurance that she should have been sent to an insane asylum for taking her helpless family into that wild country. She located 320 acres as homesteads for herself and mother, walking nine miles from the land office, through mud and water, through the forest where no attempt has been made at road making. The settlers round about turned out and built them a house, and then work for them commenced in earnest. She, with the help of her oldest boy of twelve years, grubbed and cleared ten acres of ground, made rails out of the timber and fenced it, cut the growing trees and manufactured them into pickets and posts, and made a picket fence enclosing the house and two acres of ground: raised their provisions, or, if able to purchase anything, it was at the further cost of walking nine miles to the nearest market and carrying it home on her back. And, with all this, she found time to nurse the sick and so make some little money, with which she bought pigs, chickens, cows, and a team of oxen—which she pronounces a luxury. Since going on her claim, her mother died and bu one year of her pioneer life had passed when her oldest son shot himself, so that amputation of a leg was necessary. That left the work for many months all for herself and daughter of ten years. Thus she labored with the sorrow of death in her cottage, and the trouble of sickness and its attendant expenses. With all these reverses, she writes "We have never really been in want of the necessities, although we have not strictly adhered to the latest fashion."

From Colorado, a case is reported of resolute and enduring courage. A widow with three little children, the oldest but 10 years of age, took 160 acres of mountain land. A man tried to take her claim from her, and, by intimidating her, hoped to drive her off. He commanded her to leave, but she quietly went to work to build her little house by getting together a few logs and covering them with her wagon sheet. And there, in her improvised cabin, with no protection but God's watchful care, she slept with her three little ones. And while she slept, the man built a better cabin than hers, and in the morning came with a team and ploughed around her cabin.

She resolutely walked after him and planted the ground as he ploughed. Again he left, declaring he "would come back and get her out of that.", She then, with the help of her oldest boy, dragged poles and branches from the mountain side and built a fence around the plowed ground. True to his word, her persecutor came back, bringing with him a mob of men of his own type. to help him, as against this one lone woman and her babes. She, with all the dignity of a major of an army, commanded a halt, and ordered the men not to come within her enclosure. They looked on with amazement; evidently she was not the kind of Woman they had been in the habit of dealing with. They saw in her face an assurance in the justice of her cause that could not be shaken—a spirit that could not be broken —a resolution as steadfast as the mountains of her chosen home. And they left and troubled her no more. And there, by unspeakable labor, in the seclusion of her home for which she fought so bravely, she holds her land and supports her little family.

These stirring tales of woman's endurance, of her bold, arduous, hazardous undertakings—yielding to no imposing force, but pushing straight on towards the goal of her hopes—a *home*, are not complete without a glimpse of the heart-life, of the loves and hopes that impel her, of the hidden sorrow which her new life is veiling more closely, of her brave, steadfast devotion to the one object of her life, that enables her, alone, to ring the knell of old associations, and make for herself new friends and a new home in the wild forests of the great West.

> "The bravest battle that ever was fought?
>   Shall I tell you where and when?
> On the maps of the world you will find it not;
>   'Twas fought by the mothers of men.
>
> Nay. not with cannon or battle shot,
>   With sword or nobler pen :
> Nay, not with eloquent word or thought,
>   From mouths of wonderful men.
>
> But deep in a walled up woman's heart—
>   Of woman that would not yield,
> But bravely, silently bore her part—
>   Lo ! there is that battle field."

THE WOMEN
IN THE
ALLIANCE MOVEMENT

Annie L. Diggs

Sincerely Yours
Mary E. Lease.

THE WOMEN IN THE ALLIANCE MOVEMENT.

BY ANNIE L. DIGGS.

THE women prominent in the great farmer manifesto of
this present time were long preparing for their part; not
consciously, not by any manner of means even divining that
there would be a part to play. In the many thousands of
isolated farm homes the early morning, the noonday, and the
evening-time work went on with a dreary monotony which
resulted in that startling report of the physicians that American farms were recruiting stations from whence more women
went to insane asylums than from any other walk in life.

Farm life for women is a treadmill. The eternal climb
must be kept up though the altitude never heightens. For
more than a quarter of a century these churning, washing,
ironing, baking, darning, sewing, cooking, scrubbing, drudg-
ing women, whose toilsome, dreary lives were unrelieved by
the slight incident or by-play of town life, felt that their
treadmills slipped cogs. Climb as they would, they slipped
down two steps while they climbed one. They were not
keeping pace with the women of the towns and cities. The
industry which once led in the march toward independence
and prosperity, was steadily falling behind as to remunera-
tion. Something was wrong.

The Grange came on — a most noble order, of untold
service and solace to erstwhile cheerless lives. Pathetic the
heart-hunger for the beauty side of life. The Grange blossomed forth in "Floras" and "Pomonas." There was a
season of sociability, with much good cookery, enchanting
jellies, ethereal angel cakes, and flower-decked tables. There
was much burnishing of bright-witted women — not always
listeners, often essayists. Sometimes, indeed, leaders of discussion and earnest talk about middlemen, the home market,
the railroad problem, and such other matters as would have
shed light on the cause of the farmer's declining prosperity
had not wary politicians sniffed danger, and, under specious
pretence of "keeping out politics lest it kill the Grange,"

161

MRS. MARION TODD.

tabooed free speech and thus adroitly injected the fatalest of policies. The Grange is dead. Long live the Grange born again — the Alliance! this time not to be frightened out of politics or choked of utterance; born this time to do far more than talk — to vote.

The Granger sisters through the intervening years, climbing laboriously, patiently, felt their treadmill cogs a slipping three steps down to one step up. Reincarnate in the Alliance the whilom Floras and Pomonas became secretaries and lecturers. The worn and weary treadmillers are anxious, troubled. They have no heart for poetry or play. Life is work unremitting. There is no time for ransacking of heathen mythologies for fashions with which to trig out modern goddesses. Instead of mythologic lore, they read " Seven Financial Conspiracies," " Looking Backward," " Progress and Poverty." Alas! of this last word they know much and fear more — fear for their children's future. These once frolicking Floras and playful Pomonas turn with all the fierceness of the primal mother-nature to protect their younglings from devouring, devastating plutocracy.

Politics for the farmer had been recreation, relaxation, or even exhilaration, according to the varying degree of his interest, or of honor flatteringly bestowed by town committeemen upon a " solid yeoman " at caucus or convention. The flush of pride over being selected to make a nominating speech, or the sense of importance consequent upon being placed on a resolution committee to acquiesce in the prepared document conveniently at hand — these high honors lightened much muddy plowing and hot harvest work.

But the farmers' wives participated in no such ecstacies. Hence for them no blinding party ties. And therefore when investigation turned on the light, the women spoke right out in meeting, demanding explanation for the non-appearance of the home market for the farm products, which their good husbands had been prophesying and promising would follow the upbuilding of protected industries. These women in the Alliance, grown apt in keeping close accounts from long economy, cast eyes over the long account of promises of officials managing public business, and said, "Promise and performance do not balance." "Of what value are convention honors, or even elected eloquence in national Capitol, if homelessness must be our children's heritage?"

Carlyle's Menads, hungrier than American women are *as yet*, penetrated the French Assembly "to the shamefulest interruption of public speaking" with cries of, "*Du pain! pas tant de longs discours!*" Our Alliance women spake the same in English: "Bread! not so much discoursing!" "Less eloquence and more justice!"

Strangely enough, the women of the South, where women, and men's thought about women, are most conservative, were first to go into the Alliance, and in many instances were most clear of thought and vigorous of speech. Though never venturing upon the platform, they contributed much to the inspiration and tenacity of the Alliance.

In several states, notably Texas, Georgia, Michigan, California, Colorado, and Nebraska, women have been useful and prominent in the farmer movement, which indeed is now widened and blended with the cause of labor other than that of the farm.

Kansas, however, furnished by far the largest quota of active, aggressive women, inasmuch as Kansas was the theatre where the initial act of the great labor drama was played. This drama, which, please God, must not grow into tragedy, is fully set on the world stage, and the curtain will never ring down nor the lights be turned off, until there be ushered in the eternal era of justice to the men and women who toil.

The great political victory of the people of Kansas would not have been won without the help of the women of the Alliance. Women who never dreamed of becoming public speakers, grew eloquent in their zeal and fervor. Farmers' wives and daughters rose earlier and worked later to gain

MRS. S. E. V. EMERY.

EVA McDONALD-VALESH.

FANNIE R. VICKREY.

MRS. BETTIE GAY.

time to cook the picnic dinners, to paint the mottoes on the banners, to practice with the glee clubs, to march in procession. Josh Billings' saying that "wimmin is everywhere," was literally true in that wonderful picnicking, speech-making Alliance summer of 1890.

Kansas politics was no longer a "dirty pool." That marvellous campaign was a great thrilling crusade. It was religious to the core. Instinctively the women knew that the salvation of their homes, and more even, the salvation of the republic, depended upon the outcome of that test struggle. Every word, every thought, every act, was a prayer for victory, and for the triumph of right. Victory was compelled to come.

Narrow ignoramuses long ago stumbled upon the truth, "The home is woman's sphere." Ignoramus said, " Women should cook and gossip, and rock cradles, and darn socks " — merely these and nothing more. Whereas the whole truth is, women should watch and work in all things which shape and mould the home, whether "money," "land" or "transportation." So now Alliance women look at politics and trace the swift relation to the home — their special sphere. They say, "Our homes are threatened by the dirty pool. The pool must go."

Before this question of the salvation of the imperilled homes of the nation, all other questions, whether of "prohibition" or "suffrage," pale into relative inconsequence. For where shall temperance or high thought of franchise be taught the children, by whose breath the world is saved, if sacred hearth fires shall go out? The overtopping, all-embracing moral question of the age is this for which the Alliance came. Upon such great ethical foundation is the labor movement of to-day building itself. How could women do otherwise than be in and of it?

Easily first among the Kansas women who rose to prominence as a platform speaker for the political party which grew out of the Alliance, is Mrs. Mary E. Lease.

An Irishwoman by birth, Mrs. Lease is typically fervid, impulsive, and heroic. All the hatred of oppression and scorn of oppressors, which every true son and daughter of Erin feels, found vent in Mrs. Lease's public utterances as she denounced the greedy governing class which has grown rich and powerful at the expense of the impoverished and helpless multitude.

Mrs. Lease came to America when quite a little girl. Her
father went into the Union army and died at Andersonville.
She was educated a Catholic, but thought herself out of that
communion, and is now not over-weighted with reverence
for the clergy of any sect. She not infrequently rouses
their ire by her stinging taunts as to their divergence from
the path marked out by their professed Master, whose first
concern was for the poor and needy.

Mrs. Lease's home is at Wichita, Kan. Her husband is
a pharmacist. Her children are exceptionally bright and
lovely. Her eldest son, grown to young manhood, bids fair
to follow his distinguished mother on the platform.

A most trying experience of farm life on a Western claim
taught Mrs. Lease the inside story of the farmers' declining
prosperity. Turning from unprofitable farming, she began
the study of law, in which she was engaged when the Union
Labor campaign of 1888 claimed her services as a speaker.
During this campaign she only gained a local notoriety.
Further study, larger opportunity, and the bugle call of the
Alliance movement roused her latent powers, and in the
campaign of 1890 she made speeches so full of fiery eloquence,
of righteous wrath, and fierce denunciation of the oppressors
and betrayers of the people, that she became the delight of
the people of the new party, and the detestation of the followers of the old. Seldom, if ever, was a woman so vilified
and so misrepresented by malignant newspaper attacks. A
woman of other quality would have sunk under the ava-
lanche. She was quite competent to cope with all that was
visited upon her. Indeed, the abuse did her much service.
The people but loved her the more for the enemies she made.

Her career on the public platform since that memorable
campaign has been one of uninterrupted and unparalleled
success. Her chiefest distinguishing gift is her powerful
voice; deep and resonant, its effect is startling and controlling. Her speeches are philippics. She hurls sentences as
Jove hurled thunderbolts. Her personal appearance upon the
platform is most commanding. She is tall and stately in
bearing, well meriting the title bestowed upon her at St.
Louis by General Weaver, when he introduced her to a
wildly welcoming audience as "Our Queen Mary." Queen
of women orators she truly is. She has the characteristic
combination which marks the beautiful Irishwomen, of black

hair, fair complexion, and blue eyes, — sad blue eyes that seem to see and feel the weight and woe of all the world.

Her style and subject matter of discourse are distinctively hers. She is neither classifiable nor comparable. Her torrent of speech is made up of terse, strong sentences. These she launches with resistless force at the defenceless head of whatever may be the objective point of her attack.. Hers is a nature which compels rather than persuades.

Already the story of the wondrous part she has played in the people's struggle for justice has reached other countries than our own.

Mrs. Lease will be constantly engaged in speaking for the People's Party through the coming summer and fall.

In the to-be-written history of this great epoch, Mrs. Mary E. Lease will have a most conspicuous place.

MRS. S. E. V. EMERY.

Placid, lovable, loving mother of all the other women in this great reform is Mrs. Sarah Emery. What Elizabeth Cady Stanton is to equal suffrage and to her reverent suffrage disciples, such is Mrs. Emery to the Home Crusade and her most devoted co-crusaders.

It is doubtful if any other one factor has contributed more to the spread of the financial doctrines of the People's Party than Mrs. Emery's little book, " Seven Financial Conspiracies." It was surely an inspiration of the módern sort — the putting in so clear, concise, and brief a form the epitomized story of the nation's finances since the civil war. The low price and simple style of the little book made it available and effective. It was read more extensively than any other work of its class. It was one of those " poisonous " books which Ex-Governor Geo. T. Anthony, now the Republican nominee for congressman-at-large from Kansas, in a public speech berated his fellow Republicans and Democrats for having " *allowed* the Alliance men to get behind closed doors and read."

Ex-Governor John P. St. John seems to have found meat rather than poison in the book. He said: "I learned more in relation to the financial history of our country during the past thirty years by carefully reading Mrs. Emery's 'Seven Financial Conspiracies' than I had ever known before."

Mrs. Emery was born May 12, 1838, at Phelps, Ontario County, New York. Her father was a widely informed, warm-hearted man. He espoused the doctrines of the Universalists, in those days the extreme of heresy, and was subjected to much contumely therefor. The animating spirit of early Universalism was love — love all-conquering, love that refused to believe that evil or pain could eternally endure. The breath of life from earliest childhood for this strong, mother-hearted woman was loving kindliness, tender solicitude, and entire hopefulness that all ills could be cured. Writing of her father, she says: " In my sympathy for the oppressed, in my love for justice to my fellow-men, I see my father's spirit, and the same benign influence that inspired my childish heart leads me on to-day and strengthens my devotion to the great cause of humanity."

During the years of her young womanhood, Mrs. Emery alternated between teaching and attending school. In Sunday schools and temperance societies she has always been an efficient worker. As a matter of course, she is an equal suffragist.

In 1881 Mrs. Emery was elected delegate-at-large to the State Greenback Convention of Michigan, the first woman thus honored from her state. Since that time she has been sent as delegate to national conventions of the Greenback and Union Labor parties. She was also a delegate to the Conference of Industrial Organizations at St. Louis, February 22 of this year.

Mrs. Emery began her career as a public speaker in 1880. Returning from the State Greenback Convention, she said to her husband: " When I saw that little band of men, I said in my heart, Surely these are the people chosen of God to perpetuate the principles established by our fathers, and, though despised and ridiculed, my lot must be cast with them. I feel that I must go and preach deliverance to the toiling captives of our land."

Her first meeting was held in a country schoolhouse; and though the house was crowded, there was not one person present sufficiently in sympathy with her views to be willing to preside. With entire confidence in the righteousness of her message, she proceeded calmly to expound the new political doctrine. She was listened to with profound and respectful attention, and at the close of her address an old

gentleman stepped forward and stated that he had voted the
Republican ticket ever since there had been a Republican
Party, but he should never vote it again.

Mrs. Emery makes no effort at oratory or elocutionary
style. She is none the less effective, and is credited with
making converts wherever she speaks.

She is widely known and is much beloved. Her sweet
spirit has shaped a face of benign loveliness. She is very tall
and proportionately large. She has all the wholesomeness
of perfect health and the soft color of youth in her fresh,
fair face. If the whole human race were to call upon her
for kindly attention and for sympathy, she has enough to go
around.

Mrs. Emery is one of the associate editors of the *New
Forum*, a People's Party paper just started at St. Louis.
Her home is at Lansing, Mich. She is now speaking in
Oregon, and will continue on the platform during the summer and fall. Indeed, she will doubtless be at work speaking and writing for the prisoners of poverty as long as life
shall last.

MRS. FANNY RANDOLPH VICKREY.

Mrs. Fanny Randolph Vickrey, of Emporia, Kan., could
not help being a reformer of the aggressive type. She has
it i' the blood. With Quaker-Abolitionist-Greenback ancestry, with Kansas for a native state, with a glad, free girlhood passed on a broad prairie farm — with these blessings
supplemented by a course in one of the fine co-educational
institutions of her native state, and all this crowned by marriage with a noble, generous-minded man who glories in his
wife's ability, it is not more than to be expected that Mrs.
Vickrey should be a sympathetic and active worker in the
Alliance.

In 1884 Mrs. Vickrey, then Miss Randolph, was nominated by the Greenback Party of Kansas for state superintendent of public instruction. Her fitness for that position
was acknowledged even by the opposition press. A leading
Republican paper of the state said of her: "She is a capable
teacher, and possesses elocutionary skill, which should make
her a pleasing and effective public speaker. Her force of
character indicates executive ability; and while, of course, she
cannot hope to be elected, we hazard no public interest in

saying she possesses exceptionally fine qualifications for the important duties of the office."

She did her first speech-making in the summer of 1890, borne on by the spirit of the popular crusade for " equal rights to all and special privileges to none." Her voice is rich and mellow. Her large-featured, frank, handsome face, with clear brown eyes, and her tall, graceful figure, enlist admiration, which ripens into high regard for her intelligence and worth.

She is equally as noticeable in social life as in reform work. She is a Prohibitionist, a Woman Suffragist, a Single-Taxer; and if there be good things and true for the benefaction of humankind which Mrs. Vickrey does not yet see, she is liable to call for them in the near future.

MRS. BETTIE GAY.

A companion to Mrs. Emery in stature and fine physique, Mrs. Bettie Gay of Texas is somewhat contrasting as to physiognomy. Her hair and eyes are black. The thought lines in her strong, fine face betoken a character of heroic type. There is no lack of kindly expression, but the intellectual woman greets you first. A woman so innately superior that her calm self-poise is quite lost to self-consciousness.

Mrs. Gay was born in Alabama. Her parents moved to Texas while she was a child. She was married to Hon. R. K. Gay, also an Alabamian, at an early age. Her husband was a cultivated man who had travelled extensively, and from him she gained her fondness for the literature of philosophy and science.

After the war, Mrs. Gay, like many Southern ladies who became impoverished thereby, took up a burden of unaccustomed work. She not only performed all her household duties, but helped her husband in the field work, and also sold their farm products in open market. In 1880 her husband died, leaving her with a mortgaged farm and a half-grown son. Then it was that her extraordinary qualities, her industry and her business ability, were tested to the utmost. In addition to her farm work she took in sewing. With all of her work she would snatch a little time for her beloved books. She raised and started in the world six boys and three girls, none of them having any claim of relationship upon her. She was always ready to drop her own work and go to the bedside of a sick neighbor. The entire community where she has lived so many years speak in grateful praise of her benevolence and personal service.

As a result of her indomitable energy and her executive ability, she raised the mortgage from her home, paid other outstanding debts, and educated her son. Her magnificent plantation of seventeen hundred and seventy-six acres is managed by her son, Hon. Bates Gay, who is prominent in local politics of the new school.

Mrs. Gay receives a large daily mail of letters and newspapers, to which she gives systematic attention. She is a frequent contributor to the press of her state, and writes with much force and clearness.

Mrs. Gay is broad in her religious views. Her interest is rather with deeds than creeds. She is a Woman Suffragist and a Prohibitionist. She is a leading spirit in the Alliance. Her judgment is relied upon. She has given liberal sums to furthur the interest of the order.

Hers is a history of effort and achievement which would have been expected from New England and a preceding generation rather than from the South and these later times.

Mrs. Gay contributed the excellent article on "Women in the Alliance" in N. A. Dunning's "History of the Alliance," from which the following is taken as serving to show her estimate of the benefits women have both given and received from membership in that great order.

"Through the educational influence of the Alliance, the prejudice against woman's progress is being removed, and within the last five years much has been accomplished in that direction. Women are now recognized as a prominent factor in all social and political movements. In the meetings of the Alliance she comes in contact with educated reformers, whose sympathies she always has. Her presence has a tendency to control the strong tempers of many of the members, and places a premium on politeness and gentility. She goads the stupid and ignorant to a study of the principles of reform, and adds an element to the organization without which it would be a failure. Being placed upon an equality with men, and her usefulness being recognized by the organization in all its work, she is proud of her womanhood, and is better prepared to face the stern realities of life. She is better prepared to raise and educate her offspring by teaching the responsibility of citizenship and their duty to society."

Another extract from the same article shows the advanced thought of Mrs. Gay as to woman's rightful place in the world.

" What we need, above all things else, is a better womanhood — a womanhood with the courage of conviction, armed with intelligence and the greatest virtues of her sex, acknowledging no master and accepting no compromise. When her enemies shall have laid down their arms, and her proper position in society is recognized, she will be prepared to take upon herself the responsibilities of life, and civilization will be advanced to that point where intellect instead of brute force will rule the world. When this work is accomplished, avarice, greed, and passion will cease to control the minds of the people, and we can proclaim, ' Peace on earth, good will toward men.' "

EVA MCDONALD—VALESH.

The jauntiest, sauciest, prettiest little woman in the whole coterie of women in the Alliance is piquant little Eva McDonald-Valesh. A fun-loving, jolly, prankish elf of a woman, quite as much at home on an improvised store-box platform on the street corner, speaking earnestly to her toil-hardened brother Knights of Labor, as in the drawing-room, radiating sparkling wit and repartee. All places and all experiences fall naturally within Mrs. Valesh's versatile sphere. Her career as a public speaker, covering a period of about two years, has been one of brilliant and efficient service to the cause of political reform. She was state lecturer of the Minnesota Alliance, and has spoken in several states, never failing to captivate her audiences. Her youthful appearance is quite in contrast to the maturity of her thought. She is conversational rather than elocutionary in style. Her voice is clear and strong. She uses apt illustrations, strong statement, and good logic.

At the state convention of the People's Party of Ohio, held at Springfield in the summer of 1891, she was the principal speaker at the evening mass meeting. Her address was rapturously applauded. In the course of her remarks she referred to the opposition to woman on the rostrum, saying that she hoped to be able to speak for woman's cause as long as there were homeless, voiceless women, helpless to cope with the hard conditions of life. This she intended to do regardless of the prejudice that would relegate her to the four square walls of home. At this point a gray-haired convert, won by the power and pathos of her plea, called out, " You are at home now ; you are in the sphere for which God designed you."

Mrs. Valesh is as efficient with her pen as on the platform. She has been a self-supporting newspaper writer for several years, and has written several strong papers on economic topics which have been widely noticed. Her noteworthy contribution to the May ARENA exhibits her vigorous style as well as her power of analysis.

A little more than a year ago she was married to Mr. Frank Valesh, a superior young man, prominent in labor organizations, and in the employ of the Bureau of Labor Statistics at St. Paul, Minn., where they now live.

The crowning glory of motherhood has recently come to this bright, brave little woman. If the new little man does not admire his mother as he grows to years of comprehension, he will be exceptional among her large circle of devoted friends.

MRS. MARION TODD.

One thinks of a choice poem, of a sweet song, of delicate perfume, of all things gracious and true, in the presence of Marion Todd. Such exquisite, subtle charm of personality as is hers is only gained by a life of unselfishness and of high culture.

Mrs. Todd was born in New York, of New England parentage. Her mother was a woman of much intelligence and great brilliancy. She was her daughter's high exemplar. Her father was Abner Kneeland Marsh, a Universalist preacher. He made the education of his daughter a matter of chief concern, thus enabling her at a very early age to take a position as teacher in a public school, which vocation she pursued until she was married to Mr. Benjamin Todd of Massachusetts. Her husband was a man of rare attainments, a fine public speaker, and an ardent advocate of an enlargement of woman's sphere of action. Under such hospitable conditions it became easy and natural for the young wife to take her place beside her husband in his public work. She made her first speech during the first year of her married life. Temperance, woman suffrage, and politics have successively engaged her service on the platform.

In 1879 Mrs. Todd entered the Hastings Law College, remaining two years, after which she easily passed the ordeal of examination before the Supreme Court of California. She then opened an office in San Francisco, and was a successful practitioner.

Mrs. Todd had made a specialty of the study of finance some years prior to taking up law. Her researches led her to see the monstrosity of our national legislation on the money question. In 1882 she was nominated by the Greenback Party of California as attorney-general, and ran ahead of her ticket.

In 1880 Mrs. Todd was left a widow with one child, now a most accomplished and lovely young woman, above all things proud of and devoted to her gentle-mannered mother.

Mrs. Todd left California in 1890 and went to Chicago, where she edited the Chicago *Express*, a reform paper of national circulation. She is the author of three books: one on the tariff, one on suffrage; and the third, " Pizarro and John Sherman," is a work on finance of great value. All three have had large sale.

Mrs. Todd, like the other women speakers and writers of the rising political movement, believes that homelessness threatens the masses of the American people, and that the danger is so imminent as to demand unanimity of action in order to arrest the encroachments and shake off the domination of corporate power. Hence, though an ardent prohibitionist and woman suffragist, she would, for the immediate future, leave those great questions to philanthropic and educational methods of propagandism — at least so far as national politics is concerned.

At the famous Cincinnati conference of industrial reformers on the 20th of May, 1891, Mrs. Todd was chosen to present the chairman, Senator Peffer, with a floral testimonial. Without the least time for preparation, her presentation speech was a marvellous combination of poetic, graceful utterance, and of profound thought. Her perfect readiness, her attractive personality, rendered the episode a pleasing picture, always to remain in the memory of those present.

Mrs. Todd will be one of the principal speakers in the coming campaign.

In the far West are many capable, earnest women, enlisted in the Home Crusade. Mrs. Annette Nye of California, writer and general promoter, is of the splendid Wardell family.

Mrs. Sophia Hardin of South Dakota occupies the responsible position of secretary of the State Alliance.

Mrs. Elizabeth Wardell, wife of Alonzo Wardell of South Dakota, is an able writer and an untiring worker in Alliance ranks.

Mrs. Emma Ghent Curtis of Colorado is a prolific writer of good verse, full of thought and high purpose. She is also author of " The Fate of a Fool," an interesting story bearing on the condition of the toilers of the country.

Mrs. Emma De Voe of Illinois, a most elegant and attractive woman, is a platform speaker of growing prominence.

These and hosts of others are busy working out manifest destiny toward a higher civilization. Even thus at the South are numberless enthusiastic Alliance women, who, for this time, must be unnamed. The past decade has marked wonderful progress among the Southern women. The advent of their charming and distinctive personality into larger circles of activity has added much to the history of American women. Among the most accomplished in Alliance circles is Mrs. E. R. Davidson of Georgia, niece of Hon. L. F. Livingston. She is a newspaper writer of growing power and popularity.

Mrs. Harry Brown of Atlanta, Ga., is of the Georgia Gorman family. A most engaging young woman, whom her friends delight to call the pet of her Alliance. She can ride her fine horses or write dainty, descriptive letters for her husband's paper, both with equal grace and ease.

Mrs. Dr. Dabbs of Texas demonstrated at the St. Louis conference, where she was a delegate, that she could bear her part in public discussion of a controverted question with her most practiced and ready Southern brethren.

Mrs. Ben Terrell of Texas, wife of the first lecturer of the National Alliance, has been her husband's constant companion on his lecture tours, and has thus become widely known and loved.

Miss Bessie Dwyer, a remarkably versatile and talented

young lady, recently come from Texas to Washington, is a writer on the *National Economist*, the official organ of the National Alliance.

It is a great inspiration to have a great ancestry. To be much expected of is to induce much performance. This is true either of a man or a state. Kansas was a well-born state — well fathered and mothered. New England colonized and pre-empted her for freedom and for progress. Consider her record: Kansas has nine men in the national Congress, all woman suffragists — not merely acquiescent, but reverent, believing that woman should be enfranchised in justice to herself and for safety to the state.

Susan B. Anthony gauges the wives of men by the estimate which their husbands hold of womankind. Her rule proves itself in the case of the Kansas congressmen. Their wives are all suffragists. Mr. Broderick, one of the representatives, and one of the two Republicans from Kansas, is a widower; but his three intelligent, accomplished daughters make it a matter of conscience to vote at municipal elections, at their home in Holton, and to vote for the *best* men for mayor and councilmen, thus making *party* subservient to merit.

Seven of the nine Kansas congressmen are of the new political faith which seeks to provide ways and means whereby each member of the nation's family may have fair chance to work for life, liberty, and happiness. These men are fresh from the rank and file of toilers, most of them practical farmers, whose wives have shared their labors and their hardships. And now that official duties have transferred them to the most beautiful city on the continent, the family unity is preserved, and the good-wives share their enlarged experience. What manner of women are they? Let us see.

Mrs. Jerry Simpson, born in England, is a delicate little woman devoted to her husband and their one child, a bright boy of thirteen. What a deal of hard, faithful work this little body has done! mostly by will power, by sheer determination and ambition to do the duty next at hand. One hard season, while Jerry raised the crops, she milked twenty cows with no other help than her eight-year-old boy. She churned twice a day with a dash churn, and sold three hundred pounds of butter. She takes naturally and easily to Washington life. She delights in strolling through the lovely parks, often expressing a wish that old neighbors and friends might have a resting spell, and share the charms of existence at Washington. Mrs. Simpson is a great reader of the newspapers, and keeps well posted on current events.

Mrs. J. G. Otis bears a close resemblance to Mrs. Grover Cleveland. The double attraction of a handsome face and a kindly spirit have made her a favorite in the farmer organizations to which she has belonged. She was the Flora of her grange for twelve years. She has read papers of much value before the State Dairy Association, the Grange, and the Alliance. She is vice-president of her county Alliance.

It is doubtful if Baby Ruth Cleveland is a daintier morsel of humanity than the blue-eyed Otis baby, born since coming to Washington. Certain it is, the advent of Baby Otis has been much "resolved" about in Kansas Alliances, and many congratulations have been sent the wee girl that she is come to share with three brothers and one sister the mother-love and care of so noble and true a woman as Mrs. Otis.

Mrs. Ben Clover, with hindrances and farm duties which could not be even temporarily set aside, remained at home, working harder than ever with the butter and all business of the farm, endeavoring to free the dear home place from mortgage. Round and rosy, the incarnation of good sense and constant cheeriness, you almost scent sweet clover in her presence. Mrs. Clover is a neighborhood mother, on hand in time of sickness or other need. She is much counselled with in the Alliance, and was the first woman ever sent as delegate to the Supreme Council of the National Farmers' Alliance.

Mrs. Senator Peffer is another embodiment of gentle, refined womanhood — a very genius of home and all things motherwise. She is large, stately, and placid faced. Her husband credits her with much heroism. Her mother-wit and calm courage saved his life from a marauding band of bushwhackers in Missouri in the dreadful days when brothers South and brothers North were crazed with loss of sense that they were all children of one God, and citizens of one dear native land. Mrs. Peffer is an Episcopalian. She does much quiet visiting and helping of the poor about her. Of books, she loves best Scott and Dickens, and the old English writers. And of all mothers, her admiring sons and daughters think her the wisest and best.

Mrs. Wm. Baker's eight children would of course good-naturedly but firmly dispute the Peffer children's claim as to the best woman in the world. The eldest Miss Baker taught school in Kansas before coming to Washington. She is so fair of face that were she on dress parade in decollété society, — which she will never be, — her fresh beauty, quick wit, and naive manners would be newspaperized *ad nauseam*. Mrs. Baker had more than the ordinary educational advantages of the girls of her time. She was the daughter of a well-to-do merchant at Centerville, Penn., and knew nothing of farm life until she married and went pioneering in the West. She took her books and music, and made the prairie home in Western Kansas one of refinement despite the hard work and hard times.

The beamingest personage of the entire delegation of Kansas women at Washington is Mrs. John Davis. Her presence radiates peace and good will. She is a superior woman, English by birth, a sister of Major Powell, of the United States Geological Survey. She is a Universalist in religion; not of the sect specially, but a believer that real religion is universal. She has done considerable literary work, was a long-time-ago contributor to an illustrated periodical published at Chicago. She is in demand in women's clubs and organizations both philanthropic and educational. Since coming to Washington she has made much effort toward getting the claim of " Anna Ella Carroll " considered by Congress.

It is worth much to call upon this gentlewoman and see her beaming satisfaction as she shows you the pictures of her three bright daughters and her six great, manly sons — a most notable group of photographs, the originals each busy and successful in some useful world work, each of the half-dozen boys a woman suffragist and promoter of the political Home Crusade.

To mention all the helpful Kansas women of the Alliance, even to catalogue them, would be to fill the pages of THE ARENA. What hardship to the writer not to be able to say more than a line of so fine a character as Mrs. Anna C. Wait, vice-president of the Kansas Equal Suffrage Association and co-editor with her husband for so many years of the *Lincoln Beacon*, always a progressive paper, now a People's Party advocate!

There is Mrs. Florence Olmstead, a county superintendent

of schools, and composer of a book of Alliance songs which helped to sing the people into power; Mrs. Pack, editor of the *Farmer's Wife*, organ of the Woman's National Alliance; Mrs. McLallin, wife of the president of the National Reform Press Association — the helpfulest and cheerfulest of sensible, well-informed women; Mrs. Fannie McCormick, candidate for superintendent of public instruction on the People's Party state ticket of 1890; Mrs. Anna Champe, co-editor with her husband of a People's Party and prohibition paper, and besides these a world of sensible, helpful farmer women and capable, pretty country schoolma'ams, world without end — all Alliance workers.

Consider this Kansas record, oh supercilious sneerer at "strong-minded" women. Most of these women have opened their mouths and spake before many people; they have sat in counsel with bodies of men, among whom were their husbands and sons. And oh, Ultima Thule of "unwomanliness," they have voted — actually cast ballot, thereby saying in quietest of human way that virtue shall dethrone vice in municipal government. All these heretical things have they done, and yet are womanliest, gentlest of women, the best of homekeepers, the loyalest of wives, the carefulest of mothers.

What answer to this, oh, most bombastic cavillers — you who would shield woman from the demoralizing ballot? What answer, most ridiculous of theorists, who tremble lest any sort of man-made laws be mightier than nature's laws, who writhe lest statutes should change the loving, loyal mother-nature of woman? Let not such preposterous theorist come into the presence of the six stalwart sons of halo-faced Mrs. Davis and suggest that their most revered mother is "unsexed" because of ballot box and politics.

Thus splendidly do the *facts* about women in politics refute the frivolous *theories* of timorous or hostile objectors. The women prominent as active, responsible factors in the political arena are those who are characterized by strong common sense, high ideals, and lofty patriotism. When such as these cast ballot throughout the nation,

> "Then shall their voice of sovereign choice
> Swell the deep bass of duty done,
> And strike the key of time to be
> When God and man shall speak as one."

"KATE"

THE "GOOD ANGEL" OF OKLAHOMA

A. J. McKelway

Kate Barnard is to Oklahoma what Jane Addams is to Chicago, its First Citizen

"KATE"

THE "GOOD ANGEL" OF OKLAHOMA

BY A. J. McKELWAY

ILLUSTRATED WITH REPRODUCTIONS OF PHOTOGRAPHS

EVERYBODY in Oklahoma calls her "Kate." If the stranger from the East asks a citizen of Guthrie where Miss Barnard's office is, a puzzled expression will first appear, then the difficulty will be relieved as he replies, "Oh! You mean Kate." For Kate Barnard is to Oklahoma what Jane Addams is to Chicago, its First Citizen.

She was born in Nebraska, twenty-seven years ago, of Southern parentage. But the mother died at the daughter's birth, and the little girl's life was one of hardship and poverty. At first cared for by her relatives, she was later put on the 160 acres of Oklahoma land which her father had claimed, to hold the homestead while he made a living in the near-by city. The burden of loneliness and responsibility which her young heart bore, instead of embittering her life, has given her the warmest sympathy for the unfortunate, especially for the children of the poor. Later she was sent to a convent, then taught in the public schools, and with the building up of the family fortune in that land of opportunity she went to Oklahoma City to keep house for her father. A devout Catholic, she frequently brought to her father-confessors the ambition she had of wider service, but was as often met with the old-fashioned advice, gen-

587

shod them and bought
books for them and packed
them off to school. Her
success stirred the city, and
it recognized her capacity at
once. The Provident Asso-
ciation, of business men,
and the Ministerial Alliance
had been doing charity
work, independently, in a
desultory fashion. They
came together in the United
Provident Association, elected Kate matron, and pro-
vided an income of $600 a
month for her disbursement.

*Stranded home-seekers in the
bottom-land*

*The beginning of a tenement district
in a new country*

*She knows the game and plays it well, and it is for humanity
that she is playing it*

erally the best that can be
given, that her place was
that of housekeeper in her
father's home. But she
made an application to be
put in charge of the exhibit
which the thriving young
city of Oklahoma was to
make at the St. Louis Ex-
position, and was given the
appointment over 350 com-
petitors. At St. Louis she
attracted the attention of
other exhibitors, and re-
ceived flattering offers to
do similar work at the
Portland Exposition.

But she received the sage
advice from a newspaper
man, who had some knowl-
edge of the world, that there was room for an
unexampled career of usefulness in Oklahoma,
city and territory. He advised her to gather
some of her girl friends about her as the nucleus
of a charity organization, and find first some
employment for the hundreds of stranded people
who had found their way to the newly opened
lands and newly built cities of Oklahoma. She
took this advice, and after making some investi-
gations into the condition of the unemployed, she
wrote one vivid statement for the newspapers
that brought to her doors in one day ten thousand garments and stacks of furniture. She
found 400 children, many of them living in tents,
all of them destitute, and she clothed them and

But she went at the business scientifically.
The unemployed, the men without a trade, were
organized into a Federal Union, and thus, while
finding work for 400 men, she became identified
with the American Federation of Labor. She
was given a seat in the Trades' Council of the
city and was made a delegate to the State Federation of Labor.

While matron of the association she became
the controlling spirit in the political life of Oklahoma City. She was the only one who could
vote the slum independently of the saloon, and,
if need be, against the saloon. "Hello, boys.
Where are you going?" she would say to a
group of barroom bums, towed to the polls by

a saloonkeeper. And while the saloonkeeper looked helplessly on, she would remind them that she had sent John's little girl to school, and had nursed Tom's wife through the spell of pneumonia, and had found a decent suit of clothes for Jim, and had gotten work for them all, in fact had helped to raise the wage-scale for work on the streets from $1.25 to $2.25 a day. And then she would tell the boys that they must vote against the bad candidate for mayor and for the good one, because the good one was a friend of hers, and the boys would follow her meekly to the ballot-box. Thus she elected first a Republican mayor, and then a Democratic mayor, each time by a majority of 700.

And now she began to take an interest in the affairs of the new state that was struggling for existence and recognition. She is no small part of the history of the state thus far. She was sent as a delegate to a convention where were gathered the representatives of the Farmers' Union, the State Federation of Labor, and the

Railroad Orders. She made her first public speech at this convention, a plea for the insertion of a compulsory-education and an anti-child-labor section in the new constitution. The convention included these two demands in the twenty-four which they outlined. It was quietly agreed that any candidate for delegate to the constitutional convention would be defeated who did not accede to the twenty-four demands.

Jesse Dunn, chairman of the Democratic Committee, was smart enough to recognize the power which Kate was beginning to wield. He sent her word that he would like to have her ideas in framing the Democratic platform, and so Kate wrote six of the planks on which the party was to appeal to the people in the critical period of constitution-making. He also advised individual candidates for the constitutional convention to agree to the twenty-four demands. The Republican party was divided on the question of statehood, the appetite end of the party being already close to the pie counter through

Floaters from the large cities

The poor and unfortunate, white and black and red, looked to her for relief

PETER STEWART
President United Mine Workers of America,
District No. 21

O. C. STRODE
Chairman Brotherhood of Locomotive Firemen
and Engineers

T. J. HERON
Chairman legislative
board of Interna-
tional Brotherhood
of Boilermakers and
Iron Shipbuilders

D. A. ANDERSON
Chairman legislative
board of Brother-
hood of Railway
Trainmen

G. E. WARREN
Secretary legislative
committee Oklahoma
Federation of Labor

A. A. GORDON
Secretary state leg-
islative board of
Brotherhood of
Railway Trainmen

J. L. BRITTAN
President legislative
board of state Fed-
eration of Labor

CORA F. SILER
Official stenographer to state
commissioner of labor

CHAS. L. DAUGHERTY
State commissioner of labor

KATE BARNARD

PETER HENRETTY
Vice-president legislative board of
state Federation of Labor

KATE BARNARD AND HER "BOYS"

*Kate takes no stock in woman's suffrage. She says that the boys have always done
what she asked them to do without her needing any vote for herself*

federal appointment. Oklahoma was considered a Republican community anyway, and
the "demands" were generally smiled at by
Republican candidates. So "the word was
put out" on Friday night before election day to
elect Democrats to the convention. And Kate
had made a campaign of the state for the child-
labor and compulsory-education reforms, and
had grown to be a most effective campaign
orator. And when the votes were counted it
was found that nine Republicans had been
elected to the constitutional convention, and
ninety-eight Democrats.

That convention of Farmers' Unionists and
Labor Unionists had appointed a legislative
committee to see that the demands were put
into the constitution. Kate addressed the convention on her two hobbies of compulsory education and the abolition of child-labor, and
added a third, the establishment of a state department of charities. The committee which
considered this last proposition recommended
a section in which the office of commissioner
of charities and corrections was spoken of as
"his or her" office. The convention instantly
saw the point, the section was adopted *vivâ*

590

voce, and the delegates crowded around Kate
and congratulated her as the first commissioner
to be elected for the new state. She was entirely unprepared for this demonstration, and
insisted, lest interested motives should be
charged to her, that the salary should be reduced from $2,500 to $1,500 if she was to run
for office. Again the Democrats were wise
enough to pay her the compliment of a nomination at the primaries, without opposition. The
Republican convention came within a few votes
of nominating her also, but finally selected a
Miss Tomlinson as the nominee, to make the
ticket complete. And Kate proceeded to make
whirlwind campaigns for the constitution and
the Democratic party, and her reputation as a
campaign speaker had now become so great that
three or four thousand people would gather
together anywhere when she was advertised to
speak. In fact, it became a common trick for
campaigners not so gifted to promise that Kate
would also make an address, and it often happened that she was billed to speak at the same
time at towns three hundred miles apart.

Governor Franz, candidate for governor on
the Republican ticket, was wise enough not to
accept the frequent challenges to a joint debate
with Kate. When it happened that they spoke
from the same platform, he would retire before
Kate could begin. But the candidate for attorney-general challenged her to a joint debate'
and the state was on tiptoe with excitement.
The meeting was held in the heart of the coal
regions, and before a crowd of Hungarian
miners who could understand neither speaker.
But Kate had been down into the mines, had
seen to it that the demands of the miners for protection were embodied in the constitution, and
they knew she was their friend. So when she
finished speaking they not only hooted the other
speaker from the platform, but threatened him
with instantaneous damage to his person if he
did not leave at once. The whole state laughed
over the affair, and he was literally laughed out
of the state, finding a consolation office somewhere in Alaska. For the Republican ticket
was snowed under in the election, and Kate received a majority of 56,000 votes and led the
ticket on the Democratic side by 6,000 votes.
The constitution was adopted by a popular majority of 108,000. In Oklahoma City she received 1,500 majority, though the city voted the
Republican ticket by 900 majority.

Of course there were other reasons for the
victory of the Democratic party, but Kate was
several reasons herself. She was thoroughly
trusted by the two largest classes of voters, the
farmers and the labor-union men. And she
was the favorite speaker on the Democratic side.

Lithe, graceful, petite, with dark hair and skin
and flashing eyes, and a rapid-fire articulation
that was the despair of the reporters, she painted pictures of the wrongs of childhood, of the
sufferings of miners without the protection of
law, of the needs of the orphans, of the iniquity
of sending juvenile criminals to the jails and
stockades, thrilling her vast audiences with her
earnest eloquence; and she made the advocacy
of these reforms that should have been equally

MISS KATE BARNARD

*Lithe, graceful, petite, with dark hair and skin
and flashing eyes, and a rapid-fire articulation
that was the despair of the reporters, she
painted pictures of the wrongs of childhood, of
the sufferings of miners without the protection
of law, of the iniquity of sending juvenile criminals to the jails and stockades, thrilling her
vast audiences with her earnest eloquence*

the platform of both parties an asset of the
Democratic party in the campaign, because it
had been wise enough to take her up and give
her what she asked.

When the President signed the bill that made
Oklahoma a state, she was inaugurated along
with the other state officers and given offices in
the Senate Building. And now some of her
Democratic allies, feeling the need of economy
in the public service, affected to believe that
the Commissioner of Charities and Corrections

SOME OF THE CHILDREN RESCUED BY "KATE"

*She found four hundred children, many of them living in tents, all
of them destitute, and she clothed them, and shod them and bought
books for them and packed them off to school*

was an ornament, of course, but of no practical use in the administration of the affairs of the state, and that an initial appropriation of $6,000 was too much by far for her department. So Kate had to get into action again. It was amazing how soon she whipped the fight for magnifying her office. One day a senator would introduce a bill providing for the military instead of the industrial training of juvenile delinquents. Kate would find that there was a job in the bill for a man who had already been a failure in the same scheme, and in a few hours the bill was as dead as Hector. Then another measure would be introduced by some well-meaning member of the House, and the clerk would hardly be through reading the bill before a letter would be delivered to the astonished

legislator calling attention to the fact that the constitution arranged for the management of that business from the Department of Charities. Even the Speaker of the House, who had been elected by a big majority, there being only nineteen members of the House not of his party, found himself facing an insurgent majority, in opposing an adequate appropriation for Kate's department. Speaker Murray left the chair and took the floor, announcing that he would oppose any appropriation for the department except the salary of the commissioner and of the stenographer. This was Tuesday, February 18. But the Saturday and Monday preceding 78 members of the House had called on Kate and pledged their support. The storm broke over the astonished Speaker's head.

Tillotson led with an attack on the Speaker's motives; Ashby styled Kate the "Good Angel of Oklahoma"; Ellis showed by comparative figures the reasonableness of the appropriation asked for; Skeen, the Speaker's brother-in-law, made a strong speech in favor of the bill; while Jones, the leader of the Republican minority, declared that the Democrats could not appropriate Kate, that she belonged to the state, that the poor and unfortunate, white and black and red, looked to her for relief, and he pledged the minority of nineteen to give her $10,000 more than she had asked for if she needed it. Then the two "watchdogs of the treasury" moved to give $1,000 more than Kate had asked for, and this motion carried, as did the whole bill outlining the work of the department, with five dissenting votes.

It is perhaps well for Speaker Cannon or any future czar of the House of Representatives that Kate has not yet turned her attention to national affairs.

And the spirit of the New State is incarnate in Miss Kate Barnard, commissioner of charities and corrections. The best of everything is none too good for Oklahoma. Where the experience of other states has blazed the way of reform, let that experience be placed at the state's disposal. And if a path needs to be blazed for the first time, let Oklahoma lead the way!

Judge Ben Lindsey, of Denver, Colorado, is the chief authority on the juvenile-court system, which he did so much to inaugurate and popularize. So Judge Lindsey must come to Guthrie and tell the legislature all about the system, and write the juvenile-court bill for Oklahoma, and come again to explain the details of the bill to the committees of the House and Senate, and, if need be, lobby the bill through. And Dr. Barrows, of prison-reform fame, must come from New York to help inaugurate the penal system for the new state, that it may start right in the treatment of its criminals, and one hears the members of the Farmers' Union in the legislature talking glibly about the indeterminate sentence and the court of rehabilitation. And Dr. Alexander Johnson, of the National Conference of Charities and Corrections, must come from Philadelphia to lay out a plan for the care and treatment of the feeble-minded. And Mr. Hastings H. Hart came from Chicago as the authority on homes for orphan children. While a secretary of the National Child Labor Committee is sent for from Atlanta to write the child-labor and compulsory statutes for the new state. And all help in the preparation of the bill defining the duties of the new commissioner. And nobody that was sent for refused to come.

As the bills are prepared, they are submitted to the legislative committee of the old combination, the Farmers' and the Labor Unions. Thus endorsed, the bills are assured of a majority vote in the House. It is easy to explain why Kate takes no stock in woman's suffrage. She says that the boys have always done what she asked them to do without her needing any vote for herself.

The politicians come and go through the state offices and call on the Governor and the Lieutenant-Governor and the Speaker. But they make a mistake when they do not stop to shake hands with Kate, if they want something done that is worth while. And through her little office on the top floor there pours a steady stream of people all day long, people whom she has met in her campaigns over the state, or people who want to meet her— farmers, merchants, club-women, preachers, teachers. Now a delegation of miners come to look at the mine-inspection bill, and to be assured by Kate that it was all right, and that Pete, the mine inspector, was straight. Now a committee of laundry-girls, who complain of their long hours. And Kate sends some of them on to visit their senator or representative before they return home, and tell what the people at home want done for the children or the miners or the insane or the consumptives. She knows the game and plays it well, and it is for humanity that she is playing it.

Oklahoma is making history for itself, perhaps in some respects for the nation. Some enthusiasts go so far as to say that it is the new birthplace of democracy. Already some of its ideas are spreading to the border states. But the one who sits on the throne of influence and power at this history-making time is a woman, and everybody calls her "Kate."

JULIA RICHMAN

Addie R. Altman

Julia Richman at the Age of Thirty-two

JULIA RICHMAN

BY

MRS. ADDIE R. ALTMAN

ULIA RICHMAN, of whose life I have been asked to write a sketch, was not exactly a handsome woman, but when she entered a room or stood upon a platform her appearance alone gave an impression of authority. She was a woman of whom it could be fitly said, "She was born to command."

Julia Richman was born in New York City, October 12, 1855. She was one of a family of five children, two older and two younger than herself. A glorious heritage of brains came to her, for her ancestry was a long line of rabbies and teachers, whose graves are in the old cemetery in the city of Prague, in Bohemia. These graves can be seen today by anyone interested, and can be traced back in an unbroken line to the year 1604, just a twelvemonth before the Mayflower landed on Plymouth Rock with the Puritan ancestors of our American aristocracy. This is not alone hearsay evidence, for the cemetery and the graves were visited by Julia Richman on her first European trip. Hers, consequently, was a birthright of brains. God gives to us all brains, but it is the individual who must use this God-given gift to his or her own or to the world's benefit, and Julia Richman did this. She was not a so-called "wonder-child"; on the contrary, in her case, "coming events did not cast their shadows before."

15

When she was five years old the family moved to a small country place, where all the inhabitants were acquainted and friendly. The little Julia was known as "Richman's tom-boy." Except for her glorious eyes, she was a plain-looking child, with freckles and red hair—truly red at that time, though it turned into a beautiful brown later. She was wild as an Indian, always getting into trouble and, not learning by experience, would get into the same trouble over and over again. We say of a quick tongue that it is the making or the marring of an individual; in later years her tongue, or to put it in another form, her gift of power of speech was her making. As a child, however, this quickness and impulsiveness of speech without the requisite mental balance caused annoyance to others and distress to herself. The distress was due to punishment, for the children of the Richman family were not spoiled by lack of the rod or switch or any other old thing. Her quickness of speech, combined with the equally quick temper that accompanies red hair, almost invariably was a great trial to every one, and very often her father said, most pathetically, "Julie, Julie, where will your tongue land you?" The poor man did not live to see "where," for he was accidentally drowned when Julia was just out of her 'teens.

Dolls interested her to a degree, books also, though there were not many books for children fifty years ago; but her joy was in wading brooks, climbing trees, clambering over or crawling under fences, no matter if her clothes were ruined thereby, and going to the "store," that wonderful place in a small village that combines the post-office with every necessity of life. Her favorite place for reading was up in the bough of some tree, where she was at peace with herself and the world, and where she could not always be found when wanted.

16

When she was eight years old she was sent to the post-office one day to get the newspaper, which came daily by train. It was in the days of the Civil War, and while waiting for the distribution of the mail she overheard the conversation of two men and caught the words, "Atlanta has fallen!" She knew as little about what that meant as any other young child, with this difference—that even then she showed what afterward was one of her greatest characteristics—the ability to hear things, to absorb them, to immediately make them her own and put them to the best possible use for either her own advantage or that of others. After receiving her newspaper from the postmaster, she opened it and walked down the street reading or pretending to read the news. Two men met her, one of whom, named Nichols, was a member of the School Board. The latter said, "What's the news, little one?" "Atlanta has fallen," answered Julia solemnly.

"Well," said Mr. Nichols, turning to his companion, "I always heard that Richman had smart children, and I believe it now when I see a youngster like that reading news of the war."

When about twelve years old, Julia had a companion of her own, a neighbor. The two girls did not always agree, for Julia even then was intolerant of stupidity or even slowness of thought. She herself was always quick, observant, alert, bright and inclined to be domineering. The other girl, whom we will call Amy, was pretty, was the only daughter of a rich man, but was slow in learning and backward in arithmetic, while Julia was a born mathematician. On one occasion, though many similar ones had preceded it, Julia was told to help Amy with her examples. The result was rather remarkable, inasmuch as it was prophetic. Julia at twelve was not the most patient teacher—that quality came later—and Amy was not the brightest pupil.

17

so the combination was rather unfortunate. Soon the arithmetic flew across the table and Amy was told with the utmost scorn that she was stupid. Between sobs, Amy said: "I can't help it if I am stupid, can I? Anyhow, I don't have to learn if I don't want to. I'm pretty and my father is rich and I'm going to get married when I am eighteen years old!" Then followed a torrent of words from Julia to the effect that if Amy's only idea in life was "to get married," no wonder she could not learn, etc., etc., and the closing words, which I can distinctly recall, were: "I am not pretty, my father isn't rich and I am not going to marry, but before I die all New York will know my name!" As I said before, the words were prophetic and were fulfilled in both cases. Amy married at eighteen, has a family of six children and is still living. And Julia? We know of her career, and if New York and the communities of many large cities did not know something about her I would not be telling you now about her and her work.

Efficiency was one of her strongest characteristics, and to this attribute much of her success was due. She herself often said she had been taught efficiency when quite a child. As was often the case in large families many, many years ago, where there was but one maid of all work, the Richman children were required to assist in various ways. The mother was an exceptional woman, had great ability, was a thorough housekeeper, and it was imperative for the children to do whatever was required of them with the utmost precision. This was learned by them all at any early age, because the punishment that followed any carelessness was made to "fit the crime."

One day Julia was told to set the table for dinner. When the task was completed—and it was a task for a child to set a table for seven people—Julia surveyed the work with much pride and satisfaction and called

18

to her mother to come and inspect it. The mother looked, saw that everything was in its proper place, that nothing had been forgotten, and told the child so, but added: "The tablecloth is not straight, for one side hangs down much further than the other. Now, remove everything from the table, put the things back in the cupboard, straighten the cloth and set the table again." I know you are sorry for the child, yet was it not best to teach exactness? Whether this was the best way to teach it, is immaterial. The lesson was indelibly impressed upon her memory, and in telling the story, which Miss Richman frequently did, she always declared this was her first lesson in that efficiency which remained with her through life, and which aided her in doing everything she undertook to the best of her ability. When a child she was taught to sew, but she ripped as much as she sewed, for she had not the patience needed for good needlework. In the course of the years she sewed as well as she did everything else, and her favorite answer when surprise was expressed that she sewed so well was: "My mother could never teach me to sew, but everything I sewed poorly she made me rip and do over again, and *that* taught me how to sew."

The family moved back to New York in 1866, and Julia was educated in the Normal College and the School of Pedagogy in that city. Memorizing came easily to her. She did not spend much time in studying, yet she acquired knowledge readily, because of her great powers of observation and her retentive memory. Long before graduating, she had announced her determination to teach school. There was considerable discussion about it in the family, for in those days there were very few Jewish girls who went out to work. The home and the duty connected with it, of helping the mother, were traditional, and the fathers

19

of families did not approve of outside work for their daughters. But Julia, with the firmness that even then began to assert itself, overruled all objections and spent the summer after her graduation in seeking a position.

It may be of interest for me to say here that the once powerful "Tweed Ring," connected with the Democratic organization in New York City known as Tammany Hall, was the power that ruled the schools, and it was mainly by Democratic political influence that a young girl or boy could get a position as teacher. This was her first step in public—to interview people who had the so-called "pull." She went alone, interviewed many prominent men, was sent from one man to another, and finally, through indomitable perseverance, succeeded in getting an appointment, which was then ratified by the Board of Education.

At seventeen she began to teach in the Grammar Department of one of the largest schools in New York City. A month or two later her father wished her to volunteer as Sabbath School teacher in the temple of which he had been a founder in the year 1848, and of which he was then a trustee. The congregation had a number of very wealthy members, and their sons were not always well behaved. A class was assigned to her which contained the usual quota of unruly boys. For a few months she taught them. One boy was particularly and constantly troublesome, and she had threatened to report him; but as this had no effect, she carried out the threat. The reply of the Sabbath School superintendent, no doubt intended to be conciliatory, was: "You must do the best you can, but we cannot be severe with him, as he is the son of one of our richest members." This attitude of the superintendent to shield the boy because he happened to belong to a wealthy family aroused all her sense of indignation.

and she immediately resigned her position. She could not be persuaded to go back, but that day the seed was sown which in after years bore the great fruit of her labors in the Council of Jewish Women, in the Chautauqua and in every direction where she could benefit or improve the Sabbath School system or establish the teaching of ethics. Her interest in this work continued to the end of her life, as is shown by her uncompleted book on Ethics.

She was a very successful teacher. I will quote a few words from an address read before the Albany section of the Council of Jewish Women, soon after her death. "Her record from the day of her appointment as a teacher to that of her death is one of untiring and successful labor in the service of the New York school system." After teaching eleven years, at the age of twenty-eight she became school principal, the first Normal College graduate to acquire that position and the first Jewess to obtain it.

She was an indefatigable worker, and her great ambition was to do good. She sought for other work outside of school in any and every direction where she could be useful. When the Council of Jewish Women first organized, she took charge of one of the three circles for the study of the Bible, which were formed in New York. She was a capable leader, but had to give up the work because it conflicted with school duties. Then she became identified with the Jewish Chautauqua, and for a number of years addressed them at their annual meetings in Atlantic City. She also wrote pamphlets useful in their work. She was a tireless worker in the Educational Alliance and in the early days of the Young Women's Hebrew Association, and in both of these institutions her advice was always sought and usually followed.

21

One of her trips abroad—I think it was in 1892—was to England in order to visit the principal schools in London and compare the English educational system in the public schools with the American methods. In London she became acquainted with Mr. Claude Montefiore, and a friendship ensued which lasted until her death. Through Mr. Montefiore, she met and was entertained by many distinguished English ladies, chief among them being Lady Montefiore, Lady Somerset, Baroness de Rothschild and Lady Magnus, the well-known writer. During this visit, in a conversation upon religious subjects with Mr. Montefiore, she suggested to him the advantages that he could give to the public if he would publish the Bible stories as he had told them to his own child. The idea appealed to him, and the "Montefiore Bible for Home Study" was the result. Her personality made a strong and compelling appeal to all toward whom it was directed. Her manner of presenting her side of any argument rarely failed to convince, and it was said of her: "She knew how to arouse the interest and stimulate the mind of the youngest child as well as to stir the thoughts of mature intellects."

In the summer of 1903, while she was traveling in Europe, a vacancy occurred in the Board of School Superintendents. At the special meeting which was held in order to make a new appointment, it was unanimously decided to offer the position to Miss Richman upon her return. This was done, yet she hesitated about accepting it because she had planned many changes in her own school. Finally, she concluded to accept, for she felt she would have a much broader field of action and could accomplish much more. She was the first woman in New York City appointed to that office, and, being the only woman among the five district superintendents, the men gave her the privilege of selecting the district she preferred. Much to their astonishment, for she might have had the best, she chose the lower East Side, and left her uptown home to reside among the people to whose uplift she devoted her life work. She rented a house in the heart of the Ghetto, had it remodeled and modernized in every respect, and made of it a social settlement for the teachers of the district, where they could meet every afternoon or evening. She also took some of the teachers into her home as residents.

Then it was that she undertook her greatest works--- those that will ever remain as a testimonial to her great discernment, to her executive ability, to her undaunted courage and her utter disregard of personal effort. She had fourteen day and night schools under her jurisdiction, and in these schools there were nearly six hundred teachers whom she had to supervise, and more than twenty-three thousand children. She visited the schools in rotation by day and in the evenings superintended her office work and interviewed parents who came to her office to consult her or to make complaints. These daily tasks were enough to tax the strength of a much younger woman, yet she managed to give considerable time to philanthropic and charitable work, for in her daily duties, or through them, she saw and recognized how very much there was to be done in those directions.

One of her notable achievements was the establishing of a special school for delinquent children, which was presided over by the best equipped teachers. Each refractory pupil received special instruction and direction by an able teacher, and many boys who had been deemed fit subjects for a reform school became honest, decent citizens. Later the Board of Education, seeing the success achieved by the delinquent classes, decided to establish special classes for feeble-minded and defective children. This action on the part of the board was due solely to Miss Richman's persistent appeals to them. Her idea was to separate these unfortunates from the other children so that they should not be subjected to the humiliation of being outstripped by others of their own age, and that each child might get the special training that it required. She was also directly responsible for the examination of children's eyes in the schools and of furnishing glasses if necessary.

The knowledge of the immorality which flourished in her district and to which the little children fell victims was a great grief to her. With untiring zeal, she worked to bring to justice those fiends in human guise who were responsible for the unspeakable conditions. It was through the testimony gathered by her that the Gerry Society* obtained many convictions of the men known as "cadets." In the pursuit of this object she went into the vilest places, fearless because of her purity of mind and strength of character, and many young girls, yes, children, too, owe to her influence and efforts their escape from a life of degradation. Seward Park, in the vicinity of several schools, had become a gathering place for the loafers of the neighborhood, and it was a center of contamination. For four years she labored with the city officials for the cleaning up of this plague spot, but in vain. At last, under the administration of Park Commissioner Smith, she succeeded. With the assistance of the police, she organized raids upon Seward Park in school hours, so as to gather in all the children of school age and have them give account of themselves to the proper authorities. Over two hundred and fifty truants were brought

*Society for the Prevention of Cruelty to Children.

up within a very short time, and the good effect of constant surveillance upon them was incalculable.

She was one of the organizers of and one of the hardest workers in the establishment of "The Consumptives' Outdoor Home" in New York. This was accomplished under many difficulties, but nothing ever deterred her. She knew so well the ill effects of the crowded tenements, with their lack of air and light, and she watched the rapid strides of the terrible white plague. It was at the same time that the city had begun to abolish the ferryboat system between New York and Long Island. Many old ferryboats were tied up at the docks, and the sight of these gave her the idea. She awakened the interest of influential people and a ferryboat was obtained and placed at her disposal. Then the decks were fitted up with couches, beds, hammocks and awnings, a kitchen and a nurse's room were furnished, and the floating home for consumptives was established and still exists.

She was a powerful adviser in the work of the North American Civic League for Immigrants, and many improvements in their mode of dealing with those unhappy people on Ellis Island were due to her suggestions. Her interest and labors in the Juvenile Court never waned, for, to her mind, nothing deserved more encouragement than to aid the children. She established physical culture clubs, literary and debating clubs, for both girls and boys, and any number of "Julia Richman" societies, clubs and athletic leagues flourish on the East Side. The young people esteemed it a great honor when she visited them, which she did whenever time permitted. She was a factor in the National Educational Association, and was invited to lecture upon educational matters in various cities of the United States. Boston, Chicago, Louisville, Minneapolis, Albany and many smaller towns often sent

25

for her to address conventions held there. She also wrote educational articles for magazines.

You may wonder how and where she found time to accomplish all these things and many others of which I have not told you. It seemed simple to her because she did it all so gradually. She was never hurried, never flurried; everything was arranged like clockwork and everything was systematized. Now, add to this perfect health, no nerves, promptness and regularity, and you have the secret. It was aptly said of her, "She was a severe taskmaster with others, but infinitely more severe with herself." The confidence reposed in her ability to "do things" by men and women of every station in life was so great that her suggestions were acted upon by all her co-workers, and the purses of many whose names rank high in the financial and also the social world of New York City were ever open to her to further her works. During the last year of her life she gave much time and thought to the widely discussed question of teaching sex hygiene in the public schools. No one knew better than she did how necessary it was for the children, particularly the children of the slums, to be taught a new standard of morality and to give them an understanding of what a pure life means. She was distinctly in favor of its being taught, but in the right way; and she personally raised funds to pay for lectures to her teachers in order that they might learn the proper method of presenting the subject to the pupils.

Her last public appearance was in May, 1912, five weeks before her death. It was on the occasion of the memorial services held in Carnegie Hall in memory of Mr. and Mrs. Isidor Straus. She had been a very intimate friend of Mrs. Straus for more than twenty years, and the committee on arrangements called upon her as the one best qualified to eulogize the woman who pre-

26

ferred death with her husband on the ill-fated Titanic to life without him. Julia Richman was the only woman speaker that Sunday, and her remarkable address will always remain in the memory of the thousands who heard it.

In the early spring of 1912 she decided to resign her position on the Board of School Superintendents when the autumn term began, "in order," as she said, "to give some younger woman a chance." She had many plans for the following winter's work. She expected to devote much more time to the betterment of social conditions on the East Side and to use her boundless influence in the cause of child welfare. She hoped to give many lectures, and had promised to write a book. This promise was given to the Macmillan Publishing Company, one of the largest book publishing houses in New York, who had requested her to write a book for them to be called "Forty Years in the New York Public Schools." She looked forward with much pleasure to writing this book, and expected to begin the work during the summer vacation, which she planned to spend in Switzerland. Alas, for her plans and hopes! for before she reached Switzerland she had been called on her last long journey.

On the sixth day of June she sailed for Europe, in apparently good health and in excellent spirits. The day before the steamer landed in Cherbourg she was taken ill and was carried from the steamer to the train leaving for Paris. She was rapidly conveyed from the station in Paris to the American Hospital, where an immediate operation for appendicitis was imperative. Her friends, Prof. and Mrs. Richard Gottheil, of New York, who remained with her to the end, told her of her condition and she prepared for the operation without any fear. The operation seemed successful and she rallied wonderfully, but on the fourth day complications arose and five days later all was over. Thus, in the prime of life, at the age of fifty-six, was ended her career of usefulness to the public and of service to her people. Three weeks later the remains arrived in New York and the last sad rites took place in the Temple Ahawath Chesed, where she had ever been a devout worshipper.

A memorial service was held on October 12, her birthday. The program was arranged by a committee composed of members of the Board of Education and of the Jewish Educational Alliance, and the designated place was the public school that she had made famous by her many innovations and their unqualified success. Sixteen organizations were represented, in each of which she had been a director, and a number of other organizations where she had been a more or less active worker. Nine addresses were made by prominent judges, lawyers and professors. A beautiful and touching feature was the delegation of children from the schools of the district, who marched in slowly and solemnly to the strains of Chopin's "Funeral March." Later they sang some of her favorite hymns. The boys had black bands on their coat sleeves and the girls wore white dresses with black sashes. The Hon. Egerton Winthrop, Jr., President of the Board of Education, presided, and in the course of his address promised that the Board of Education would raise a monument to the memory of the departed superintendent which would be imperishable and everlasting. The promise was fulfilled a few months later, when the memorial took the form of a new high school, which is called "The Julia Richman High School."

* * *

In the limited space which was allotted for this paper I have endeavored to sketch the life and work of a woman who devoted forty years to the good of humanity. The Talmud says:

'Tis not our knowledge God desires;
It is our best that He requires.

It is our best that God requires, and Julia Richman gave her best. She gave all her thoughts, all her ability, all her powers to the work of uplifting her people, to the advancement of education and philanthropy, to the improvement of the condition of the poor, to the welfare of unfortunates. From teacher to principal, from principal to district superintendent, for forty years she was identified with the struggles, with the opposition and with the final success of public movements on humanistic lines.

She was not what is called a "superwoman"; she was merely an indefatigable worker who never spared herself. She was just a woman like the rest of us, with faults and failings. She had her detractors, too, as all must have who rise to prominence; but no harsh criticism ever daunted her and she persevered in every undertaking until her purpose was achieved. No matter how high or inaccessible might be the Mountain of Difficulty, if she could not climb over the intervening obstacles she would go any distance to get around them if she was convinced in her own mind that the object to be obtained was worthy of any effort whatsoever. And her whole heart and soul were in everything she did.

In Memoriam

JULIA RICHMAN

Come all who serve the city, all who serve
  The glorious golden City of our dream,
With true heart-service that can never swerve,
  How faint soe'r the strength, or far the gleam:
Come sorrow proudly for our comrade passed
  Into the silence: one who served indeed
In all things, even unto the least and last,
  Spending herself to meet the momen't need.
Share memories of that strong, illumined face,
  Keen speech, and courage springing to the test,
And all the fervor of the ancient race
  That finds its longed-for East in this young West,—
Be this the sum, the last word best of all:
She built her life into the city wall.

                  —HELEN GRAY CONE.

"THE AWAKENING" BY KATE CHOPIN

Robert Cantwell

THE AWAKENING

by Kate Chopin

Kate Chopin described the Louisiana community in which she lived as "a rambling little French village of one street, with the Catholic church at one end, and our plantation at the other, and Red River flowing through everybody's back-yard." It was of the Creoles in such communities that she wrote. Often her stories turned upon acts of rebellion. This was particularly true of The Awakening, *and it owed much of its fame to the excited controversy which arose over its unconventionality. The St. Louis* Republic *roared that the book committed "unutterable crimes against polite society" and "should be labeled 'poison.'" Scores of critics joined in, warning mothers not to let their daughters read it, and Mrs. Chopin—with grim humor—wrote in her own defense, "I never dreamed of Mrs. Pontellier making such a mess of things and working out her own damnation as she did. If I had had the slightest intimation of such a thing I would have excluded her from the company. But when I found out what she was up to, the play was half over and it was then too late." Recent critics—like our reviewer—have been much kinder to* The Awakening, *one calling it "probably as near to a* Madame Bovary *as the period produced." But the contemporary criticism, though making the book famous, struck—as one of her defenders put it—"deep at the author's heart, even killing her desire to write."*

Reviewed by ROBERT CANTWELL

MRS. Kate Chopin's *The Awakening* seems to me to be the finest novel of its sort written by an American, and to rank among the world's masterpieces of short fiction. She wrote only this one major work, published five years before her death in 1904, though she also produced a number of exquisite short stories. Born Katherine O'Flaherty in St. Louis in 1851, she was the daughter of an Irish immigrant who prospered as a merchant and builder. On her mother's side she was a descendant of one of those intricate French clans who linked St. Louis with Louisiana, continued to speak French, and maintained only a formal diplomatic relationship with the United States.

At twenty-one she married Oscar Chopin, a cotton broker of New Orleans, the son of another far-flung French family which, however, carried its dislike of American ways almost to the point of non-recognition. The Chopin family lived in New Orleans and on plantations on Cane River near Natchitoches, but the family home remained at Chateau Thierry in France, the bulk of the family fortune was in French railroads, and its Louisiana residence was little more than extended colonial exile. While Kate and Oscar were on their honeymoon in Europe, the Franco-Prussian War broke out—"What an uproar! What an excitement!"—and on the stairs of the hotel at Heidelberg she came face to face with Von Moltke himself. The great man seemed to regard her with a peculiarly penetrating glance. He should have, if he didn't. She was an observer of uncannily intuitive insight.

Living as a young society matron in New Orleans, she bore Oscar Chopin six children before she was thirty. They left the city for Cane River plantations in 1880. One of these had once been owned by the original of Simon Legree in *Uncle Tom's Cabin*—one of the many originals—a gloomy and desolate place, avoided by the Negroes and white people alike. Her husband's father, a physician who gave up medicine after his marriage to an heiress, had been notorious for his mistreatment of the Negroes there in slave-owning days. After the death of Oscar Chopin in 1883, his widow returned to St. Louis, where she lived until her death. Her first novel, *At Fault*, was published by a St. Louis firm in 1890. It is now excessively rare. I have not read it; but it is said to deal, in part, with the story of Simon Legree in modern psychological terms.

Between 1889 and 1901, Kate Chopin enjoyed a slight vogue in the days of enthusiasm for regional and dialect literature, publishing in *Scribners*, the *Atlantic*, and *Century* her tales of the Louisiana Cajuns, later collected in *Bayou Folk* and *A Night in Acadie*. She occasionally figures in literary histories on the strength of these, almost always linked with people like Mary Murphree of Tennessee. Some of her stories are wonderful; a few like *Désirée's Baby*, which tells of a country girl who learns from the birth of her child that she is of Negro blood, are unforgettable; but they are fragmentary, and her mastery of the Cajun idiom is an example of her facility and her inclination toward prevailing literary trends rather than of her ability to distill imaginatively the life she herself had known. They more often seem translations of experiences from the sophisticated world into the backwoods than evocations of that backwoods life itself. Mrs. Chopin had an extraordinary distaste for the elementary mechanics of fiction—getting people into and out of rooms, the *he saids* and *she saids* of romance. She tended to skip over them entirely if possible, and the result is a lack of continuity, and a broken effect of many-faceted brilliance rather than a sustained narrative control—an impression which often results from a writer's attempt to take over a subject and a setting not his own.

But *The Awakening* is a great novel. In his history of American writers, Van Wyck Brooks refers to it as an almost perfect piece of work. The "almost" in that characterization is significant. Turgenev is the novelist whom Mrs. Chopin most strongly suggests, and where the novel falls short it is Turgenev's fault—the book is too good a work on the Turgenev pattern to be true to Louisiana in its quietly melodramatic conclusion. Mrs. Chopin also tried to emulate George Washington Cable's stories of New Orleans' Creole society. According to Daniel Rankin, in *Kate Chopin and Her Creole Stories*, she thought Cable misrepresented Creole life; nevertheless, she tried to equal the almost incredible charm and vivacity of Cable's French-American conversations, the rattling inconsequent talk, and the high-spirited worldly humor that is so magically free of malice. Mrs. Chopin did well enough, better than anyone except Cable himself, but the achievement was still secondary, and not her own native gift.

That gift was rather a heightened sensuous awareness, awake and alive. The novel opens on Grand Isle, then the Newport or the Saratoga of New Orleans, in a midsummer langour: the parrot, which could speak a little French, chattering on the verandah, *Allez vous-en, That's all right!* to the drowsy wives of New Orleans businessmen who are lounging on wicker chairs or in hammocks while their husbands pretend to be busy in Carondelet Street in the city; the two little girls next door practicing duets from *Zampa* (wonderful background music, incidentally, for a novel which is filled with music). The story concerns Mrs. Edna Pontellier, a girl of Mississippi and Kentucky plantation background and Protestant upbringing, whose marriage to a wealthy French businessman of New Orleans has separated her from her own family. Her two children occupy her in an uneven, impulsive way, alternately passionately loved, or missed with intense longing, or forgotten—"Their absence was a sort of relief, though she did not admit this, even to herself." Profoundly restless, susceptible to music to the point of tears, or to radiant happiness at some casual, unstudied loveliness of the scene, and innocently candid to the point of cruelty in her dissatisfaction, she is nevertheless not possessed or driven by any profound motive to tragedy. It is rather that the atmosphere itself is the motive, a summer like a green meadow, through which she seems to herself to move "idly, aimlessly, unthinking and unguided." She falls in love with a young Frenchman of good family who, however, remains a gentleman, and takes himself off to Mexico to prevent any scandal coming her way. But the emotional currents that have been set in motion are too powerful, and in the New Orleans winter Mrs. Pontellier finds herself involved with the 1890 equivalent of *café society*, and an affair with a professional homebreaker—an affair that leads to a tragicomic separation from her practical, sensible, bewildered husband, as she transports her belongings to an adjacent house which she had gloomily fitted up for her residence without telling him why. And it leads ultimately to her suicide, almost as much a matter of impulse and dream-like susceptibility as the summer had been.

In any such novel as this any false notes in the creation of atmosphere would be disastrous, but there are none. The sensuous warmth of Mrs. Chopin's writing was controlled by economy rather than detachment: the world of Grande Isle emerges in sunshades, cool muslin dresses, drowsy muffled voices, croquet, water oaks, the sound of a band playing in a hotel across the water:

> . . . the strains reached them faintly, tempered by the distance. There were strange, rare odors abroad—the tangle of the sea smell and damp, new-plowed earth, mingled with the heavy perfume of a field of white blossoms somewhere near. But the night sat lightly upon the sea and the land. There was no weight of darkness; there were no shadows. The white light of the moon had fallen upon the world like the mystery and softness of sleep.

The world of New Orleans emerges through items of provincial elegance: the Pontellier house on Esplanade, cut glass, silver, damask, the opera, the race track, an untimely visit from Edna's father, a Confederate colonel, an expert at concocting strong drinks, who, with little sense of humor and of the fitness of things, relates sombre episodes "of those dark and bitter days, in which he had acted a conspicuous part and always formed the central figure." Even more, that life is visualized in instances where Edna's husband leaves her to spend the evening at his club, after a domestic disagreement having to do with her neglect of her social responsibilities and the fact that the fish was scorched at dinner:

> . . . that evening Edna finished her dinner alone, with forced deliberation. Her face was flushed and her eyes flamed with some inward fire that lighted them. . . . After finishing her dinner she went to her room, having instructed the boy to tell any other callers that she was indisposed. She went and stood at an open window and looked out upon the deep tangle of the garden below. All the mystery and witchcraft of the night seemed to have gathered there amid the perfumes of the dusky and tortuous outlines of the flowers and foliage.

After she has given herself to her lover:

> There was with her an overwhelming feeling of irresponsibility. There was the shock of the unexpected and the unaccustomed. There was her husband's reproach looking at her from the external things around her which he had provided for her external existence. There was Robert's reproach making itself felt by a quicker, fiercer, more overpowering love, which had awakened within her toward him. Above all, there was understanding. She felt as if a mist had been lifted from her eyes, enabling her to look upon and comprehend the significance of life, that monster made up of beauty and brutality. But among the conflicting sensations which assailed her, there was neither shame nor remorse.

The extraordinary economy with which Mrs. Chopin achieved her effects is suggested in the scene where Mrs. Pontellier packs up her belongings and moves to the nearby house she has fitted up, her lover walking with her:

> She seemed disheartened, and had nothing to say. She took his arm, which he had offered her, holding up the weight of her satin train with the other hand. She looked down, noticing the black line of his leg moving in and out so close against the yellow shimmer of her gown. There was the whistle of a railway train somewhere in the distance, and the midnight bells were ringing. They met no one in their short walk.

Mrs. Chopin's novel met with an intensely adverse critical reception. It was brought out by Hubert Stone, the son of a founder of the

Associated Press, who had launched his new publishing company in Chicago in an attempt to break the stranglehold that New York editors and publishers at the turn of the century had fastened on American letters. Stone's editorial level was very high, and for a few years the books coming out of Chicago were immeasurably superior to the standard New York product. But they were what is politely referred to as "in advance of their time," and often labored under other disadvantages as well. In *The Awakening* one sizeable block of type, perhaps through the efforts of some resolute proofreader determined not to let time advance, is calmly reprinted, and the reader finds himself going over again what he had read a short time before. *The Awakening* became popular, but the critical comments were so savage that Mrs. Chopin was compelled to issue a statement saying she did not identify herself with Mrs. Pontellier, and did not mean that she approved of the conduct of her character. The book was banned from library circulation, and the author refused admittance to the St. Louis Arts Society. Mrs. Chopin was disgusted, and, apart from a few short stories, wrote nothing more.

A WOMAN IN
STEEL
—Rebecca Lukens (1794-1854)

❦

ROBERT W. WOLCOTT

A Newcomen Address

"Were American Newcomen to do naught else, our work is well done if we succeed in sharing with America a strengthened inspiration to continue the struggle towards a nobler Civilization—through wider knowledge and understanding of the hopes, ambitions, and deeds of leaders in the past who have upheld Civilization's material progress. As we look backward, let us look forward."

—CHARLES PENROSE

Senior Vice President
for North America
The Newcomen Society
of England

This statement, crystallizing a broad purpose of the Society, was first read at the Newcomen Meeting at New York World's Fair on August 5, 1939, when American Newcomen were guests of The British Government

A WOMAN IN STEEL
—Rebecca Lukens (1794-1854)

"REBECCA LUKENS found inspiration and wisdom
in her environment. It was but natural that her
community should profit thereby. Those traditions still are conserved in a business now in continuous existence during over one hundred and
thirty years—in the famed Chester Valley. A
business which at this present moment is doing
its bit in the National Defense."

—ROBERT W. WOLCOTT

"CHESTER COUNTY in America challenges imagination. Its charm is wide-known. Sturdy oak on steep hillside bordering Brandywine's banks is emblem of generations of sturdy Americans, on farm and in village, who have lived and worked and died in this famous Chester Valley. Their lives have been spent within shadow of its hills. It is a country of the fox and the hunting horn, of rich tilled fields, of gristmills by waterfalls, of rolling meadows and woodland, of winding streams. William Penn knew these fields, rode beside these streams. Here in eastern Pennsylvania, quiet farmhouses and country churches paint their own picture of a wholesome, outdoor life. Farming and livestock and bees are the central interest. Many of the houses date back to colonial times, many of the land-deeds bear Royal grant. Washington and his troops fought over this land; Valley Forge is a neighbor. American History first opened its pages near here. The Liberty Bell rang within day's journey away, by horse. Time was more leisurely then.

"Such a countryside of a century ago, in this same Chester Valley, was the picturesque background of REBECCA LUKENS—about whose useful, dramatic, distinctive life it is my privilege to tell you tonight: of this *Woman in Steel*."

—ROBERT W. WOLCOTT

THE NEWCOMEN SOCIETY
AMERICAN BRANCH

A WOMAN IN STEEL

—*Rebecca Lukens (1794-1854)*

By
ROBERT W. WOLCOTT
Member of The Newcomen Society
President
Lukens Steel Company

A Newcomen Address

1940

This Newcomen Address, based upon con-
temporary records in possession of Lukens Steel
Company, was delivered at a Newcomen Dinner,
held in Mr. Wolcott's honor, at Union League
Club of New York, on December 12, 1940

❧

SET UP, PRINTED AND BOUND
IN THE UNITED STATES OF AMERICA
AT
THE PRINCETON UNIVERSITY PRESS

THE NEWCOMEN SOCIETY OF ENGLAND

THE NEWCOMEN SOCIETY OF ENGLAND *was founded at London shortly after the First World War, to encourage and promote research and study of* material *History, that of Material Civilization, including the history of: Industry, Transportation, Communication, the Utilities, Mining, Economics, Finance, and Banking. Engineering provides a basis for these human activities.*

With headquarters at The Science Museum, South Kensington, in London, the British membership includes industrialists, engineers, physicists, educators, historians, and technologists distinguished for their services in various parts of The British Empire.

The Society takes its name from Thomas Newcomen (1663-1729), the British Engineer, whose valuable contributions in improvements to the newly invented Steam Engine brought him lasting fame in the field of the mechanic arts. Newcomen, in partnership with the famous Thomas Savery (1650-1715), developed the Newcomen Engines, whose period of use was from 1712 to 1775. It was in 1764, while working on a model of Newcomen's engine, that James Watt first conceived the idea of a condensing engine: the Watt Engine.

The "Transactions" of The Newcomen Society, issued annually at London, constitute an unique and most valuable contribution to the history of Material Civilization. These annual volumes find their way to technical and university libraries throughout the World.

In 1923, through the initiative and efforts of The American Founder, the late L. F. Loree of New York, aided by a small group of well-known American industrialists, bankers, railroad presidents, historians, engineers, and educators, there was founded the American Branch of The Newcomen Society of England. The American Newcomen has its headquarters in those of The American Society of Mechanical Engineers at New York, one of whose officers is the Joint Honorary Corresponding Secretary for North America, in Newcomen Society.

Two principal events in the yearly program of American Newcomen are: the Annual American Dinner at New York, held simultaneously with the British Dinner at London and with exchange of cable greetings; and the "National Pilgrimage" to points of historic interest concerned with the beginnings of industry, or transportation, or the mechanic arts in America. Papers presented at the Annual Dinners are read simultaneously at London and New York.

A collateral objective of American Newcomen is to provide another informal link in the friendly and intimate relations between the United States and Great Britain. American Newcomen has three Honorary Members.

American Newcomen comprises in its membership many American leaders in the fields of finance, industry, transportation, communication, the utilities, history, science, engineering, university education, and technology. The Newcomen Society of England enjoys international reputation in the value of its papers and meetings, which are based upon exhaustive scientific research in these special fields of History.

Biographical Sketch
of The Author

At "Rokeby" on Buck Run in Chester County in Pennsylvania, in the Year 1793 began the Iron production which is background of the operations of Lukens Steel Company presided over by ROBERT W. WOLCOTT. This Newcomen Address is a true recital of the amazing executive achievements of his children's great-great-grandmother, REBECCA LUKENS (1794-1854), who headed the Lukens' operations from 1823 until 1847. At the age of 30 she became the outstanding woman-executive of the age in the United States. Since leaving Lehigh University, Mr. Wolcott has continuously been identified with Engineering and the Steel Industry. Has been President of Lukens Steel Company since 1925. Is widely known through his industry. Is a Director of American Iron and Steel Institute. Is a member of the Philadelphia Committee, in The Newcomen Society of England. The traditions of his company's operations at Coatesville in Chester County, dating back to the "Brandywine Mill" of Isaac Pennock and the leadership of Dr. Charles Lukens who became junior partner in 1813, are rooted in those early days when blast furnaces were built against a hillside, along a wooded stream, in picturesque valleys where Ironmaster and his men lived in contentment and mutual understanding. Out of such traditions emerged sinews of America's strength

A WOMAN IN STEEL

—*Rebecca Lukens (1794-1854)*

❦ ❦

CHESTER COUNTY provides colorful background for *an intimate lifestory* which it is my purpose to share with you tonight. Because of the lapse of time this recital can at best be but made up of fragments. However, there is much we can supply by reading between the lines; by interpreting the story *in terms of its surroundings.* These happy surroundings are those of Chester County and its famous Chester Valley—a land of true beauty, rich in history, fertile in productivity.

Chester *in Old England,* famed walled town of Plantagenet and Tudor reigns, with her towers and gateways, her halls and battlements, her abbey and cloisters, her cathedral and chapter-house, gave her name to *the Chester County of America.* This was back in late 17th Century days when Pennsylvania was yet a Province. From Old Chester, a heritage was gained. Tradition was born. Character was derived.

Amid such surroundings in America was the heroine of our story born—in 1794. Amid such surroundings was she reared. She learned of this heritage from Old England; of these traditions! Character for her was inbred. Her life clearly shows all this.

Chester County in America challenges imagination. Its charm is wide-known. Sturdy oak on steep hillside bordering Brandywine's banks is emblem of generations of sturdy Americans, on farm and in village, who have lived and worked and died in this famous Chester Valley. Their lives have been spent within shadow of its hills. It is a country of the fox and the hunting horn, of rich tilled fields, of gristmills by waterfalls, of rolling meadows and woodland, of winding streams. William Penn knew these fields, rode beside these streams. Here in Eastern Pennsylvania, quiet farmhouses and country churches paint their own picture of a wholesome, outdoor life. Farming and livestock are the central interest. Many of the houses date back to colonial times, many of the land-deeds bear Penn's grant. Washington and his troops fought over this land; Valley Forge is a neighbor. American History first opened its pages near here. The Liberty Bell rang within day's journey away, by horse.

Nor is rare beauty lacking in these wooded hillsides and broad meadows. Many a time have you who are here to-night had glimpses of this valley from your car window aboard the *"Broadway Limited."* You have looked down upon its beauty from high aloft when flying westwards to the setting sun, bound for California overnight.

Such a countryside of a century ago, in this same Chester Valley, was the picturesque background of Rebecca Lukens—about whose useful, dramatic, distinctive life it is my privilege to tell you tonight: of this Woman in Steel.

REBECCA LUKENS

(1794-1854)

"A Woman in Steel"

"Mistress of Brandywine." Heroine of this story. Shepherdess both of simple, countryside husbandry and of the intricacies of 19th Century iron-manufacturing. Much of her early life was spent in the saddle. She loved reading; Shakespeare was a favorite during long candlelight evenings at "Brandywine House." Stagecoaches ran during her childhood. She saw a first steam railroad penetrate into her Valley. Water Power was a high gift. She welcomed progress; she herself was part of that progress —in Steel. Her's were many interests; many friends. The outdoors beckoned her. Devoted wife and mother, her husband's death, when she was 30, brought a challenge which she met—and she became the outstanding woman-executive of her time in the United States

And that we may have broader understanding of what her problems were and of the fulness of her courage in attacking them, let me first sketch briefly the beginnings and early growth of the iron industry, child of her own family, which she was called upon alone to direct and conserve—she a woman wholly unfamiliar with executive responsibilities, unfamiliar with business practices. Indeed, Rebecca Lukens was destined to be confronted by and to survive the Panic of 1837.

In our brief review of beginnings and early growth, we shall encounter the names of four Chester County pioneers: Jesse Kersey, Moses Coates, Isaac Pennock, and Charles Lukens. Each plays his part in the unfolding of our story:

ॐ ॐ

Jesse Kersey, born at York in the Province of Pennsylvania in 1768, is the first name we encounter. This picturesque personality, apprenticed at the age of 15 to a potter, came to East Caln Township in Chester County in 1789 and opened a school. He had turned from moulding in clay to moulding in character. Within a year he married Elizabeth, daughter of Moses Coates. Kersey, a devout Quaker, set out in the Autumn of 1795, when cornfields were giving a golden harvest, to undertake a missionary visit to adjoining States, visiting Maryland, Virginia, and North Carolina. Our next record of him appears in his purchase of a farm, in 1797, near what today is Downingtown in the Chester Valley.

The century turned and again we find Kersey, this time aboard ship bound for England and Ireland, where he preached during 1804 and 1805.

In 1810, just 130 years ago, he performed undoubtedly the most worldly accomplishment of his life when he founded a town (later to be known as Coatesville in honor of Moses Coates) and established the business over which your speaker today presides. It was located on a part of Moses Coates' farm, near to the early Federal turnpike connecting Philadelphia and Lancaster. The plant spread itself out along the banks of the historic Brandywine. The early business was known as *"The Brandywine Iron Works and Nail Factory."* Here were the beginnings of the present *Lukens Steel Company.*

With Quaker acumen, Jesse Kersey looked about him for a partner experienced in iron production, a man whose skill was known in his industry. He found such a one in Isaac Pennock, a successful Ironmaster who had owned and operated the Federal Slitting Mill on Buck Run some five miles distant. The actual date of establishment, both of town and new industry at Coates Villa (later Coatesville) was Seventh month, Second, 1810. Or, as we would say: July 2, 1810.

Perhaps there is something significant that all this took place just at a time of year when the Chester Valley is at its height of productivity and beauty. The adjacent fields of grain were ripening for a harvest.

Isaac Pennock had come of distinguished ancestry, engaged in farming. There was little manufacture in those days. His father in 1792 had deeded him 300 acres of rich farmland; despite which fact the son decided to go into the iron business. We may be able to understand how shocked was the father at this decision to abandon a good Chester County farm "when wheat was selling at 3 dollars a bushel." It was in September 1793 that Isaac Pennock started up his slitting mill on Buck Run. Retrospect

[13]

appears fully to justify the decision of this good farmer-Quaker, Pennock, to turn Ironmaster.

❧ ❧

We now have encountered Jesse Kersey, Moses Coates, and Isaac Pennock; we find the town of Coatesville established; and the Iron Industry there beginning to flourish under the aegis of the aforementioned Isaac Pennock. In 1817, Pennock became sole owner.

A fourth personality is to enter our story, as preamble to the entrance of Rebecca Lukens—A Woman in Steel.

That fourth figure is Charles Lukens, the son-in-law of Isaac Pennock and husband of Rebecca Pennock. To Charles Lukens, about this same time, 1817, the Ironmaster Pennock leased the iron works; with an understanding that it would be left to Rebecca Pennock, his daughter, upon the father's death. Rebecca Pennock, now become *Rebecca Lukens*, is none other than our heroine.

❧ ❧

The Family Bible, still preserved, has this record: "Rebecca Pennock was born the 6th of the 1 mo. 1794, daughter of Isaac and Martha Pennock." For purposes of this informal history of a quite amazing woman of a century ago, we shall know her herein as Rebecca Lukens (1794-1854), the wife of and later the widow of the said Charles Lukens of Chester County, Ironmaster.

It would have been impossible for Rebecca Lukens in her earlier years, spent at home in a glorious countryside, to have escaped the influence of that wonderful valley in which she lived. Hardly could she have ignored the quiet beauty of farmland and village and winding stream, of the

[14]

very oaks and steep hillside which I pictured to you at the outset.

Rebecca Lukens found inspiration in the march of the seasons. She lived close to the land; much of her early life was spent in the saddle. Life had a simplicity and a directness. The seasons brought inspiration. Sunset's glow upon drifted snowfields; early April and seed time; wheat fields bronzed by July's sun; harvest and frost; November's leaden skies and a carpet of browned leaves on forest's floor; the joys of Christmas and her children's delight in all which Christmas holds. We can understand how truly Rebecca Lukens was a Christian. We can understand how these influences brought to her a kindliness that bound to her in affectionate esteem the men who worked in this Iron Industry which she directed.

Rebecca Lukens found inspiration and wisdom in her environment. It was but natural that her community should profit thereby. Those traditions still are conserved in a business now in continuous existence during over one hundred and thirty years—in the famed Chester Valley. A business which at this present moment is doing its bit in the National Defense.

❦ ❦

We find much of the woman herself in the opening sentences of Rebecca Lukens' *autobiography*, written for the benefit of her children at a time when her husband's death had cast upon her both the shadow of bereavement and the spur of necessity personally to take over the direction of the iron works. Here is what she wrote, and it shows her grip upon the realities of life and her sympathies toward life:

"I have latterly often thought I would pen a sketch of my life which might be interesting to my children when their mother

[15]

should slumber in the grave, and in delineating the events which have marked its course draw for them a portrait of the noble, the exalted being to whom they owe their existence now I trust a Saint in a better world. They will be made acquainted by this with all the incidents which have varied the flight of thirty summers. Of the wild and romantic reveries of youth, the pure and perfect happiness of a short period of more mature life, and the feelings agonized and harrowed to phrensy which followed those few brief years of bliss. My design is not merely to gratify their curiosity but if possible to improve them by an instructive lesson by warning them of those errors in which my own inexperience and warmth both of imagination and feelings too often led me and by holding up to their view the bright example of their father incite them to follow in his steps the path of every noble, every sublime virtue. In the fate of their mother they will learn the instability of earthly happiness and of the danger of making for themselves a paradise of bliss and vainly thinking the worshiped *idol* which absorbed all their thoughts and made this earth their Heaven should long be permitted to receive the worship due only to their Creator. In bitter sorrow have I learned this lesson and fain would I guard you my beloved girls from the fatal error. But, as I wish not to be led into digressions, I will begin my narrative from the earliest years of life which memory can furnish me with incidents to relate."

᭡ ᭡

You will understand how interwoven into the history of this old company, Lukens Steel Company, is the life-story of this young woman who, at the age of 30 with five children, one still unborn, was called upon to shoulder the complete responsibility and management of an iron rolling mill. She was the sole head, succeeding her late husband, Charles Lukens, to whom she was passionately devoted. This was in 1825.

You will understand too how her memory is cherished by that company; how the oldest inhabitants in the

Chester Valley still speak of anecdotes of her told to them by their grandfathers.

It is related that once, while standing in front of *"Brandywine House,"* the iron works mansion, with Joseph Webb, her uncle, Rebecca Lukens spoke of a possibility of a steam railroad being projected along the Chester Valley. "How would they span that chasm?" asked Webb. "By a high bridge, of course," replied the niece.

This was spoken, prophetically, in days when small stone bridges over narrow streams were considered engineering feats—in stagecoach days. Rebecca Lukens lived to see her high bridge an accomplished fact, in 1833. On the last day of February, 1834, the first train of cars passed over it, introducing undreamed possibilities for Rebecca Lukens and her iron works. Previously, her market had been restricted to within a radius of 50 to 75 miles, unless shipments were made by water from Philadelphia, 38 miles away, or from Wilmington, in the State of Delaware, 26 miles away. It might be remarked that when the iron works began to use coal, the mill hauled it from Columbia, on the Susquehanna River, 42 miles away. Teaming to Philadelphia cost four dollars a short ton. The dirt roads were rough. These were days of toll gates and kindly taverns. Highway robbers were not unknown.

❦ ❦

When Charles Lukens died in the Summer of 1825, it was just at the time he had commenced rolling Boiler Plate. Of this, Rebecca Lukens wrote:

"My husband had just commenced the Boiler Plate Business and secured sufficient workmen to carry it on. This was a new branch in Pennsylvania and he was sanguine in his hopes of success. It was his dying request that he wished me to continue and I promised to comply."

Added to the overwhelming shock of her husband's death was Rebecca Lukens' physical condition at the time. Their youngest daughter was born the following December. Yet this Woman in Steel took over; and with a success that amazed! She wrote at the time: "Necessity is a stern taskmistress; and my every responsibility gave me courage. I had my promise made to my husband. I had my duty to my children."

꧁ ꧂

Twelve years later, Rebecca Lukens, Ironmaster, was confronted by the Panic of 1837. The following is quoted from a letter to an old and dear friend, dated "Brandywine 5 Mo. 22nd, 1837." In it Rebecca Lukens wrote:

"Mother is returning this afternoon and I could not let such an opportunity pass without addressing a few lines to thee. The difficulties of the times throw a gloom on everything. All is paralyzed—business at a stand. I have as yet lost nothing but am in constant fear, and have even forbidden my agents to sell, not knowing who would be safe to trust.

"George's agent in New York has suspended, but he thinks there will be no eventual loss, though his agent's notes returning unpaid are sadly deranging George's business.

"I have stopped rolling for a few weeks, and set my men to repairing the race dam, &, having a heavy stock manufactured already, I do not wish to increase it until times are more settled; but shall take advantage of the first gleam of sunshine to resume.

"We do not know how to do without a circulating medium. Every one that has a dollar in silver hoards it up as if he never expects to see another, and our cautious people as yet are affraid of your small notes."

Rebecca Lukens continued at the helm until 1849, when her son-in-law, Charles Huston, husband of her younger daughter Isabella, was taken into the firm. However, Rebecca Lukens maintained a guidance over the business until her death, in her beloved Chester Valley, on December 10th, 1854. The outstanding woman business executive of her times had passed.

❦ ❦

As we conclude this fragmentary recital of a very human story; as we withdraw from the enchantment of a country-side Rebecca Lukens loved and I have labored to picture to you; as we leave behind us these events of a century ago concerned with the heroine of this memoir of courage and enterprise—as we conclude, it seems appropriate that I should pause in order to bear witness to the contributions which Rebecca Lukens made to the progress of what has grown to be one of the greatest of American industries: The Steel Industry.

Little could she perceive to what growth that industry was to attain within the span of 100 years. Yet in the simple directness, faith, sincerity, and earnestness of her life; in the prudence, judgment, and courage of her decisions and their humanity; and in her undaunted determination to carry on—she serves as an example after the passing of nearly ten decades. These indeed were contributions, rockbedded in the eternal and priceless values of character. She had known what suffering is, and out of that suffering arose strength and understanding and determination.

Yes, Rebecca Lukens, Ironmaster and Christian, contributed to the development of American Industry at its best; and for those contributions it is my privilege and right, as her successor of another century in the post of President of Lukens Steel Company in the historic Chester Valley of Pennsylvania, to bear witness to the attainments of this *Woman in Steel*.

THE END

ॐ

The National Newcomen Dinner of The Newcomen Society of England, held at Union League Club of New York on December 12, 1940 in honor of Mr. Wolcott, was under the direction of American Newcomen's permanent New York Committee, whose roster is given on the following pages:

THE NEWCOMEN SOCIETY
AMERICAN BRANCH

❧

American Founder
L. F. LOREE (*1858–1940*)

Office Bearers for North America
DR. CHARLES PENROSE, *Senior Vice-President for North America*
JAMES R. LEAVELL, *Junior Vice-President for North America*

American Members of Council (*London*)
RALPH BUDD   DR. THOMAS W. MARTIN
MAJOR GENERAL JAMES G. HARBORD, K.C.M.G., D.S.M.,
United States Army (*Ret.*)
J. B. ENNIS   DR. L. K. SILLCOX

Joint Honorary Corresponding Secretaries for the United States
F. N. JEAN GINDORFF   GEORGE A. STETSON
63 Wall Street   29 West 39th Street
New York, N.Y.   New York, N.Y.

American Chaplain
THE BISHOP OF BETHLEHEM

American Treasurer
WILLIAM M. VERMILYE
Vice-President
The National City Bank of New York

Committee for North America
NEWCOMB CARLTON, *Chairman*
DR. WILLIAM CARTER DICKERMAN
COLONEL C. E. DAVIES, *Past-President*
SIR EDWARD BEATTY, G.B.E., K.C., LLD, DCL
—*and the Chairmen of regional committees in U.S.A.*

❧

Honorary Members (American Newcomen)
THE RIGHT HONORABLE SIR RONALD LINDSAY, P.C., G.C.M.G.,
K.C.B., C.V.O.
Formerly, His Britannic Majesty's Ambassador to the
United States of America
SIR GERALD CAMPBELL, K.C.M.G.
His Britannic Majesty's High Commissioner in Canada
for the United Kingdom
SIR LOUIS BEALE, K.C.M.G., C.B.E., LL.D.
Formerly, Commissioner-General for His Majesty's Government
in the United Kingdom, New York World's Fair 1939
Member, The Anglo-French Purchasing Board in the United States

THE NEWCOMEN SOCIETY
AMERICAN BRANCH

❦

Historical Advisory Committee

Chairman

DR. JOSEPH W. ROE
Professor Emeritus of Industrial Engineering, New York University
Visiting Professor, Yale University

Vice-Chairman

DR. DEXTER S. KIMBALL
Dean Emeritus of Sibley College of Engineering, Cornell University

❦

DR. ISAIAH BOWMAN
President, Johns Hopkins University

DR. KARL T. COMPTON
President, Massachusetts Institute of Technology

DR. HARVEY N. DAVIS
President, Stevens Institute of Technology
Past-President, The American Society of Mechanical Engineers

JAMES K. FINCH
Renwick Professor of Civil Engineering, Columbia University

DR. RALPH H. GABRIEL
Larned Professor of American History, Yale University

DR. ARTHUR M. GREENE, JR.
Dean Emeritus of Engineering, Princeton University

PROFESSOR FRED V. LARKIN
Director of Mechanical Engineering, Lehigh University

GEORGE A. ORROK
Consulting Engineer, New York

DR. L. K. SILLCOX
First Vice-President, New York Air Brake Company

DR. ABBOTT PAYSON USHER
Professor of Economics, Harvard University

DR. THOMAS JEFFERSON WERTENBAKER
Edwards Professor of American History, Princeton University

❦

F. N. JEAN GINDORFF, *ex-officio*

GEORGE A. STETSON, *ex-officio*

"The Old Mill"
—in Rebecca Lukens' time

"THE HISTORY *of what today is Lukens Steel Company actually goes back to 1793, or only twelve years after Cornwallis' surrender at Yorktown, which brought the Revolutionary War to a virtual end. Prior to that period, the working of iron was not permitted by the British Crown. The Act of Parliament of 1750 made it unlawful 'to encourage the importation of pig and bar iron from His Majesty's colonies into Great Britain. The erection is prohibited of any mill or engine for slitting or rolling iron, or any plate making forge to work with a tilt-hammer, or any furnace for making steel in any of the colonies.' Despite the British ban against iron making on this Continent the industry was surreptitiously carried on with lookouts posted to warn of the approach of British agents and officers. Threat of fine and imprisonment did not prevent the pioneers of American iron and steel from keeping their home forges burning."* In these words, "The Iron Age" *traced early beginnings of Lukens Steel Company on the banks of the historic Brandywine, describing, in the issue of July 4, 1935, the heritage of "One hundred and twenty-five years of continuous making of iron and steel under an uninterrupted line of family ownership and management. That, we believe, is a unique record in the Steel Industry of America."*

꙲ ꙲

*"The roads you travel
so briskly lead out
of dim antiquity, and
you study the past
chiefly because of its
bearing on the living
present and its
promise for the future."*

—Major General James G. Harbord,
K.C.M.G., D.S.M., U.S. Army (*Ret.*)
*American Member of Council
at London, The Newcomen Society*

꙲

LADY WITH THE HATCHET

James L. Dwyer

THE LADY WITH THE HATCHET

BY JAMES L. DWYER

IN 1800 Kentucky was in the throes of a great revival. The mountaineers, exhibiting the effects of frontier cookery on the dour temperament inherited from their Scotch and North-Irish ancestors, were ripe for the army of wandering evangelists who took the State by storm, exorcising demons, and spreading terror. No monument at Gasper River marks the spot, but here, during the upheaval, for the first time in America a whole countryside met to worship God with yells, writhings and convulsions. Thus was born a highly characteristic American institution —the camp-meeting.

Forty-six years later the same great State and the same Scotch-Irish primates produced a second cosmic phenomenon in Carrie Nation, corn-fed Joan of Arc and Mother of Prohibition. It has been said of her that she was insane. She probably was. But there is a difference in the Republic between being merely crazy and being crazy on the subject of religion, the difference, to wit, between confinement in a psychopathic ward and freedom to harangue the multitude. So Carrie was allowed to run at large—a fact of immense historical importance, since even the briefest examination of the effects of her crusade offers proof positive that the cause of Prohibition owes as much to her as to any other agent of God, male or female, clerical or lay.

Her father was George Moore, a moderately well off slave-owner and zealous Campbellite. The Moores were frequently on the move—the Civil War found them in Missouri and later in Texas, whence they returned to Kentucky. Carrie's girlhood, described in her autobiography, was

unhappy: "My parents regarded me as hard headed." When she was ten the twig was definitely bent toward a holy life by two important religious experiences. Like so many other moral crusaders she once knew evil ways, and as a child, it seems, she lied to escape punishment, and stole food from the pantry and ribbons for her dolls. Fortunately, a little book was given to her, telling how a child who began with such small sins would inevitably end on the gallows. At once, she was overcome with shame and remorse, and from that day on she never sinned again. Her "conversion"—a necessary Campbellite rite— soon followed. She was taken to an icy stream and totally immersed, and "the little Carrie who walked into that water was different from the one who walked out."

As a maiden she was lofty of soul and pure of heart. Although not averse to the attentions of young men she permitted no nonsense.

> I see young ladies and gentlemen who entertain each other with their silly jokes and gigglings that are disgusting. When I had company I always directed the conversation so that my friend would teach me something, or I would teach him. I would read the poets, and Scott's writings, and history, . . . mythology and the Bible. . . . I would go to country dances. . . . But my native modesty prevented me from ever dancing a round dance with a gentleman. I cannot think this hugging match compatible with a true woman.

How, then, came such a violet to give herself to a man, even in marriage? It happened this way. In 1865 Charles Gloyd, a young physician of some education and refinement, was boarding with the Moores. In a rash moment the young doctor caught the daughter of the house unaware and kissed her. This sealed his doom, for the horrified virgin at once threw up her hands to her face, repeating over and over, "I am ruined!" Obviously, there were not many courses left open to Dr. Gloyd. He did the honorable thing, however, and—ruined himself.

The match turned out badly from the start. Says Carrie of her love: "When Dr. Gloyd came up to marry me I noticed with pain that his countenance was changed. . . . I did not find Dr. Gloyd the lover I expected. He was kind, but seemed to want to be away from me; he used to sit and read, when I was so hungry for his caresses and love." Eventually, Gloyd took to drinking heavily and to spending most of his time at his Masonic lodge. To a woman like the then Mrs. Gloyd the secrecy which Freemasonry imposed on her husband was torture. "Thus," she said, "is confidence destroyed in the sacred precincts of the home." One can imagine the curtain lectures and the supper-table philippics which the doctor had to suffer. His nights at home, therefore, became less and less frequent, and he sank deeper into Rum and Masonry. At last, a few weeks after the birth of her daughter Charlien, Carrie abandoned him to the devil. Gloyd, by this time a hopeless alcoholic, died within six months, and the widow went to the home of her parents, nursing an intense and growing hatred of drink and secret orders.

Soon Carrie again left home to live with Gloyd's widowed mother. For four years she supported Charlien and the elder Mrs. Gloyd by teaching, until some original ideas on pronunciation got her into trouble with the school board. Her position gone, she resolved to marry again and prayed to God for a husband. The answer to her prayers was David Nation, aged fifty, a preacher, lawyer, and Union veteran. But here again there was a hitch. Carrie's severely Christian life and over-zealous churchly interests were offensive even to her minister husband. At one period it was her pleasure to sit in a front pew while

he addressed his flock and to pass audible judgment on his efforts. When she felt he had said enough she would remark. "That will be about all for today, David!" So in 1901 Brother David divorced her, charging cruelty and desertion, after living with her twenty-four years.

Shortly after their marriage the Nations bought a cotton plantation in the San Bernard river region, Texas. This proved disastrous. They were soon in want, the Rev. Mr. Nation was forced to resume his law practice, and Carrie took charge of a small hotel in Columbia. In the meantime there was Charlien to worry over, then about twelve.

This, my only child, was peculiar, . . . the result of a drunken father and a distracted mother. . . . She seemed to have taken a positive dislike to Christianity. . . . I used to pray to God to save her soul at any cost. I often prayed for bodily affliction on her, if that was what would make her love and serve God. Anything for her eternal salvation.

The bodily affliction arrived. Charlien became stricken with an erosive disease, severe and lingering, which kept her in hospitals for many months. Carrie, however, attributed this to the parentage of Gloyd and not to the power of prayer.

II

Soon after, the Nations moved to Richmond, Texas, where in 1884 Carrie received the baptism of the Holy Ghost. At a Methodist Conference she began to feel very strange. A halo appeared above the minister, ecstasy possessed her, an angel seemed to be speaking and the church and all in it ascending to heaven. When it was over she inquired if others had felt anything extraordinary. None had, so she concluded that this was a visitation of the Holy Spirit on herself alone, and announced to all present that she was consecrated. Visions, warnings, and miracles followed. One night a heavenly presence filled her room; next day when a fire threatened her hotel she allowed nothing to be carried out, confident that the vision was a guarantee of protection. During a drought she successfully prayed for rain. She walked with God. But she did not walk with the church authorities—both Methodists and Episcopalians dropped her as a Sunday-school teacher for insisting on unorthodox instruction. Whereupon she started a class of her own, gathering about thirty children who did not belong to the "regular" churches. Sometimes she held session in a graveyard. "I wished by this to impress the little ones with the purpose of the Gospel."

The year 1892 brought the Nations to Medicine Lodge, a Kansas short grass town and the home of Sockless Jerry Simpson. Greater fame awaited it, for here Carrie's mission took definite form, and here she received the Call that was to put her on the front page of every newspaper in the land. It was several years before the Call came. Indeed, her beginnings in Medicine Lodge were most inauspicious. Her testimony concerning the Holy Ghost failed to impress her fellow Campbellites, and even elicited the pastor's opinion that she was not sound in the faith. Matters were not helped when she found this same pastor idling in front of a questionable drug store and rebuked him for "sitting in the seat of the scornful." Finally, her constant rows and bickerings in church got her cast out as a "stumbling-block and disturber of the peace." That is, they told her she was cast out, but she continued to occupy her pew.

Before long she was appointed Jail Evangelist in a newly organized branch of the W. C. T. U., her duty being to annoy the inmates of the neighboring bastilles. This was congenial, but the more important aims of the society soon claimed her full attention. Kansas, of course, had gone legally dry by virtue of the heavy farmer vote. This, inevitably, meant two things: the saloons paid a nominal monthly fine in lieu of a license fee, and the drug stores began to do an enormous prescription business.

Everybody was happy—but Carrie. She saw that the Demon Rum, though like her-

self officially cast out, still occupied his pew, and she resolved to oust him once and for all. Novel plans occurred to her. She dug up an old hand organ and serenaded the various dives, choosing W. C. T. U. battle songs not calculated to fill her listeners with cheer. Since she was now a town character little heed was paid to her, least of all by the town drunkards. More heroic measures were needed, so, keying herself up, she entered a saloon for the first time in her life. The proprietor, Mart Strong, seized her by the shoulders and cried, "Get out of here, you crazy woman!" But Carrie, with the fire of God leaping within her, brushed him aside and lifted up her voice in lusty song:

Who hath sorrow? Who hath woe?
They who dare not answer no;
They whose feet to sin incline
While they tarry at the wine.

Chorus:

They who tarry at the wine cup,
They who tarry at the wine cup,
They who tarry at the wine cup,
They have sorrow, they have woe.

There were four more verses. As the last died away Jim Gano, the constable, uttered a wistful desire—a desire that within three years was to be echoed and re-echoed by police, magistrates, and office-holders throughout the republic. "I wish," he said, "I could take you off the streets."

Emboldened, Carrie invaded other joints; other women, inflamed by her railings and infected with her savage zeal, followed her. The lawbreakers grew uneasy. In Henry Durst's place she threw herself on her knees, prayed long and hysterically, and informed Durst that he was going to hell. Most amusing was her adventure in Hank O'Bryan's dive:

I smelled the horrid drink and went in. A man by the name of Grogan was there, half drunk, and I said: "You have a dive here. . . . Let me see what you have in the back room." He took me to a very small room with a table covered with empty bottles, and in one corner sat a man, Mr. Smith. Grogan introduced me and he, Mr. Smith, looked terrified and astonished. I took one of the bottles and asked what it had contained. He replied: "Hop tea." I asked: "What name is that

on the label?" It was Anheuser-Busch, but I could
get neither of them to pronounce it. I told them
it was beer and I could take an oath it was. Grogan threw up his hands, saying, "Now, Mother
Nation, if you get me into trouble I will do something desperate." When I said I would not tell
on them the look of gladness on their faces was
pitiful to see. I said: "I am going to pray God to
have mercy on you. Kneel down." Like two
obedient little children, they knelt. Some may
laugh at this but I was deeply affected.

Her crusade in Medicine Lodge ended
when, at the head of her train, she entered
the drug store of O. L. Day and overturned
a whiskey keg with loud hosannas and
resounding hymns.

She had been successful. Those "jointists"
who had not already sought other towns
were in a state of fear. Well they might
have been, for the opposition of small-
town churchwomen, organized and led by
a Christian Amazon, is truly formidable.
But as yet Carrie had done no smashing,
having confined herself to verbal abuse and
noisy prayer. When, however, the outside
world beckoned her she decided that more
ruthless tactics were needed.

III

The Call came in June, 1900, in the form of
various supernatural signs. For a long time
she seemed to be hanging by a rope over a
bottomless chasm; then she was swung to
solid ground. God stood behind her for
three days, and at length a soft, musical
voice urged her: "Go to Kiowa. I'll stand
by you." Kiowa, near the Oklahoma border and about twenty miles from Medicine
Lodge, was then slightly smaller than the
latter town but bore a reputation for its
quota of thriving saloons. Before starting
for this godless center Carrie loaded her
buggy with paper parcels. Inside each
parcel was a good-sized rock. Leaving
Medicine Lodge, she saw "in the middle
of the road a dozen or so creatures in the
forms of men. Their faces were those of
demons, and the gestures of their hands
as if they would tear me up." She invoked
heaven, and the demons scampered off
across the Kansan fields. The rest of the

trip was without incident. She arrived in
Kiowa after dark and spent the night chat-
ting with the Lord.

In the morning, laden with her packages,
she entered the nearest saloon. Pronounc-
ing doom on the place and warning the
customers to stand back, she let fly. In this
way she wrecked three saloons; not a hand
was raised to stop her. While in the first
dive she had a vision of McKinley toppling
from his chair—this meant the fall of the
Republican party, the "tool of the liquor
interests." Her smashing done, she made
an appropriate speech from a street corner.
The mayor interrupted with a request that
she pay for the damage, to which she replied with threats of fire and brimstone.
He decided to let her go. So, mounting her
buggy, she delivered this somewhat in-
congruous benediction to the crowd in
parting: "Peace on earth and good will to
men."

Probably her sex, as well as the Holy
Ghost, saved her from leaving town astride
a rail, clad in tar and feathers. As it was,
she did not go scot free. The saloon-keepers
dared not prosecute, but their friend Griffin,
the county attorney, sued her for slander;
she had accused him of not only allowing
dives to exist, but of patronizing them.
While her accusations were indeed defama-
tory they were evidently not unfounded,
for the jury awarded Griffin one dollar.
The costs, however, came to two hundred
dollars, and a judgment was secured. When
later, she came to pay this it was but a
fraction of her week's salary.

Six months elapsed before Carrie's second
expedition. Meanwhile she enjoyed her
usual visions, chief among which was one
of the Saviour and herself standing in a
blaze of glory, and she kept on disrupting
divine service by marching up and down
the church aisles, clapping her hands, and
shouting: "Hallelujah!" and "Praise the
Lord!" Mrs. Hutchinson, State president
of the W. C. T. U.—and, incidentally, wife
of a political appointee—withheld official
sanction, but the local sisters gloated over
her. Her readiness to achieve martyrdom

was proved with the aid of several bottles of Budweiser procured from a "sneaking, degenerate druggist."

One of the bottles I took to a W. C. T. U. meeting and in the presence of the ladies I drank the contents. Then I had two of them take me down to a doctor's office. I fell limp on the sofa and said: "Doctor, what is the matter with me?" He looked at my eyes, felt my heart and pulse, shook his head and looked grave. I said: "Am I poisoned?" "Yes," said the doctor. I resorted to this to show the effect that beer has on the system.

In December, 1900, she again felt the urge to destroy—inspired, perhaps, by the emotional stimulus of Christmas. This time she selected Wichita. Arriving there at night she entered the Carey Hotel bar, the "swell" saloon of the town; the usual painting of a nude woman caught her eye and she informed the bartender that this was an insult to his mother. She ranted on for a while and, since she was unarmed, left without violence. In the morning she gathered several rocks—and the trusty iron rod she now carried under her cape when chasing the devil. "I had found out I could use a rock but once." In the Carey saloon she stoned the painting and swept the glassware off the bar. This earned her several weeks in jail, which, however, did not dampen her spirit in the slightest. On her release she immediately smashed two other saloons in company with sisters Wilhoite, Muntz, and Evans—on this occasion she first used a hatchet, which thereafter became her symbol and trademark. Locked up, the four held a continual revival meeting, which may or may not have been the reason for Carrie's speedy release on a writ of *habeas corpus*. Going directly to Enterprise, she broke up the place of one Stillings, for which she was horsewhipped and scratched by the proprietor's wife and lady friends. The town marshal escorted her to the railroad station through a gauntlet of rotten eggs.

Next on her list was Topeka, where she was jailed three times. She was now a national figure—the "Hatchet Woman of Kansas." Everywhere the press gave her prominence and eagerly awaited her next outburst. In her cell she edited a journal, the *Smasher's Mail*. Offers from lecture agencies and lyceum bureaus poured in, "one as high as $800 a week, a palace car and a maid." These she at first refused, having a horror of anything that savored of the stage. But later, convinced of the wide missionary field that lay before her, she yielded to the promise of James Furlong, former manager of Patti, that he would pay the fines necessary to secure her release if she would come under his wing. Her success was immediate and enormous; within a few years she became rich.

IV

The reaction of the public was characteristic. Hitherto there had been feeble attempts by her victims to have her adjudged insane. These now ceased. Many citizens felt she was "in it for what she got out of it," others advised that she be put in jail and kept there, and judges frequently accused her of advertising herself through the courts. But the overwhelming proof of her sanity was her earning power. Insane people do not make several hundreds a week, reasoned the Americano: "She's no fool." Here it can be said for Carrie that the frequent cries of commercialism that pursued her were ungrounded. Her messianic obsession and the actual use she made of her money seem to answer all such charges. She gave liberally to various moral causes: in Kansas City, Kansas, she endowed a Home for Drunkards' Wives (which closed for lack of these rum widows); and any panhandler wise enough to pose as a repentant sinner was generously rewarded by her. Though a born showwoman she had little business sense; more than once she was mulcted of large sums by bogus temperance workers. When she accepted bookings in burlesque theatres and drinking halls she likened herself to Christ among the publicans. If she were well paid for carrying the Word to these sinners, it was but further proof of God's favor. There is no doubt that like many another nuisance she was sincere—completely, hopelessly sincere.

Moreover, a fair estimate must allow her other qualities less dubious than sincerity. There were limits to her narrowness. A Southerner, she was without the Southern rancor toward the Negro. She had high regard for the Jews, and except for Christian Science, which she dubbed witchcraft, she was tolerant of other creeds. And though she would have elected a Kaffir President on a Prohibition ticket, this same zeal for her cause led her to discover much sham and corruption in politics and to form shrewd judgments thereon. The disparity between the public utterances and private views of Great Men did not escape her, nor did the loftiness of office dazzle her. "Government," she said, "like dead fish, stinks worse at the head." Roosevelt she denounced as blood-thirsty, reckless and extravagant. Of the late minister plenipotentiary from heaven and lineal descendant of Adam and Eve she asserted: "Bryan was for Bryan and what Bryan could get for Bryan." Indeed, her blasphemous assaults aroused something like popular fury against her when she undertook a too ardent defense of Csolgosz, McKinley's assassin. In Rochester, N. Y., at the time, a delicious irony of circumstance forced her to hide in a saloon from a large and dangerous mob.

Contrary to the general impression, Carrie smashed but one legally operated saloon. The exception was a Texas groggery named in her honor; this was too much for her. Her convictions outside Kansas, about thirty in all, resulted from disturbing the peace, drawing a crowd, and like charges. A well advertised tornado, she swept from Coney Island to San Francisco, from Texas to the Maritime Provinces. She harangued train and steamship passengers, Baptist congregations, girls in segregated districts, a few drunks gathered about a bar.

A saloon-keeper in Kentucky pursued and belabored her with a chair, another in Maine knocked her head against a stone

pillar; admirers in her home State gave her a medal inscribed: "To the Bravest Woman in Kansas." In Washington she burst into the Senate chamber and shouted: "Treason, anarchy and conspiracy! Discuss these!" Seated in a Pittsburgh street car she espied a man wearing a Masonic pin and remarked to the car in general: "That man . . . belongs to an order who swear to have their tongues cut out, their throats ripped across, their hearts torn out and given to the beasts, their bowels taken out and burned to ashes. Such oaths originate in hell."

In Sacramento she visited the California legislature in joint session and in a loud voice revealed the members' caches of liquor. "In the bill-filing room . . . liquors are kept, also in the sergeant-at-arms' room; in room 56 is a safe where bottles of beer and whiskey are kept . . . ." and so on. The law-makers received this like a "lot of bad boys caught stealing watermelons," and the session was adjourned. She swooped down on colleges, to the delight of undergraduates and the consternation of deans. She found that the Yale students were being ruined body and soul by the alcoholic sauces served with their food, or so they told her, and at Harvard she saw professors brazenly smoking cigarettes.

One day she entered a New York bar where the famous John L. Sullivan was tarrying at the wine cup. A clash of Titans? No. The Boston Strong Boy, terror of the ring and tyrant of the grog-shop, discreetly withdrew into a back room, there to sit quietly until the coast was clear. His wisdom is attested by a description in *Current Literature* for April, 1901:

Mrs. Nation is quite fierce when aroused. Her face . . . becomes distorted with wrath, and she is not pleasant to look upon or to deal with. . . . She . . . can talk your arm off if you will let her. . . . When she sets out to get contributions she cannot be shaken off. . . . She is nearly six feet tall, weighs about 175 pounds, has iron-gray hair, small and very black eyes and a strong arm.

Other celebrities were less fortunate than Sullivan. Once successful in bearding a politician in his office or home she was not easily got rid of. If the prominent one,

thus cornered, had any sense he would call!
the police wagon without further delay;
if not, he would call it some minutes later
and pray to God it had a fast horse.

Hostile audiences never fazed her. When
heckling became serious she would simply
lean over the platform and talk to those
immediately about her in a low, earnest
voice; the hecklers, realizing they were
wasting breath, would usually subside.
Sometimes this device would not work—
in a cheap burlesque theatre she was apt to
be drowned out. On such occasions she
would denounce the crowd as hell hounds
and sots and stalk off. A forceful speaker,
her imagery was vivid and her rhetoric
vigorously effective, with a King James
flavor decidedly heartier than the sancti-
monious billingsgate of the average evan-
gelical baboon. She enjoyed the most vehement and tireless tongue a woman ever
had, and her invective would have paralyzed a fishwife. A smartly dressed woman
was a "manikin on which to hang the
filthy rags of fashion," clubmen were
"diamond-studded, gold-fobbed rummies
whose bodies are reeking masses of corruption," judges were addressed as "your dis-
honor," a policeman who bundled her into
the "hoodlum wagon" was denounced as
a "beer-soaked, whiskey-swilled, saturn-
faced man," and in one jail she saluted the
warden and his wife as "Ahab and Jezebel."

A report of her interview with Gov.
Stanley of Kansas appeared in the New
York *Times:*

"Do you think my method is right?" she asked.
"No, I do not," the governor replied.
"Well, governor, have you a better one?"
"No, I don't think I have," he finally replied.
"What can I do? I am powerless. . . ."
"If necessary, call out the militia," was Mrs.
Nation's prompt reply. As she proceeded she became more vehement and . . . pointing her finger
at him, called him lawbreaker and perjurer without the least show of fear. He tried to make reply,
but she gave him no chance, the words of invective proceeding from her in a rush that would not
be stemmed. Finally Gov. Stanley volunteered:
"You get the prosecuting attorneys of the different counties to put the joint-keepers in jail, and
I will use my power as governor to keep them
there." This . . . transformed Mrs. Nation. She
fairly beamed with joy.

Carrie's influence was felt far beyond
Kansas. As a matter of sober record, it extended all over this great Christian Republic; that New York and other large
cities ridiculed her in no way alters the
fact. The city dweller enjoys many a good
laugh at his country cousin, but while he
is thus merrily employed the countryman
is busy stuffing the statute books with
anti-cigarette laws, prohibition laws, and
other such lunacies. Carrie, it is true, fell
flat in the cities, but in the cow States,
where superannuated socks are used to
cure abscesses, and where the late William
Jennings is believed to be promenading the
streets of Paradise with St. Paul—in these
wide regions her work produced tangible
results. Following her raids in Topeka the
Review of Reviews stated: "The people of
Kansas have had time to consider Mrs.
Nation's position carefully and tens of
thousands are indorsing it." The Rochester
Democrat (N. Y.) observed: "She is unquestionably a stirrer-up of dry bones."
According to the Springfield *Republican:*
"Kansas lawyers there are who support
her . . . and say she cannot be punished.
. . . She is a distinct moral force. . . ." And
at her death, ten years later, the New York
Evening Post commented thus: "Since she
appeared on the scene a Prohibition wave
has swept through the Southern and
Western States, and the anti-saloon movement has gained thousands of voters, with
the result that scores of new excise laws
have appeared." These quotations are
typical.

V

Messiahs are wont to take a great deal on
their shoulders. Carrie's burden, by the
will of God, was the United States. This
she divined by a mystical interpretation of
her name, based on an early misspelling of
her father's to which she later adhered; it
is at once ingenious and awful.

I do not belong to the "can't" family. When I
was born my father wrote my name Carry Amelia
Moore, then later it was Nation, which is more
still. C. A. N. are the initials of my name, then

C. (see!) A. Nation! And altogether. Carry A. Nation! This is no accident, but providence.

The job of carrying a nation was somewhat ramified, embracing such evils as smoking, "lodgism," and feminine immodesty in dress. "I have the right," she said, "to take cigars and cigarettes from men's mouths, and they ought not to be allowed to injure themselves." She inspired Lucy Page Gaston, pythoness of the Anti-Cigarette League, to write to Roosevelt inquiring if it were true, as reported, that he was guilty of the vice; and these two old busybodies received a solemn assurance from a secretary that, really, the president had never smoked a cigarette in his life. Masonry she fought by publishing one of the numerous "exposés" of that order; and in the matter of women's dress she contented herself with lecturing bedizened victims encountered on the street. One other concern of hers was the purity of little boys. How many little boys were accustomed to read the *Hatchet*, a monthly edited by her in 1906, is not known, but they had other habits of which she did not approve and against which she issued a sinister editorial, of such nature that the postal authorities suppressed the July number and summoned her to Washington. Her dealings with the young were characteristically severe, as revealed by her encounter one Summer night in Kansas:

As I was going down to a neighbor's one dark night I heard low voices of parties sitting by the roadside. I got a lantern. I found them to be those of a young man of Medicine Lodge and a young girl visiting there. I warned them, telling the young boy to act toward the girl as he would toward his sister. I told the girl that ruin would be her fate; and she hid her face, and soon both of them ran down the alley.

A far more powerful weapon than her hatchet, or even her tongue, was publicity. To read about Carrie Nation was to read about the bar-room, a form of continual advertising that could not have been otherwise than harmful to the latter. Although the country was not then ready for Volstead, nobody had a good word for the saloon, for which, consequently, any publicity was adverse publicity. The saloon-keeper was a pariah who thrived in the shade; the brewers and distillers let him fight his own battles, in the main, smugly confident that more genteel vendors of their wares would replace him were he driven from the street corners. Few dreamed that when he finally walked the plank the whole business would be dumped overboard with him—that the cry, "The saloon must go!" was but the thin end of the wedge whose broad base is the Eighteenth Amendment. This wedge is now driven home, and to Carrie Nation belongs much of the credit for inserting it where it was most effective—the South and Middle-West. She forced Kansas to pretend to live up to its pretensions, thereby making it a model for other theocratically ambitious States, and in general focussed public attention on the liquor traffic to a greater extent than a whole host of temperance workers before her had been able to achieve.

Early in 1911 she entered a sanatorium in Leavenworth, where she died of paresis the following June. Her death, unattended by relatives or friends, was strangely peaceful. Told the end was near, she smiled; and when, some days before, she had observed a doctor smoking, she merely remarked, "I have done what I could to eradicate the evil." She had expressed the wish that the words, "She hath done what she could" be inscribed on her tombstone.

Others might provide her with different epitaphs. A psycho-analyst, no doubt, after tearing her to pieces would find her crammed with all sorts of psychoses and neuroses; certainly, some of her anti-social activities are obvious indications, while others are immensely suggestive. Such a post mortem is not for the layman, but one may be permitted the gloomy observation that Carrie was a lifelong inebriate. Her ungovernable lust for righteousness led her to deplorable excesses; the murderous broth distilled by theological moonshiners in the backwoods maddened her brain; she never knew when to stop.

POETESS OF PASSION

Miriam Allen de Ford

POETESS OF PASSION

BY MIRIAM ALLEN DE FORD

IN THE first week of June, 1918, Big
Bertha was pounding Paris. Lee Meriwether of St. Louis, special assistant to
the American Ambassador, was arranging
for the removal from the city of such
Americans as desired to leave. Into his office there marched determinedly one
morning a small, plump woman in the
sixties, her blonde hair faded to gray. She
announced herself as Ella Wheeler Wilcox.

"I had to see you personally," she said.
"I want to leave Paris. I was talking to
Mr. Wilcox last night, and he told me to
go to Tours."

"Your husband is in Tours?" inquired
Mr. Meriwether politely.

The lady fixed him with a glance of
scorn.

"My husband," she retorted icily, "died
two years ago. He comes to see me every
night and talks to me on the ouija board."

Six months later Mr. Wilcox ordered his
wife to return to Paris, but this time his
commands were refused by a callous government. Ella went to England instead,
where she suffered a nervous breakdown.
Then she returned to America and on October 30, 1919, she died at her beloved
home in Short Beach, Connecticut, at the
age of sixty-four. She had undertaken the
aforementioned trip to Europe as a representative of the Red Star, the animals' Red
Cross. Her friends opposed her going, but
she had "astral orders" from her dead husband, which were law with her.

Although it was not until after Robert
Wilcox's death that his widow became an
avowed spiritualist, she had had leanings
toward the metaphysical from her childhood. Like other precocious children in
commonplace homes, she felt superior to
her family, and her later researches into
the supernatural gave her an easy explanation. "Being an old soul myself, reincarnated many more times than any other
member of my family, I knew the truth of
spiritual things not revealed to them." She
swallowed the New Thought and Theos-
ophy in her stride, and lent a welcoming
ear to every whisper from the Unknown.
"The palm," she said categorically, "even
as the Bible tells us, contains the whole
character. It never lies."

When Ella Wheeler Wilcox went to
join her adored Robert in Summerland,
the Hearst papers, for which she had been
writing for more than thirty years, gave
her an appropriate send-off. She had, said
one of them, "a greater personal following
than probably any other writer in the
United States." The strange thing is that
it was true. The Wisconsin farm girl who
had started her literary career by "out-
Swinburning Swinburne and out-Whit-
maning Whitman," and ended it with
very tame platitudes of the Dorothy Dix
variety, reached an enormous public. She
was the darling of readers just a cut above
the disciples of Eddie Guest and a trifle
below the admirers of Laurence Hope. In
the eighties and nineties every parlor table

435

which did not hold a copy of the Rubaiyat carried Ella Wheeler Wilcox's celebrated "Poems of Passion."

The verses which so thrilled and outraged our parents sound sadly flabby today. Mrs. Wilcox's outré ideas on sex barely extended to the theses that true love without marriage is better than marriage without true love; that illegitimate children are not to blame for their obscure birth; and that wives should reciprocate the affection of their husbands. In 1897, when her narrative poem, "Three Women," appeared, young ladies gasped to read that the hero

Drew her face up to his, on her frightened
   lips pressed
Wild caresses of passion that startled and
   shocked, . . .
While his iron arms welded her bosom to
   his.
"Well, that bruise on your lips tells the
   story!"

II

Mrs. Wilcox claimed, and with obvious truth, that her "literary proclivities and mental powers were influenced by reading Ouida, Mary J. Holmes, and Mrs. Southworth." Her one year at the University of Wisconsin, undertaken to please her ambitious mother, seems to have taught her nothing of genuine literature; she says herself that her head was "full of nonsense," and that she would not study. As a matter of fact, she felt that she had been born with all the knowledge she needed. "My literary career was in large measure begun before my birth through prenatal influences. . . . My mother committed to memory whole cantos of Byron, Moore, and Scott, and mentally devoured the plays of Shakespeare." With such an equipment, she needed no help from such dreary places as schools or colleges. When

she was only nine years old she listened with contempt to the earth-bound conversation of her elders. "I recollect just how crude and limited their minds seemed to me." She herself never had any doubt of her genius, though she was well aware that "the English highbrow critics (like the American) have had little use for me." She would have had nothing but contempt for the later commentator who said that her verses were to the world of real poetry what the novels of Marie Corelli were to the world of real fiction.

At the beginning of her journalistic career an editor wrote to her: "Give us heartwails; that is what our readers like." And "heart-wails" she continued to produce. "Poets," she said proudly, "are given their voices to be heralds of greater lives beyond." And she knew very well the source of her almost incredible popularity: "If I chance to be a popular poet it is because I have loved God and life and people, and expressed sentiments which found echoes in other hearts."

Nevertheless, one may trace in her vainglorious autobiographical pages a certain disappointment and resentment. Privately, it seems, she would have been content with a more select group of worshippers. Apparently she never came into contact with a first-rate mind; the celebrities whom she lists as her friends were all second-raters or worse, and she spent her life as a grimly inflated frog in a very small puddle. She endeavored to console herself by melancholy croakings. "I have written many real poems of literary and artistic value." "I was recognized from the age of eight to fourteen as a child prodigy." "A college education does not seem to me the most desirable thing for a woman."

She considered her series of very pedestrian sonnets on Heloïse as her best work

—as they undoubtedly are—and never got
over the hurt of their lack of recognition
by the highbrow critics. Publicly she ascribed this failure to jealousy of her fame
among the lowly; but deep down in her
heart she knew better. When in addition
to this dissatisfaction she lost first her only
child and then her patient, adoring husband of thirty-two years, she was desperate
for comfort, and turned to "the divine
power and the divinity within us." As far
back as 1901 she was already proclaiming,

> Though life has given me a heaping meas-
> ure
> Of all the best gifts, and many a cup of
> pleasure,

still she thought "of death as some delightful journey, That I shall take when
all my tasks are done."

About twenty years ago Ella Wheeler
Wilcox was being hailed or attacked as a
Socialist. But in this both her friends and
critics were mistaken. To be sure, she had
delivered herself of a poem entitled "The
Workers," in which occurred some rather
incendiary if muddled stanzas:

> There is growth in Revolution, if the word
> is understood;
> It is one with Evolution, up from self to
> brotherhood; . . .

> God is calling to the masses, to the peasant
> and the peer;
> He is calling to all classes that the crucial
> hour is near;
> For each rotting throne must tremble and
> fall broken in the dust,
> With the leaders who dissemble and betray
> the people's trust.

> Still the voice of God is calling; and above
> the wreck I see
> And beyond the gloom appalling, the great
> Government-to-Be.
> From the ruins it has risen, and my soul is
> overjoyed,
> For the school supplants the prison, and
> there are no unemployed.

But there is nothing in these pious
banalities which is beyond the orbit of
William Randolph Hearst; the agonies of
the silent majority of misery really meant
very little to her. As a matter of fact, she
was more Tory than Liberal. Her récipé
for poverty was not revolution, but religion.

If any troubled soul facing financial need
reads these lines, let me urge PRAYER
WITHOUT CEASING for light and
STRENGTH TO SEE THE PATH TO
INDEPENDENCE, and constant quiet assertions of the POWER within that Soul
to bring its rightful share of God's opu-
lence. Then go forth and seek, and the way
will open.

She was not even a good feminist.
Though she earned plenty of money herself, she put into the mouth of the heroine
of one of her narrative poems a diatribe
against the economic independence of
married women:

> I hold it the truth that no woman can be
> An excellent wife and an excellent mother,
> And leave enough purpose and time for
> another
> Profession outside. And our sex was not
> made
> To jostle with men in the great mart of
> trade.
> The wage-earning women, who talk of
> their sphere,
> Have thrown the domestic machine out of
> gear.
> They point to their fast swelling ranks
> overjoyed,
> Forgetting the army of men unemployed.
> The banner of Feminine "Rights" when
> unfurled
> Means a flag of distress to the rest of the
> world.
> And poor Cupid, distressed by such follies
> and crimes,
> Sits weeping, alone, in the Land of Hard
> Times.

It is not of record that she refused any
royalties because she was the wife of a
wealthy man who was able to retire before

middle age from his position as sales manager for a wholesale silverware firm.

Woman, to her, was a higher and finer species of being than the mere male, a naturally pure and delicate spirit whose mission was to draw recalcitrant man up to her lofty plane. "Do not thrust upon the man's mind continually," she advised her sisters, "the idea that you are a vastly higher order of being than he is. *He will reach your standard much sooner if you come half way.*" But coming half way did not mean joining him in his low tastes. "Let him never doubt your abhorrence of vulgarity and your distaste for the familiarity that breeds contempt."

III

It is fortunate for Ella that she died before the onset of Prohibition and the hotcha era. Though she never seems to have been active in the dry cause, she had the traditional horror of the farm woman for alcohol, that wicked vice of the big town. "He grew wild," she laments of one of her characters, "took to drink; spent a week at a time in the city."

And the sight of a cigarette between a woman's lips drove her to frenzy. "I am confident," she announced, with the superlative confidence of all her beliefs, "the habit vitiates the blood, injures the digestion, and makes the breath offensive. . . . A woman who expects ever to bring children into the world is little better than a criminal to form such a habit, . . . giving [the unborn child] hour by hour the impression of her mental and physical conditions."

She never doubted the power of prenatal influence, which, *via* Byron and Shakespeare, she confided to the world had bestowed upon her her "literary career." "From reincarnated sources and through prenatal causes" she drew, she felt, all her powers and achievements. She carried with her on a trip around the world her sublime parochial faith. When an Algerian in the Kabyl Mountains surprised her by his artistic ability, she ascribed his talent immediately to the influence of "past lives." She tried to indoctrinate a Singhalese Buddhist nun with "a little healthful New Thought"; "but the good nun, like a large majority of our good Christians, could not at once come into an understanding of these ideas." The plight of Eurasians in the Orient troubled her greatly; but she was comforted by the vengeful thought that their erring fathers would, in the next incarnation, "probably be Eurasians themselves" as a fitting punishment. Her interest in her travels was limited by their metaphysical attractions; California, to her, was "that center of spiritual research," where lived "the Rosicrucians, a noble and intellectual company of people." Even Kansas City was glorified by the presence of Unity, the New Thought Society, made up of "beautiful souls who conserve their lives for this purpose," and to whom she appealed for "the word of strength and healing" whenever she or her husband became ill.

There was too much of the shrewd Middle-Westerner in Ella, however, to leave her continually in this state of nebulous piety. She had a good eye for the supply to popular demand. When "Poems of Passion" shook the nation with horror and ecstasy (the New York *Sun* likened them to "the songs of half-tipsy wantons," and the Chicago *Herald* hoped that she would now "relapse into 'Poems of Decency'"), she was hurt by the criticism but charmed by the sensation she had caused.

She followed up this feverish book of verse with "Poems of Pleasure" and "Poems of Power," and gave to her forgotten novels such Southworthian titles as "A Double Life," "An Erring Woman's Love," and "Sweet Danger."

None of them, unfortunately, lived up to the promise of the title, but she had consolidated a faithful public which insured her a large sale for every bound volume, and a devout audience for her huge output of palpitating verse and prose in the Hearst newspapers. She wrote in words they could understand. They, too, had a stake in poetry when their favorite poet brought to the service of the Muse such fearless songs as

We have fricasseed chicken and strawberry cake
For our dinner today.

IV

And so for pleasant years of maturity, until the sudden death of her husband disrupted her world and set her seeking for another into which she was soon to follow him, she settled down happily in her beloved Bungalow in Connecticut, full of shimmering draperies and cozy corners and with its walls hidden by miscellaneous loot of a world-wide tour; pleased by her vast following, her comfortable income, her admiring husband, the letters and visits and dinners that symbolized the adulation of her public and almost deceived her into belief in her literary greatness and lasting fame. There was the Sound to swim in, much to the horror of her mother, who came from Wisconsin to live with her, and who, before she lapsed into senility, used to declaim with disgust that in her day ladies would not have exposed themselves in the indecent bathing-suits of the early 1900's. There were young people, especially young girls, of whom Ella was always fond, to come as guests

and to sit at her feet while she read and talked.

There was dear Robert, who after his retirement seems to have had no hobby except adoring his wife. There were always cats, animals to which Ella was partial: "I have all my life found wonderful companionship in cats." As she neared sixty she began to be anxious about her health; she was underweight even for her five feet three and a half, and instead of writing to Unity about it she consumed a gallon of milk daily, and soon recovered the pleasing curves which she loved to exhibit in American Indian costume at masquerade parties.

It was a happy life. If only the highbrow critics had been able to overcome their jealousy and acknowledge her rightful place in the world of poesy, she would have been supremely content. Still, she knew that genius often had to wait for posterity to acclaim its greatness. There were the comforting examples of Keats and Blake.

Anyway, the common people, whose hearts and minds were sound and unspoiled by envy, adored her. She died knowing in her heart that some of the poems she had written would live forever.

Perhaps, in that half-world of literature where she was queen, some of them will. She had a gift for concise platitude. Perhaps our children, when they become of age, will be quoting that folk-masterpiece, which was so overwhelmingly popular that a lunatic ex-convict tried in vain to claim it for his own:

Laugh and the world laughs with you;
Weep and you weep alone;
For the sad old earth must borrow its mirth,
But has trouble enough of its own.

LAURA JEAN LIBBEY

Louis Gold

LAURA JEAN LIBBEY

BY LOUIS GOLD

NEARLY a quarter of a century ago, when I was seventeen, I was typist for a while for Laura Jean Libbey, and she dictated to me a long series of plays and articles. I had called at her husband's law office in answer to an advertisement. He accepted me, apparently, on my appearance, for he asked me none of the usual questions regarding my experience and references, and not even my name. I was sent to his home in the Park Slope section of Brooklyn and told simply that his wife needed my services. At the start I did not know who she was and she did not reveal her identity. I knew her only as Mrs. Stilwell.

She was at that time about forty-two years old, and inclined to stoutness. Her complexion was florid, her nose aquiline, and her lips full and firm. She carried herself with dignity, and spoke in a pleasant, unhesitating contralto voice. Her hair puzzled me; it was short, perhaps six inches long, and showed a curious riot of colors, except at the back, where it was a fine dark brown. In her younger days, I learned later, it had been chestnut all over, and she had worn it in a mass of curls piled over her forehead, and rather long in the back.

I took dictation from her for a few days, wondering who she might be, and then I began to suspect that she was Laura Jean Libbey, for I had read a number of her novels when I was a few years younger, and I recognized her style. She was surprised and pleased that I had discovered her identity, and asked if the picture in the front parlor had caused me to guess who she was. When I told her I had not seen the picture she made me go down to look at it. It was a full-sized oil painting by Benjamin Eggleston, and showed her in a dazzling white satin dress and pearl necklace. She was in her early twenties when it was done. She was very proud of it, and showed me favorable articles in the newspapers regarding it.

Laura Jean Libbey wrote her first romance when she was seventeen, in the early eighties. When she completed it, she took the manuscript to New York, walking over the Brooklyn Bridge with a friend. She presented the work to a publisher who said it was wonderful, and gave her $25 for it. She was overjoyed and decided to celebrate the event in a fitting manner. She had a very strict upbringing and had not been able to get much candy. Near the Brooklyn Bridge was a confectionery store. She bought five pounds of marshmallows, and on the way home, with the aid of her friend, finished them. Both girls had severe attacks of indigestion.

The style of her first book and of all the succeeding ones was essentially the same; they showed the mentality of seventeen, and were addressed mainly to an audience of the same age. Miss Libbey claimed to be the first author of the paperbound novels that were once so popular, and she told me that all the subsequent writers of them, such as Charles Garvice, Bertha M. Clay, Mrs. E. D. E. N. Southworth, Charlotte Braeme and Caroline Hart, were her imitators and plagiarized her stories, and that a good many dramatists used her plots. The plan of action was always the same, and it could be said of her books what Cabell says of women, that their names alone varied. A virtuous young man met a similarly blessed young girl and there was love at first sight, which was displeasing to the villain or villainess, or both. From then on the characters moved on joined circles or figures of eight; where the lines of movements met there was a collision, with favorable or undesirable consequences; then they separated and again circled until another meeting. This was repeated for two hundred pages, when the lovers were abruptly united, misunderstandings were cleared up, the bad characters suddenly discomfited, and the book ended happily. The conclusion was always a wedding.

Only once did she write a story with an unhappy ending; the storm of protesting letters she received discouraged her from making another such blunder. In this story the poor girl died of a broken heart, and was buried in a lonely grave. One night, during a terrible snow-storm, the hero, who had learned where she was buried, dragged himself to the grave and wept bitterly over it. He was found the next day, frozen dead, and was buried beside his sweetheart.

In her novels the bride of the hero was always a virgin, even though she had married the villain of the story. Miss Libbey often had to stretch probability to extremes to accomplish this. Sometimes the villain-husband was jailed immediately after the ceremony, or kidnapped, or had to flee from the police, and the separation continued until his first wife, from whom

he had not had a legal separation, appeared on the scene to permit a happy ending. At other times, the bride fell ill of brain-fever, which lasted until the death or exposure of her wicked husband. In every case the virtuous young man of the story was assured of a virgin bride.

It was generally impossible to judge the contents of a given story by the title, for most of them could be used, like the characters, interchangeably. There were "When His Love Grew Cold," "He Loved Her but Was Lured Away," "Had She Loved Him Less," "Was She Sweetheart or Wife?" "Beautiful Florabelle's Lover," "The Abandoned Bride," "The Loan of a Lover," and so on. The chapter headings were usually long and romantic. The following, for example, were the first three in "The Girl He Forsook":

Chapter 1. Why should Heaven let those meet who might learn to love each other, if there is an insurmountable barrier between them which can never be beaten down? I say it is cruel—it is unjust!

Chapter 2. Oh God, can nothing save us from being dispossessed—turned out into the street, with our little all, this bitterly cold Winter day?

Chapter 3. In the great battle between love and duty, which would win? He was only human.

II

Laura Jean Libbey wrote all of her novels before her mother died, when she was still unmarried. Her mother, she told me, loved to read them as she wrote the pages in her fine firm penmanship, making hardly any elisions or corrections, the story flowing from her in a steady stream. Her mother was of French extraction, of which fact she appeared to be proud. Laura Jean described her as quite an aristocratic little lady. She would never go into the dining-room in the basement of the family house, but insisted that meals be served in the back parlor. Laura Jean had been very fond of her mother and revered her memory; she showed me a photograph of a granite shaft she had erected to her in Greenwood Cemetery. But there were times when she spoke with regret of the demands that her mother had made—for example, that she remain single. She declined a number of proposals when she was young, one of them from a man who is now a noted editorial writer. She never told me anything about her father, although there was a large picture of him on the wall of her bedroom; he must have died when she was quite young.

She married a few years after her mother's death, when she was about thirty-six. Her husband, when I knew him, was a taciturn lawyer. The only other member of her family that I ever saw or heard of was a sister, somewhat older than Laura Jean. She was married, with an adult son, and often came for visits of days or even weeks. She was immensely proud of Laura, telling me constantly how popular she had been at the height of her career, and how she had been greeted and acclaimed all over this country and in Europe. I never liked the way this sister called me. It was: "Lou-ass, Lou-ass," with very definite emphasis on the second syllable.

A red tom-cat called Teddy and its mother, a coal black cat, were Laura Jean Libbey's pets. The tom-cat was rather bad tempered and often gave its mistress scratches, but that did not diminish her fondness for him. The black cat regularly presented her with a litter of kittens, all of which were taken away by the S.P.C.A.

About ten years after she had written her last novel, and before her popularity had entirely waned, Miss Libbey blossomed once more into public notice. The theatrical manager, Charles E. Blaney, who was then staging a series of melodramas, dramatized and produced one of her books, "Parted On Her Bridal Tour." She was overwhelmed with delight and immediately considered her possibilities as a dramatist, finally deciding that she could write plays as well as books. Her ambition led to my employment.

In the morning I would arrive at about half past nine. A few minutes later her husband would leave to walk to his office in the Borough Hall section of Brooklyn. Laura Jean would kiss him good-bye, usually asking him to come home early, or not to go to his club. His reply was regularly polite but non-committal.

She would dictate to me in the back parlor behind the billiard room, or in the music room on the floor above. In the former place there was a door to a stairway which went down to the kitchen. In the early part of the playwriting period, Laura Jean would now and then tip-toe over to the door, continuing to dictate to me, and pull it open quickly. Once she caught her Irish maid listening, and at other times there was a sound of scurrying feet. The maid did not continue this very long, however, for it must have been trying to be chased away at an interesting point in a play, leaving the outcome in doubt.

Usually, Laura Jean wore a house dress or apron when dictating, and nearly always stood up. She seldom paced the floor, and rarely was at a loss for words. Her usual pose was to stand with her left arm across her waist, resting her right elbow in the palm of her left hand, with her right hand at her chin. Sometimes she would stand at a window, looking out as she dictated.

She began a play by looking in the morning newspaper for names. She never made an outline or had notes, saying that she did not have the full plot in mind, but would work it out as she proceeded, just as she had written her books. She dictated for a few hours in the morning and a few hours in the afternoon, taking sometimes a holiday of an afternoon or at the end of a week. It usually took two days to write a play, and two plays a week was the rule, but occasionally there were three plays a week. Each play filled from sixty to ninety pages of legal paper s.
In a year and a half she finished in this manner about a hundred and twenty plays.

As in her books, there was a great deal of repetition, and none of the characters was drawn very clearly. As plays, they frankly bored me, for they exhibited no originality, and lacked the action of the books. Whenever I ventured to point out that she had used a given situation or joke in a previous play she said she would make the necessary changes in whichever play was produced last; she was certain that all of them would be staged.

Two jokes were her favorites, and she used them in every other play. One had to do with a widower who was chided for remarrying too soon after the death of his first wife. He answered: "Well, isn't she as dead now as she ever will be?" The other came from "Parted On Her Bridal Tour"; it was not in her book, but was put in by the man who dramatized it. A woman sat on a man's straw hat, crushing it completely. The woman then presented the hat to the man, saying: "I think I sat on your hat." The man looked at the hat and replied: "You *think* you sat on my hat? You know damn well you did!"

When the one hundred and twenty plays were all finished, she named them.

She came down one day with a list of one hundred and twenty names, similar to those of her books, and I made out the title sheets, using one name to a sheet. I thought that we would have a hard time locating the plays to which the titles belonged, but she had a quick solution for that problem. According to her instructions, I placed a title page on each play in the order in which they came to my hand without regard to the contents, and that was the way they were copyrighted. I imagine the names fitted the plays pretty well. She made a trip to Washington for the occasion, and received quite a bit of publicity, which she hoped would create a demand for the production of the plays. But in the twenty-odd years that have followed since the last of them was written, not one of them, so far as I know, has ever been produced. Perhaps the rise of the movies is to blame; they were becoming popular at the time she finished, and beginning to take over the theatres formerly devoted to melodrama.

She did very little entertaining and went out seldom. I remember there was only a single visitor in the daytime in over two years, and the maid informed me there were very few in the evenings. I imagine she would have made an entertaining hostess or guest. Once she read a paper on Ouida before a women's club, laying emphasis on Ouida's death, which she described in minute detail. After the reading, she told me, tears were streaming and handkerchiefs were wet.

After I had been working for her about a year, I asked for a raise in salary. She said she would speak to her husband. She told me later that he was opposed to it, but said that she would give me the usual check weekly and add the raise I wanted in cash, but I was not to mention it to anyone.

lived a secluded life. She hinted to me once that she had to write down to the level of her audience, but she gave many evidences that she believed in the greater part of what she wrote.

On the first day of the appearance of the articles there were two of them, with a large photograph of her taken about twenty years previously. The type was large and the two articles with the picture filled half a page. The titles were "What's the World to One Who Has No Dearie?" and "Where May Girls Who Toil Meet Men to Marry?" The articles following bore such titles as "Are Women Ever Loved Too Well?" "Do Men Cast Off by Society Make Good Husbands?" "Wiles of Wedded Flirts," "Is a Wife a Husband's Heart Partner Only?" "Can Love Become a Mockery?" "A Wife's Broken Love Dream," "Do Men Admire Gayly Attired Women?"

I considered one article so bad that I made bold to comment upon it unfavorably. It was entitled "The Heart of a Working Girl," and appeared in the *Mail* with the others. It told with pathos of the trials and tribulations of poor working girls, particularly those who had to stand behind department-store counters and wait upon snappish insulting customers. One pretty girl unwittingly made a customer angry. The floor-walker was called and in spite of the poor girl's pleadings and tears, and a pathetic story of the family dependent upon her support, with sick members and the possibility of being dispossessed, she was brutally discharged. She received her tiny pay from the cashier and staggered out of the door into the slush and snow, so crushed by the blow that she did not notice the traffic. A large automobile knocked her over. Immediately a handsome young man sprang out and picked up the poor little victim. He was overjoyed at finding her unhurt and took her to her home. He was the son of the owner of the department-store. Soon he married her. Therefore, continued the article, let not the poor working girls become disheartened, for something similar may happen to them.

Laura Jean Libbey received many letters asking for advice. They were of the kind one would expect. Some were from flippant smart-alecks, and a few were unprintable. But in order to fill up her space, she sometimes had to make up letters. These were good enough, but she made up only a few of them, leaving to her sister the job of concocting the rest.

In those days Laura Jean received a number of letters proposing marriage. One writer claimed he was the son of a former Governor of Mississippi. They all thought that she was single and that her present appearance was like the photograph at the head of her column.

Apparently the column was not successful. At first it was placed prominently in large type near the front page of the newspaper. In a very short while her picture disappeared, and the type became smaller. Page by page it retreated until it reached the last page. In a few months there were days when there was no article. Long before the end of the year, the articles disappeared altogether.

About three years ago there was a brief announcement in the Brooklyn *Daily Eagle*, occupying barely half an inch, which said that Laura Jean Libbey had died. I read a number of metropolitan newspapers. No other newspaper that I saw carried the news and I did not see any editorial comment.

Now and then there would be periods of a few days or a week when she could not think of anything or felt indisposed. On such days I showed up as usual in the morning, but left immediately after her husband did; or if he delayed his departure, occupied myself in making lines on pages or in appearing busy in some other fashion.

The bedrooms in the house were all on the third floor. There was an iron gate at the head of the stairs which went up to the ceiling and was locked every night. During a short period when she was suffering from lumbago I carried my typewriter to her bedroom, and took dictation there. Once she showed me a small box full of jewelry, mostly unset diamonds, which she kept in a small safe in the room. At the same time, perhaps purposely, she also showed me two of the longest barrelled .45 revolvers that I have ever seen, even in the movies, which were kept near the safe.

When the plays were completed, I was given an extra week's pay and told there was no further use for my services.

III

The following Winter Laura Jean Libbey appeared as a vaudeville performer at the American Theatre in West 42nd street in New York. She wore a large bonnet with wide ribbons underneath her chin. She carried a parasol and skipped to the center of the stage with stiff swaying movements. She had adopted a high-pitched falsetto voice for the stage, and with a wide fixed smile she gave humorous anecdotes of what would now be called the love racket, ending each one with a little laugh, a long indrawn breath, and a long "Ye-e-es" before going on to the next. The audience was not in a receptive

mood and there was hardly any applause. After the performance, she held a reception on the stage to greet those who came to shake hands with her. Letters could then be handed to her requesting advice on love matters, or they could be dropped into the boxes set up in different parts of the theatre. Her sister was there also, bustling about. Laura Jean never again appeared on the stage. Evidently she was not a success.

I wrote a letter to her saying that I had enjoyed her performance, and that she looked and acted youthful, girlish and splendid. She wrote back, requesting me to call at her home, which I did with alacrity, as I had lacked a steady job since I left her employ six months before. She told me she had a contract to conduct a column of love advice for a syndicate of newspapers and needed a typist again.

Shortly afterward, huge billboard advertisements, and a series of interviews in the New York *Mail* announced her appearance as a special writer for that newspaper. She was to conduct a department called "Cupid's Red Cross: First Aid to Wounded Hearts." I do not know who picked the title; it sounds a good deal like her own choice. F. P. A. was at that time conducting his column, "Always in Good Humor," in the same newspaper.

The method used in preparing these articles was different from that used for the plays. She would write them out in longhand on legal length paper, two full sheets to an article, and I would copy them on the typewriter. The written sheets, as she presented them to me, were quite neat and showed practically no corrections or erasures.

The articles, in contents and outlook, were a generation behind their times, and showed a lack of worldly knowledge that could have come only from one who had

FANNIE FARMER AND HER COOK BOOK

Zulma Steele

FANNIE FARMER AND HER COOK BOOK

By Zulma Steele

THAT kitchen-wise New England spinster, Fannie Merritt Farmer, never dreamed of the influence she was to exert upon millions of homes when she set down, in 1895, the recipes that make up her *Boston Cooking School Cook Book*. Not even the publisher to whom she took her collection of recipes foresaw a landslide in that first mouse-colored copy of the *Boston Cook Book*. Cautiously, that year of 1896, Little Brown printed 3000 copies — but with many misgivings, and at the author's expense. Then as printing after printing melted on the market they watched, amazed, while this kitchen Bible outstripped their best-selling *Quo Vadis?* and *Little Women*. It has reached today a tidy total of over 2,000,000 copies, and is still selling briskly all over the English-speaking world. It has even been translated for the blind in a Braille edition of nineteen volumes.

When Fannie Farmer wrote down her culinary secrets, however, she wasn't thinking beyond an audience of her own pupils. Fannie was then thirty-eight, and principal of a school that taught the art of cookery to genteel young ladies of Boston, and on Thursday afternoons-out to their cooks. Tradition — and the covers of Fanny Farmer candy boxes — pictures "Aunt Fannie" as an aproned old body pottering about an odoriferous kitchen. Actually, the picture has no more connection with that vigorous career-woman than have the candies which blandly took her name. For Fannie was a *lady*, in the full nineteenth century meaning of that mistreated word.

It was in the Farmers' parlor, crowded with gold chairs and inlaid tables, with whatnots and all the trappings of a Boston middleclass home, that Fannie composed her masterpiece. Her sister Cora, with an editorial eye to detail, sat at a table taking it down with a fine pen. Fannie did the dictating, striding restlessly up and down the room, her high-piled red hair and lovely transparent skin vibrating energy. A boundless physical vitality was in her tread. With each step, though, she lurched a little sideways, for Fannie Farmer was a cripple.

That paralytic limp, far from being

ZULMA STEELE *is the author of a biography of Henry Bergh, founder of the American Society for the Prevention of Cruelty to Animals, published in 1942. She has done a considerable amount of magazine writing and at one time worked for the* Reader's Digest.

a handicap, instead was the spur that drove her to fame. Born in 1857, the daughter of J. Frank Farmer, a printer and ex-newspaperman, Fannie grew up in a bookish family that spent winters in Boston, summers in Scituate. Evenings they played cribbage and skat; Sundays they attended the Unitarian church, marking the day with a taffy pull. Mother and father and the four daughters, of whom Fannie was eldest, made a happy, close-knit unit.

Then seventeen-year-old Fannie, just graduated from high-school, was stricken with the mysterious "paralysis" which maimed her for life. During the next ten years while she was in bed or barely able to putter about the house, two of her sisters became schoolteachers. The third married and bore a son, Fannie's adored nephew, Dexter Perkins. Her unworldly father, meanwhile, clinging to his hand press in the face of changing methods of printing, had lost most of his business and with it their modest income.

Fannie, with a permanent limp, came back to active life determined no one should feel sorry for her, and bound she would somehow retrieve the family fortunes. At first, she shocked neighboring gentry by taking a job "in trade," but after a few months this behind-the-counter work proved too much for her. Then for nearly a year she was mother's helper in a nearby family. Finally, she discovered her true bent by enrolling in the Boston Cooking School, graduating to become assistant head and then principal of the school for a ten-year stretch.

The Farmers marveled at Fannie's success as a teacher of cooking, for by family tradition she was far from the best cook among them. She was too apt to let the pots burn as she ran enthusiastically from one recipe to another. Her sister May surpassed her in the kitchen, while their maid-of-all-work, Maggie Murphy, amiable boss of the household, outdid them all with delicate pastries and chowders. Standards of cookery and housekeeping were high in the Farmer household, and the daughters grew up in a haze of mouth-watering odors that floated from the kitchen to envelop the house. Fresh bread was always baking or rising in the kitchen; fresh-caught fish and spicy hams steamed from the old-fashioned range to the table; cakes and cranberry pies, Parker House rolls and gossamer gingerbread — all the enticing New England specialties appeared regularly on the Farmers' table.

Into the 700-odd pages of her cook book, Fannie distilled all the priceless cooking lore of this well-nourished New England family. Other cook books may have more glamorous recipes, but Fannie covered the field of what is known in America as "good home cooking." "Her hollandaise," as one critic remarked, "may not be the finest ever heard of, but it is hollandaise." While generous with the best eggs, butter and cream, Fannie was careful to include an economical one-egg cake, along with her ten-egg

Sunshine cake. To her meat and fish recipes she added warmed-over dishes — glorified croquettes, hash and casseroles. So between the extremes of Baked Ham with Champagne Sauce and Poor Man's Pudding (rice), she missed few well-known dishes.

With Yankee practicality, Fannie set down as well the sort of homely pointers that would be passed along by anyone's New England spinster aunt to a small niece learning her way around a kitchen. "To bake," says the book (in case one wondered), "is to cook in an oven." "To boil is to cook in boiling water (212° F. at sea level)." Along with eight ways to build a fire (kerosene, gas, soft wood, hard wood, charcoal, coal, coke and alcohol), Fannie listed as well Helpful Hints to the Young Housekeeper such as "In sweeping carpets occasionally turn broom that it may wear evenly" — gleanings, perhaps, from the Farmers' meticulous Maggie, who dusted keyholes with a feather.

II

Enthusiastic Fannie Farmer, inspiring classes with her joyous philosophy, "Cooking can be fun," was a far cry from today's aseptic calory-counting dietitians. Yet to her goes credit for an innovation which revolutionized the art of cooking.

In Fannie's day cook books were apt to list the vaguest of rules. "Add flour to thicken," they directed, or "a pinch of lard." Or "butter size of an egg" — whether pullet's egg or ostrich's, they didn't specify, though naturally it made a difference. Miss Farmer herself, instructing a little girl in a class of children to use a heaping spoonful of baking powder, admonished her in the idiom of the day: "Remember, Marcia, make it as rounding as the spoon hollows."

"It will come out different every time, Aunt Fannie," the child protested. "Can't I use two *level* spoonfuls?"

Her teacher thought quickly and from that moment applied the child's notion to measurement of cup and spoon. In time other cook books followed her teaching and Fannie Farmer's system of level measurements — as elementary as the decimal system — changed cooking from a guessing game to a near-science.

It would always be the best butter, though, and the heaviest cream that Fannie leveled in spoon or cup. She was too fiercely-principled a Bostonian to stomach any compromise with quality, any dissembling. Her pupils like to remember the day a photographer came to school to take a picture for her cook book to illustrate chicken *en casserole*. Obviously, a covered casserole looks the same whether or not a chicken is in the pot. Fannie insisted, though, on a bird's being prepared according to recipe and placed in the casserole before she allowed the photographer to proceed.

In the same way, it would not occur to Fannie Farmer to stint or substitute for expensive butter and cream for a class of one hundred pupils. She simply multiplied the tablespoon of butter, the half-pint of cream, by a hundred. Schools where she taught, in consequence, lost money under her generous dictatorship.

Luckily for the Farmer fortunes, however, Fannie's cook book, as it settled down to steady sales of about 50,000 copies a year, began to bring in a comfortable income. By chance, the book appeared at a time when there was little to choose between such pamphlets as *Fifteen-Cent Dinners for Families of Six* and the 1000-page tomes by professional chefs of Paris or Delmonico's whose notions of cooking involved enormous kitchens, well-stocked pantries and, of course, a staff of six or more. *The Boston Cooking School Cook Book* was simple, comprehensive and designed for an average family of six, with not more than one servant. Fannie's all-inclusive recipes, from simple white sauce to Sauce Béarnaise, were mouth-watering and easy to follow. America's middleclass market snapped up her book by the thousands, and Fannie Farmer soon found herself not only well-to-do but famous.

Fannie's personal following enabled her to open her own school of cookery, also in Boston, in 1902. There she taught twice a week, dramatizing her lectures as she limped briskly about the demonstration platform, her red hair vivid above the white instructor's uniform. Fannie herself was careless about details of dress, but Mrs. Farmer, a fine needlewoman, turned her out for each appearance like a prima donna. Her piqué skirt hung full to the floor, protected by yards of gathered apron. Her gossamer shirtwaist had the daintiest of organdy fichus, and tiny hand-hemmed ruffles and beading embellished her collars and cuffs. An assistant and a maid or two always waited upon Miss Farmer. With her Boston sense of the fitness of things, Fannie Farmer refused to sully her own white fingertips in kneading up a flaky piecrust. Usually two hundred pupils attended, and her talks, published in the Boston Transcript, were widely reprinted. From 1905 till her death ten years later, Fannie Farmer conducted the cooking department in the *Woman's Home Companion*, having been described by the editor, Gertrude Lane, as "the finest cook in the country."

III

"Well, I'm getting to be quite a businesswoman, aren't I?" Fannie liked to say, preening herself in the family circle.

Fannie's mother and father, her sisters and the young nephew would all turn aside to smile. For while the cook book brought in a tidy sum, Fannie was as rashly openhanded with money as with recipes. She was always making bad loans. Impulsive as she was generous, Fannie was forever setting out on a trip by carriage or car, forgetful of her empty purse. When the conductor pushed her politely but firmly off the train, without ticket or money, she never failed to be surprised and indignant.

Her noncommercial ideals prevented Fannie Farmer from reaping a large profit in endorsements. She steadfastly refused to recommend products used in her school, beyond a reserved line or two in the advertisements at the back of her cook book, for Cleveland's Baking Powder, Foss' Extracts, Knox's Sparkling Calves-Foot Gelatine and Read's "Odorless" Refrigerators ("Are Perfectly Dry and Will Not Sweat").

Miss Farmer, moreover, would not enter a dish in any of the many cooking competitions she was asked to judge, for "it would be so dreadful if we won." But Maggie Murphy had no such scruples. Twice the Farmers' Maggie submitted dishes under an assumed name and walked off with first prize awarded by Miss Farmer herself.

For all her strict principles, Fannie Farmer approved of wine in recipes and with dinner. (Succeeding editions of her book, though, listed home brews, save for Prohibition years when pallid sherry flavoring had to be substituted for spirituous liquors.)

IV

Fannie Farmer's cook book, under her thumb and through succeeding printings jealously edited by her sister and niece, displayed the provincialism as well as the virtues of the Farmer family. As recently as 1930 H. L. Mencken, reviewing a new edition, criticized it as "too feminine and a shade too Yankee" — a defect "appar-

ently flowing out of the fact that it was hatched in Boston, where lower middle class British notions of cookery still prevail." While allowing it the merits of clarity, comprehensiveness and common sense, Mencken felt it dealt rather poorly with dishes of "more cultured regions," deeply deploring Fannie's recipe for soft-shell crabs as "an obscenity almost beyond belief."

Foreign frills and fancy sauces were not, it is true, welcomed at the Farmers' New England table. Ice cream, for instance, was considered a homemade delicacy to be whipped up on the back porch with a crank freezer, not tortured into odd shapes and disguised, as in one dessert of the day, to look like a lady's muff, furry to touch and taste. Boston-born Fannie looked a trifle askance at "furrin" novelties, much as, all her life, she felt a condescending sympathy for her three sisters who had the misfortune to be born out of Boston in suburban Medford. Nevertheless, she explored for new recipes in such nearby towns, as well as in New York and Atlantic City. At forty-eight she took her young nephew *by trolley* to see the world between Boston and New York, dining after the humble and uncomfortable ride at fashionable Delmonico's. Later, she made a three-months' lecture tour of the Pacific Coast, and also visited St. Louis and Texas.

Fannie found most chefs willing to reveal the secrets of their kitchens, but when balked could usually guess at ingredients with a Sherlockian tongue. Other cook books copied Fannie Farmer without so much as a by-your-leave, lifting out recipes, sometimes, with printing errors intact. When Fannie included a recipe for a Russian canape sent to her from St. Petersburg by young Dexter Perkins, the recipe she christened the "Dexter Canape" sprang up in books, magazines and newspapers all over the country.

Slowly other new dishes came into the Farmer fold, but only after thorough testing, for the family prided itself on putting out a well-tried guide that was not a compilation of other cooks' ideas. Fannie herself was slow to change, suspicious of the value of such new-fangled gadgets as the meat chopper and the telephone. For years she was the only author to submit copy to the *Woman's Home Companion* in longhand. One wonders whether she would approve the broadening influence on her cook book of her well-travelled niece, Mrs. Dexter Perkins, who edits the book today with a leaning toward such dishes as Zabaglione and Beef Stroganoff.

Indefatigable to the last, Fannie Farmer for years was the first to arrive at school — often laden with packages from the big market a mile and a half away — and the last to lock up at night. When another stroke, seven years before her death, completely paralyzed her legs, she hunched about on crutches and lectured from a wheelchair.

Though her red hair was flecked with white and her gray eyes looked at the world through pince-nez, the gallant old lady never lost her grip on a well-directed life. Forewarned of the gravity of her last illness, she gave power of attorney into the hands of her sister, who was to carry on the cook book, and calmly arranged for a visit to the hospital. She delivered her final lecture just ten days before the end. In 1915 Miss Farmer died, at fifty-eight, of Bright's Disease.

Like many another famous person, Fannie Farmer misread her place in the future. Handicapped herself, she had taught Invalid Cookery in many hospitals before there were hospital dietitians; she also had classes of trained nurses and Harvard Medical students, and worked on a diabetic diet, since outmoded by insulin. She considered her Life Work a small volume, *Food and Cooking for the Sick and Convalescent*, which sold poorly and is now out of print.

With a touch of clairvoyance she might have looked ahead down a happy vista of best-selling records that spread her gospel of the bean and the cod to a second generation of nephews and sons hungering now from foreign shores for their Aunt Fannie's New England dishes. Well, the boys can read about it, anyway. One of the phenomena of World War II is the popularity of the occasional battered copy of Fannie Farmer's *Boston Cooking School Cook Book* which turns up in the service men's camps of Africa, Italy, the Solomons, to be pored over by men sick for the smells and flavors of their home kitchens.

Women in America

FROM COLONIAL TIMES TO THE 20TH CENTURY

An Arno Press Collection

Andrews, John B. and W. D. P. Bliss. **History of Women in Trade Unions** (*Report on Conditions of Woman and Child Wage-Earners in the United States,* Vol. X; 61st Congress, 2nd Session, Senate Document No. 645). 1911

Anthony, Susan B. **An Account of the Proceedings on the Trial of Susan B. Anthony, on the Charge of Illegal Voting at the Presidential Election in November, 1872,** and on the Trial of Beverly W. Jones, Edwin T. Marsh and William B. Hall, the Inspectors of Election by Whom her Vote was Received. 1874

The Autobiography of a Happy Woman. 1915

Ayer, Harriet Hubbard. **Harriet Hubbard Ayer's Book:** A Complete and Authentic Treatise on the Laws of Health and Beauty. 1902

Barrett, Kate Waller. **Some Practical Suggestions on the Conduct of a Rescue Home.** *Including* **Life of Dr. Kate Waller Barrett** (Reprinted from *Fifty Years' Work With Girls* by Otto Wilson). [1903]

Bates, Mrs. D. B. **Incidents on Land and Water;** Or, Four Years on the Pacific Coast. 1858

Blumenthal, Walter Hart. **Women Camp Followers of the American Revolution.** 1952

Boothe, Viva B., editor. **Women in the Modern World** (*The Annals of the American Academy of Political and Social Science,* Vol. CXLIII, May 1929). 1929

Bowne, Eliza Southgate. **A Girl's Life Eighty Years Ago:** Selections from the Letters of Eliza Southgate Bowne. 1888

Brooks, Geraldine. **Dames and Daughters of Colonial Days.** 1900

Carola Woerishoffer: Her Life and Work. 1912

Clement, J[esse], editor. **Noble Deeds of American Women;** With Biographical Sketches of Some of the More Prominent. 1851

Crow, Martha Foote. **The American Country Girl.** 1915

De Leon, T[homas] C. **Belles, Beaux and Brains of the 60's.** 1909

de Wolfe, Elsie (Lady Mendl). **After All.** 1935

Dix, Dorothy (Elizabeth Meriwether Gilmer). **How to Win and Hold a Husband.** 1939

Donovan, Frances R. **The Saleslady.** 1929

Donovan, Frances R. **The Schoolma'am.** 1938

Donovan, Frances R. **The Woman Who Waits.** 1920

Eagle, Mary Kavanaugh Oldham, editor. **The Congress of Women,** Held in the Woman's Building, World's Columbian Exposition, Chicago, U.S.A., 1893. 1894

Ellet, Elizabeth F. **The Eminent and Heroic Women of America.** 1873

Ellis, Anne. **The Life of an Ordinary Woman.** 1929

[Farrar, Eliza W. R.] **The Young Lady's Friend.** By a Lady. 1836

Filene, Catherine, editor. **Careers for Women.** 1920

Finley, Ruth E. **The Lady of Godey's:** Sarah Josepha Hale. 1931 **Fragments of Autobiography.** 1974

Frost, John. **Pioneer Mothers of the West;** Or, Daring and Heroic Deeds of American Women. 1869

[Gilman], Charlotte Perkins Stetson. **In This Our World.** 1899

Goldberg, Jacob A. and Rosamond W. Goldberg. **Girls on the City Streets:** A Study of 1400 Cases of Rape. 1935

Grace H. Dodge: Her Life and Work. 1974

Greenbie, Marjorie Barstow. **My Dear Lady:** The Story of Anna Ella Carroll, the "Great Unrecognized Member of Lincoln's Cabinet." 1940

Hourwich, Andria Taylor and Gladys L. Palmer, editors. **I Am a Woman Worker:** A Scrapbook of Autobiographies. 1936

Howe, M[ark] A. De Wolfe. **Memories of a Hostess:** A Chronicle of Friendships Drawn Chiefly from the Diaries of Mrs. James T. Fields. 1922

Irwin, Inez Haynes. **Angels and Amazons:** A Hundred Years of American Women. 1934

Laughlin, Clara E. **The Work-a-Day Girl:** A Study of Some Present-Day Conditions. 1913

Lewis, Dio. **Our Girls.** 1871

Liberating the Home. 1974

Livermore, Mary A. **The Story of My Life; Or, The Sunshine and Shadow of Seventy Years . . . To Which is Added Six of Her Most Popular Lectures.** 1899

Lives to Remember. 1974

Lobsenz, Johanna. **The Older Woman in Industry.** 1929

MacLean, Annie Marion. **Wage-Earning Women.** 1910

Meginness, John F. **Biography of Frances Slocum, the Lost Sister of Wyoming:** A Complete Narrative of her Captivity of Wanderings Among the Indians. 1891

Nathan, Maud. **Once Upon a Time and Today.** 1933

[Packard, Elizabeth Parsons Ware]. **Great Disclosure of Spiritual Wickedness!!** In High Places. With an Appeal to the Government to Protect the Inalienable Rights of Married Women. 1865

Parsons, Alice Beal. **Woman's Dilemma.** 1926

Parton, James, et al. **Eminent Women of the Age:** Being Narratives of the Lives and Deeds of the Most Prominent Women of the Present Generation. 1869

Paton, Lucy Allen. **Elizabeth Cary Agassiz:** A Biography. 1919

Rayne, M[artha] L[ouise]. **What Can a Woman Do; Or, Her Position in the Business and Literary World.** 1893

Richmond, Mary E. and Fred S. Hall. **A Study of Nine Hundred and Eighty-Five Widows Known to Certain Charity Organization Societies in 1910.** 1913

Ross, Ishbel. **Ladies of the Press:** The Story of Women in Journalism by an Insider. 1936

Sex and Equality. 1974

Snyder, Charles McCool. **Dr. Mary Walker:** The Little Lady in Pants. 1962

Stow, Mrs. J. W. **Probate Confiscation:** Unjust Laws Which Govern Woman. 1878

Sumner, Helen L. **History of Women in Industry in the United**

States (*Report on Conditions of Woman and Child Wage-Earners in the United States,* Vol. IX; 61st Congress, 2nd Session, Senate Document No. 645). 1910

[Vorse, Mary H.] **Autobiography of an Elderly Woman.** 1911

Washburn, Charles. **Come into My Parlor:** A Biography of the Aristocratic Everleigh Sisters of Chicago. 1936

Women of Lowell. 1974

Woolson, Abba Gould. **Dress-Reform:** A Series of Lectures Delivered in Boston on Dress as it Affects the Health of Women. 1874

Working Girls of Cincinnati. 1974

Date Due